JULIE HAMILL

15 MINUTES WITH YOU

INTERVIEWS WITH SMITHS/MORRISSEY COLLABORATORS AND FAMOUS FANS

First Published in the UK September 2015 by FBS Publishing.
22 Dereham Road, Thetford,
Norfolk. IP25 6ER

ISBN: 978-0-9932043-2-6

Fabulous BookS

www.fbs-publishing.co.uk
Cover Photograph © Kevin Cummins
Cover design by Simon Inkpen
Text Edited by Alasdair McKenzie
Graphic design and typesetting by Scott Burditt

Paper stock used is natural, recyclable and made from wood grown in sustainable forests.
The manufacturing processes conform to environmental regulations.

Due to the different sources and methods used, including using many of the author's
own photographs, the quality of the images in this book will vary.

JULIE HAMILL

15 MINUTES WITH YOU

INTERVIEWS WITH SMITHS/MORRISSEY COLLABORATORS AND FAMOUS FANS

Why
don't you
find out
for
yourself?

I t is well documented that Morrissey has a handful of friends that he keeps close. He values his privacy and that is to be respected, especially by a fan. But for a fan like me, of thirty years, (of which there are many), it's hard not to want to know everything about him, the truth, not the fair-weather and often blackened portrayals of him in the press. I want to know for myself: Who is Morrissey? What does he really talk about? What does he eat? How does he take his tea? What makes him laugh? Is he like me?

I've never wanted to intrude, or rummage through his bins, I've just gently wanted to know how human he is, because I know I'll never get that close to this genius that has been a constant in my life, both in terms of lyrical comfort, fascination and awe. I love Morrissey, and I'm not alone. I want to make connections and find things in common between us, in an effort to feel closer. That's why I did these interviews; my curious intention always as a gentle and grateful hand-shake; never a poke in the shoulder.

A few accidents happened along the way.
1. While asking questions about Morrissey, I inadvertently discovered much more about the interviewee, and this in itself, became truly fascinating, especially 'favourite things'.
2. The only note to my mum was supposed to be from Mark Nevin. As a fan of Fairground Attraction, she asked me to get his autograph. After Mark, once I started I couldn't stop. Now she keeps all of her notes in plastic wallets in a special folder on a high shelf.

Meeting the people who have worked with or know Morrissey has been one of the most thrilling highlights of my life. I have enjoyed listening to their stories. I left each and every one of these interviews on a high. Vicarious living is under-rated. There were times I felt I was right there with them, back in time, as their eyes lit up with pride in their own production and contribution to Morrissey's legacy.

Meeting the famous fans has been incredibly rewarding. Each and every one fabulous in their own right, it was exciting to see the fame veil come down when the songs were sung. Real fans connect. Particularly Smiths/Morrissey fans. Famous or not we relish and admire like no other, an indestructible army bound together forever by Morrissey's lyrics and music. I've kept all the detail in, for my friends in the #Mozarmy. Thank you, always, for the rock solid support with the interviews, and thank you to the interviewees. Morrissey fans are the very best, and you're all great dancers.

Fifteen minutes with Moz? Only if I could spend it on his knee.

Preface by Andrew McGibbon

In 2012, I got a call from guitarist Kevin Armstrong who asked if I'd mind a certain Julie from London coming round and interviewing me over some tea and biscuits about my time with Morrissey. I was Morrissey's drummer for his first three solo albums and we recorded music together that I was deeply proud of so I was very happy to share these experiences with Julie, a fan of his for over three decades.

I enjoyed the interview so much that I was allowed to rewrite it to make it reflect what I thought I'd actually said.

In 'Fifteen Minutes With You' you'll discover other people who have associated with and been inspired by Morrissey. Some of them have been thrust into Morrissey's sepia tinted spotlight whilst being in the public eye themselves, some have been moved to contribute to his legacy, some have been paid to contribute to his legacy, others stimulated to devotion by decades of romance and rejection.

Each individual goes some way to uncovering the mystique of Moz, as Julie poses questions from a fan's-eye view. It's true that many books have been written about the unquestionable genius of Morrissey, but it's only this book that uncovers a simple fact often obscured by the academic hysteria: Morrissey is just a man who needs to be loved.

I hope you enjoy this unique and diverse collection of interviews. Julie captures the essence of each individual (and their favourite crisp flavours) perfectly. There are over twenty people who didn't say no to her invitation. You shouldn't either. You won't be 'disappointed'.

(Now go straight to page 112)

Viva Morrissey,
Andrew Paresi (McGibbon)
Morrissey's drummer, *Viva Hate, Bona Drag, Kill Uncle.*

For Gerard, Sadie, Archie, Mum, Dad, Morrissey and the #Mozarmy.

Warmest thanks to Kevin Cummins and Andrew Paresi

"Morrissey? I think he's a lovely singer. Now … what does he sing again? Ah-ha ha!"
Bridget Ward 1937 - 2014

The Interviews:

Mark Nevin

Morrissey's co-writer and guitarist on Kill Uncle

15 MINUTES WITH YOU

FEBRUARY 2012 is big coat-and-jumper weather and, despite wearing both, I'm perished walking out of Highgate tube down a wide and windy street to meet Mark Nevin. Mark is the first person to grant me a 'Fifteen Minutes', and I kind of half-expect a phone call to say he has made a mistake; that he's staying at home to polish his Brit awards. Thankfully, he is there at the bar, and his welcome is as warm as apple pie.

We talk at length about his work on *Kill Uncle*, the second studio album that contains some of Morrissey's most irreverent and experimental songs of his career. Under-rated but never under-valued, *Kill Uncle* is the album that critics got wrong and fans took to their hearts.

Mark is a musical storyteller with a warm *Jackanory* flow, and the beautiful melodies he creates are, to many, a natural fit with Morrissey's poetry on *Kill Uncle*. He fondly recalls the laughter in the band when they first heard Morrissey sing the lyrics to 'Our Frank'. *'I remember the look on Morrissey's face, delighted that he'd had this effect on us.'*

Before working with Morrissey, Mark was the writer in Fairground Attraction, penning the number one platinum album *First of A Million Kisses* [which includes the number one hit 'Perfect']. He has worked with Kirsty MacColl, Sandie Shaw and Lloyd Cole.

In addition to working on *Kill Uncle*, Morrissey/Nevin also recorded 'I Know It's Gonna Happen Someday' (a track from the follow-up album, *Your Arsenal*), as well as Smiths disco favourites 'The Loop' and 'Pregnant For The Last Time.'

He first met Morrissey by a post box in Camden. He enjoys Ready Salted crisps, David Bowie and Kid Creole. His latest album *Stand Beside Me in the Sun,* was reviewed by *Q magazine* as 'robust and ecstatic', and, like the song, he really does know where Ray Davies lives.

J. Please say your full name.

M. Mark Nevin.

J: Please describe yourself in a sentence.

M: Well I hope the questions get easier than this!

J: How about: 'One of pop's great storytellers'? Your music is arranged as a story, isn't it?

M: Yeah. My songwriting style, if you like, was started by reading short stories. I was addicted to reading William Saroyan, an American literary superstar of the 30s. I wanted to write songs like his short stories. I also love the music of The Kinks and The Beatles.

J: One of your more recent solo songs, 'The Girl On The Motorbike', is a tale of romance. Is it about your wife?

M: Yeah, it is. Louise is fantastic, she's just amazing.

J: How did she feel when you presented her with a song that you had written about her?

M: I don't know, I think she likes it. It would be irritating if she didn't!

'

J: How did Louise react when she heard 'Oh Mama'?

M: She thought it was a Beatles song and she wondered what Paul McCartney would make of it! I was like: 'What's it got to do with Paul McCartney?'

J: The whole album is fragranced with Beatles' and Kinks' influences.

M: Yeah, definitely. The story for 'I Know Where Ray Davies Lives' really happened. I was sitting in a pub and Ray walked up and said 'Is anybody sitting here?' I thought, he just wants to watch the football, so I'll just pretend I don't know it's Ray Davies. And we just sat and watched the football together.

J: It must have been difficult for you to hide the fact that one of your musical influences was sitting beside you.

M: I just thought that if I start going on about the Kinks then he'll just go home.

J: Did you always want to be in music when you were growing up?

M: Yes, ever since I saw David Bowie doing 'Starman' on 15 June 1972. I had a crappy old guitar and thought, 'That's it, I want to write a song like that.' My brother told me I shouldn't sing, and I listened to him for about twenty years.

J: What does it feel like now when one of your songs, past or present, comes on the radio?

M: It's lovely. It's great; I really like it, particularly when my solo ones get played. I'm not so keen when people say, 'I listened to your record on Spotify' and I go, 'Thanks a lot.'

J: What's your favourite song to perform?

M: I dunno, maybe 'Ray Davies' at the moment. I love doing 'Perfect', they all sing their heads off.

J: That's fantastic.

M: Oh yeah you can't go wrong, I wish I had ten more like it. For someone like Morrissey to go out and have twenty massive hits must feel amazing.

J: Well, you're not far off it, you have lots from your work with Kirsty MacColl, Morrissey, your own material, and of course, *Kill Uncle*. Would you change anything about it?

M: I find the hostility towards it amazing.

J: I think the hostility is from the critics, not the fans. It's under-rated, not under-valued.

M: It was really strange when I got asked to work with Morrissey, because he's such a shy person. It wasn't really like he said, 'Come round and have a cup of tea.' I just got a call from his drummer, who said 'Can you send Morrissey some music?' So I just sent these tapes to him. Then one day, I was putting a cassette into the letterbox on Chalk Farm Road, and there he was—he went bright red. He was so embarrassed; he didn't know what to say. And I was really nervous because he was Morrissey, you know cos I just sent these things to him and he would send postcards back. The first card that came back just said, 'Perfect.'

Then he rang me up for a conversation, but we were having a wake in our house because a friend of mine had died very suddenly and remotely in Iona. We had the wake at my house in Camden, it was quite late on, everyone pretty pissed and the phone rang. 'Mark! Mark! Phone!' someone said. Turned out it was Morrissey, he was all awkward and embarrassed and he didn't know what to say, and I was like, 'I'm sorry Morrissey, we're having a wake, my friend died.' He was like, 'Oh, I'm sorry about that.' It was really weird. I hadn't really met him, I was just sending him tapes.

J: So you sent the music to him first, then he put the words to it?

M: Yeah. We went up to Hook End Manor to record *Kill Uncle*. As I drove up, Morrissey rode past my car on his bicycle, looking just like that 'Stop Me' video. I just thought, this is surreal; here's Morrissey, dressed as Morrissey, on a bicycle.

J: Did you enjoy the recording process?

M: Yes! Then when we [the band] did the first song, 'Our Frank', we hadn't heard the lyrics, then Morrissey came along and put the guide vocal on it, they put a real Elvis echo to his voice. We were nervous, like, it was like the first day of school, and the energy around him ... you don't feel relaxed around Morrissey. Then he sang the 'frankly vulgar red pullover' bit—are we supposed to laugh or not? So we look at each other, and we're giggling uncontrollably, and I remember the look on Morrissey's face, delighted that he'd had this effect on us.

J: How were the meals at Hook End?

M: There was all this beautiful, fantastic vegetarian food, Morrissey sat at the head of the table, not saying much. So the less he said, the more nervous energy there was. So I couldn't stop talking. I begged myself, 'Stop me, please make me stop, God'. So I'd have another drink, and it would make me worse. 'Do you like eggs? I like eggs. I had eggs yesterday, I'll probably have eggs tomorrow as well ...' Everyone was talking rubbish.

J: Are you vegetarian?

M: No, I'm not, but I had to be then. There were sneaky bacon sarnies going on, but I didn't have any.

J: Were you a Smiths fan before you worked with Morrissey?

M: Oh yes. I loved Johnny's guitar playing, especially *The Queen is Dead* album. Those last two albums were incredible. They were on fine form. I remember the first time I saw them on TV (*The Oxford Roadshow*) I thought his guitar playing sounded sort of African.

J: What is your favourite Smiths song?

M: 'There Is A Light', and 'I Know It's Over'. 'There Is A Light ...' I mean, Johnny's guitar playing and Morrissey's lyrics—it's sublime. And 'Stop Me' is a great, great track. The guitar is just so great.

J: Did you ever meet Johnny?

M: Yes, the last time I saw him was at Kirsty MacColl's tribute. He was very friendly. I am a fan of his.

J: You didn't tour with Morrissey, but you went to the Madison Square Garden gig. What happened there?

M: I just went out to see a few shows, he asked me to hang out. I remember the end of the set, there were these white Rolls Royce cars that came up in lifts and the band rushed offstage, into these cars. I had to get a cab and say 'Follow the white cars' down to the Tribeca Grill for the after-show party. I was like, this is weird, cos I remember The B52s were there, REM ... Morrissey wanted me to go and do this tour with him. But I had so many things going on at the time, I had the Sweetmouth thing, I had Kirsty MacColl's *Electric Landlady* and my son (who's now 21) had just been born and was very ill. The idea of going on a world tour at that stage ... I mean, I was going to do it but they never told me when it was going to happen. I said to Jo Slee, 'Just give me a clue as to what dates we're talking about.' Eventually, she got back to me saying 'May 23rd we're rehearsing for three weeks ...' I was like, 'That's tomorrow, so you want me to start rehearsing tomorrow then go on a world

tour straight away?' They wanted me to drop everything and everybody, but I was making a video on the Tuesday.

J: Was there someone else ready to stand in for you?

M: Oh no, he definitely wanted me to do it. It happened then was I was playing with Sweetmouth and to say I was stressed was a bit of an understatement. I was really, really, really stressed. It ended up with me beating up my A&R man. It's a long story, but I felt so let down by him ... I physically attacked him, we had a fistfight outside Moles club in Bath. He [A&R man] said, 'I deserve a kicking' and I said, 'Too right you do!' I was pretty stressed out, I'd never do anything like that normally, or ever have since. It was just very unprofessionally handled. I felt betrayed by him. I needed a break. It was incredibly intense. There were all sorts of legal issues going on, I was dealing with so much.

J: You were contracted to do these Sweetmouth gigs?

M: No, but other people's lives were in the mix, and I respect that. I said, 'I don't care if it's Elvis Presley, I'm not going on tour!' Then, Morrissey wrote me a letter, it said, 'Power to your elbow, I still want to carry on writing the next album with you.'

J: Did you have codenames for all your tracks? I read that 'My Love Life' was 'Smooth Track.'

M: Yes! 'Asian Rut' was 'Idiots Funeral', 'I Know It's Gonna Happen Someday' was 'French Epic'.

J: And 'Sling Your wife'?

M: No, that's made up!

J: Oh. So onto the next album ...

M: In a way it's very annoying because I got really psyched up for *Kill Auntie* (Morrissey's working title for *Your Arsenal)*. I was disappointed with aspects of Clive's [Langer] production of the last album, because I wanted it to be really guitar-based, and he replaced my guitars with more piano. I remember there was a review in the *Melody Maker* calling it a 'boiled lettuce production'. Clive is a brilliant producer [Madness], but I wanted guitar. So when the next album with Mick Ronson came out, it was much more like I wanted it to be, and everyone was like, 'Oh, they got rid of Mark Nevin—now it sounds great!'

J: Oh no!

M: When we recorded 'I Know It's Gonna Happen Someday', poor Mick was in hospital at the time [with cancer], so I got Boz and Alain to copy exactly what I had played on the demo, note for note, so that track was pretty much produced by me.

J: Do you think by replacing guitars with pianos Clive was trying to pull the sound away from the 'Johnny Marr' sound of The Smiths?

M: Yes, most likely. Something like 'Our Frank' started out with loads of guitars, but ended up with all this piano. Clive took it all out.

J: Do you ever play any of the songs that you wrote with Morrissey in your own live set?

M: I sometimes play 'Sing Your Life' in my live set now. I like to tell a story and then sing a song, and I tell this story about how my publisher once told me that I was committing career suicide by singing my songs myself. I said, 'I don't care', and then I do 'Sing Your Life' because it is about just that, singing your life—good advice Morrissey! 'Sing your life, walk right up to the microphone and name ...'

J: What would you say to Morrissey if he walked in here right now, into this pub, and said 'All right, Mark?'

M: What would I say? I'd say, 'I'm doing an interview about you.' I saw him at Hop Farm, actually; I was with Mary Coughlin.

J: Tell me about this picture.

M: That was at my house in Camden. I think we went to see Suede that night, before they were big, at the White Horse.

J: There's a lot of booze there on the mantelpiece.

M: Yeah, lots of drinking. We'd had a few, but not Morrissey though, he always stayed sensible. He didn't really drink much at all then.

J: If you had to caption this picture, what would you put?

M: 'Legend sandwich.'

J: What's your favourite radio station?

M: Radio London.

J: What's your favourite crisp flavour?

M: Ready salted.

J: Safe. What do you make of Wotsits and Nik Naks?

M: Disgusting. Wotsits are the devil. I'd leave if you put them out.

(LtoR) Peter Hogg, Kirsty MacColl, Mark Nevin, Morrissey.

J: What's your favourite TV programme?

M: *Curb Your Enthusiasm*.

J: What's your favourite film?

M: I like a foreign film called 'Harry's Here To help'.

J: Is it a comedy?

M: It's funny, but it's not a comedy. I wish I hadn't seen it so I could see it again.

J: Why don't you just watch it again?

M: I could, but ... yeah, I suppose I could.

J: What music do you play to get a party started?

M: Lots of reggae. Anything off the Island label. Squeeze's 'Up the Junction' is a great storytelling record. As is 'She's Leaving Home' by the Beatles.

J: Favourite record of all time?

M: I'd say 'Life On Mars'. I could never listen to that song and not be blown away by it.

J: That's my karaoke song.

M: Is it? Well, next time we'll do a duet on it.

J: What's your favourite book?

M: *In Cold Blood* by Truman Capote.

J: What's your favourite pizza topping?

M: I like the 'Soho' pizza with the rocket topping. Do you go for that?

J: I do go for that. It looks odd on the menu but it's so right, a salad pizza. Favourite childhood toy?

M: Monopoly. I played the iron or the racing car. The boot is quite good as well. They're all good. I'm very good at Monopoly. A killer. Ruthless. I take it very seriously. I buy up Park lane and Mayfair and it's all over.

J: What's your favourite concert?

M: David Bowie, Ziggy Stardust, 1973/1974. My first concert was Slade supported by the Alex Harvey Band. Noddy was wearing the hat of mirrors. The second band I saw had a new band called Queen as support, and that was absolutely incredible!

J: David Bowie covered 'I Know It's Gonna Happen Someday.' How did that feel, your musical hero singing a song that you wrote with Morrissey?

M: It was amazing, fantastic.

J: Who do you think does 'I Know It's Gonna Happen' better?

M: I like the Morrissey version.

J: Would you work with Morrissey again?

M: That will never happen, but hypothetically … Well, yes, I suppose I would. I wouldn't want to go on tour, though. Not with anybody. And were it ever to happen, I would be much more proactive in the discussion about what it was we were actually doing. I'm at a different stage of life, more into my family now—this is a big night out for me, you know.

J: Can you write a note to my mum?

M: What's her name?

J: Pat.

Amy Lamé

Writer & Performer

15 **MINUTES WITH YOU**

PERFORMANCE artist Amy Lamé is a self-proclaimed 'uberfan' of The Smiths and Morrissey. Her club Duckie, the Saturday night club she co-founded in the mid nineties at The Royal Vauxhall Tavern, has Smiths and Morrissey songs at the heart of its eclectic playlist, often sandwiched between Kylie Minogue's 'Spinning Around' and Olivia Newton John's 'Xanadu'. Amy has fashioned Duckie into a unique celebration of performance, party and disco, for 'boys, girls and everyone in-between', and the club has regulars that have been going every week for the past twenty years.

Amy is also the writer of the unique and hilarious play, *Unhappy Birthday*, a one-woman play based around her teen obsession and lifelong love of Morrissey. Her out there, on-the-edge teen character is always at the very centre of events, showing the crowd that she's ready to step further down into the depths of obsession and teen love, and has every intention of taking them with her.

She featured the Morrissey track 'Come Back to Camden' as her theme song during her time as Mayoress of Camden 2010/2011, and she curated Smithsfest (to celebrate thirty years of The Smiths) for the London ICA in 2013. She writes, acts and frequently appears on television to discuss feminism, LGBT culture, music, politics, comedy and, of course, Morrissey. She stood for selection as Labour Party candidate for Dulwich and West Norwood in March 2014.

When I meet Amy it's a sunny day and she greets me with a light bouncy walk in pink Converse. Her enthusiasm is infectious and soon we're talking animatedly about favourite lyrics and gigs. Amy has a childlike energy to her that makes her a wonderful, positive and exciting person; she is not afraid to be herself, and there's no greater thrill than being caught up in her laughter. Being with Amy is akin to sliding down a helter skelter after a cheeky cider.

Her favourite drink is a Campari, she fancies a bit of Blondie and likes aubergine on a pizza. If Morrissey came to her house, she'd try to get him drunk.

J: Please say your full name.

A: My name is Amy Lamé. Said with the accent. I try to avoid 'lame.'

J: Is it your real name?

A: No, it's my stage name. My mom came up with it, so if people don't like it, I just say 'Hey, my mom gave me this name!'

J: Can you describe yourself in a sentence?

A: I'd say ... I'm a writer, performer, broadcaster and all-round chubby glamour puss.

J: You have a very unique look. Where does it come from?

A: It was never anything conscious. I always struggled to be myself and express that in every way that I can. When I'm getting dressed I stick a belt on it and turn to my partner and say, 'Is it too much?' and she always says, in the words of Luther Vandross, 'Just remember, Amy, it's never too much.'

J: Were you musical as a child?

A: I always wanted to learn how to play piano, but my parents couldn't afford one, so I had one that you blew through. I never learned any instruments, but I was very into pop music.

J: What bands were you into?

A: I was given an album as a gift when I was six, because I was a child model for this chubby girls' clothes store. I did catwalk in the shopping mall. I got paid in pop records and clothes. My mom loved this idea that I got free clothes. One of the albums they gave me was Billy Davis Jr: 'You don't have to be a star, baby, to be in my show ...'

J: Your future was mapped out from that point on.

A: Exactly. And I got Donny and Marie.

J: So you're a little bit country?

A: ... and a little bit rock n roll. I was a huge Osmond fan. It just started from there.

J: How did your tastes develop?

A: When I was ten I was given two more albums that are really important to me: one was Blondie's *Parallel Lines,* and the other was Donna Summer's *On the Radio*. I remember staring at the cover of *Parallel Lines* and thinking that her armpits are the sexiest part of her body.

J: Her armpits?

A: Yes. I was pre-pubescent, I should have thought to move over a little bit. I just used to sit with the headphones on and listen. But I didn't discover The Smiths until they broke up. Growing up in New Jersey it was guitar-Springsteen-Bon Jovi-sound and I didn't have an older sibling to show me the way.

J: You did well with what you had so far.

A: Yeah, I did! The first gig I ever went to — when I was fifteen—was The Ramones. They played in a local theatre that doubled up as a children's theatre, and behind them was the set for *Cinderella*. Honestly, people were taking drugs everywhere, The Ramones smashed up the whole place, the *Cinderella* set, the chairs, it was absolute mayhem. And I just thought 'I totally want more of this!' Then when I was sixteen I did an exchange trip to France, and the student's brother was like: 'Oh! Mais non! Ecouté!' And he put on Depeche Mode.

J: Brilliant!

A: Yeah, it totally blew my mind. I had heard of this band The Smiths and thought I'd better check them out. I went to the local record shop and saw the album *Strangeways, here we come* had just come out. So I thought, I'll buy that then go to the newsagents and read the NME (for free—I never bought it). And of course it says that The Smiths have split up. So I had just heard this band that pushes every single button from The Ramones to Blondie to Depeche Mode to The Osmonds and Donna Summer. Everything crystalised for me, and I saw my future, and then I discovered they had split up.

J: Did you hide in your room?

A: I became so preoccupied, and bought the entire back catalogue and just thought, I have to know absolutely everything about this band. The following year *Viva Hate* came out. That was my final year of high school, so kind of like a really important time. I was seventeen, my dad was into cars and I was lucky enough that he bought me a convertible Mustang. And I had *Viva Hate* on cassette.

J: What colour was the Mustang?

A: Grey, with white leather interior. I was a very lucky girl.

J: Have you ever met Morrissey? Didn't you wait outside a record shop for him?

A: He did a record signing when *Vauxhall and I* came out. I waited outside HMV. I was third in the queue. I went up to him and I said, 'Morrissey, can I ask you a question?' He said 'No.' So I was like, 'Um, okay, so ...' I gave him my CD and he signed it. It says, 'Amy, have a happy life—Morrissey.' He placed it on my left shoulder and I just walked away. It was a bizarre encounter. Did I meet Morrissey? No, not really ... but that moment was inspirational for the 'Unhappy Birthday' show.

J: So, what if he walked across the grass right here, right now, and said, 'All right, Amy?' What would you say to him?

A: I'd probably just say 'Hi! Wow! How funny meeting you here! I didn't know that there were so many Morrissey impersonators around!'

J: What are your favourite Smiths and Morrissey songs?

A: My favourite Smiths song is 'What Difference Does It Make?' All the songs bring you back to a particular place and time in your life. It's my coming out song, my identity, who I am, how I feel about myself, and the 'F-you' attitude. I have to be myself. My favourite Morrissey song—I find it harder with the solo stuff because it changes all the time. Recently I have been listening to 'I Like You' again, which kind of passed me by first time but ...

J: It's a grower, isn't it?

A: It's like an earworm, I cannot get it out of my head. After talking with Mark [Nevin], the other song I have been listening to is 'There's A Place In Hell For Me And My Friends'. I know that whole album is considered to be kind of touch and go [*Kill Uncle*], but I love the intimacy of it.

J: You are the ex-Mayoress of Camden. Is it true that you used 'Come Back To Camden' as your theme?

A: Yes! Morrissey's 'Come Back To Camden' was our unofficial Mayoral song and my tagline! I did a fundraiser ball and it was all about that song! I was appointed as purely civic and purely voluntary, so I couldn't run again. The ex-Mayor is an elected councillor and he needed a mayoress and he thought of choosing me because the focus of our year was the musical heritage of Camden.

J: How perfect.

A: We met at Duckie's dancing to The Smiths, so it seemed natural.

J: Tell me, if Morrissey came to your house, what stuff would you hide away, and what snacks would you put out?

A: Do you know what? I'd hide nothing! Leave it all out!

J: Are you vegetarian?

A: Not any more. He's really not coming, is he? I think I'd put out Twiglets. I know he doesn't like anything too spicy. Maybe just a cheese sandwich. Yes. Cheese sandwiches. And a plate of deviled eggs ... and maybe some scented candles ... We have an eclectic selection of contemporary art that he'd like. The fear would be that I'd run around and turn into an eight-year-old child picking up stuff and saying 'Look at this! Look at this!" Like my niece does when I go around and she shows me every colour of crayon.

J: Yes. You'd show him every Barbie.

A: I think I'd try to get him drunk!

J: Let's talk about your play *Unhappy Birthday*.

A: It's more of a show/gig/party, because the audience are invited as my mates—my guests—and we're all sat 'in the round' at a party, playing games.

J: How much of it is written versus improvised?

A: Well, the whole show is worked out, but it's not a set script. A lot of it is improvised because it really depends on the audience. And I have to be able to respond to that.

J: What's the premise?

A: It's my birthday, you're all invited, and we're all waiting for my other very special guest to turn up, and while we wait for Morrissey, everything happens. The show, the party, the gig. It's a non-stop Smiths set list, the music is fantastic. It's quite intense, it explores our obsession with celebrity, and then it tips from fascination to obsession into madness. I think all Morrissey fans have been there.

J: Definitely.

A: Any fan will get it. You don't have to be a Morrissey fan, but I want to meet all of the nice Morrissey fans.

J: Can I ask you some favourite things?

A: Sure!

J: What is your favourite drink?

A: Campari with soda and a splash of orange.

J: Favourite radio station?

A: BBC London or BBC6 music.

J: Favourite crisp flavour?

A: Worcester sauce.

J: NICE! Would you put them out for Morrissey with the Twiglets?

A: I'd have to check that the flavour doesn't have anchovies in. Mind you, I don't think chicken crisps have chicken in. I love prawn flavour.

J: Favourite TV programme?

A: *The Simpsons*.

J: Favourite biscuit?

A: Every biscuit!

J: Favourite tune to put on before you go out?

A: Gold FM for the awesome 60s and 70s tunes. Or Brian Matthews, *Sounds of the Sixties* on Listen Again R2 8-10 a.m.

J: Favourite childhood toy?

A: My Donny and Marie stage. You had to stick the dolls into the stage then move the lever and they moved pretending to dance.

J: Favourite pizza topping?

A: You can't beat a classic margarita. Otherwise, aubergine—I love aubergine with chilli.

J: Could you write a note to my mum?

A: Sure!

J: Thank you so much.

A: It was my pleasure.

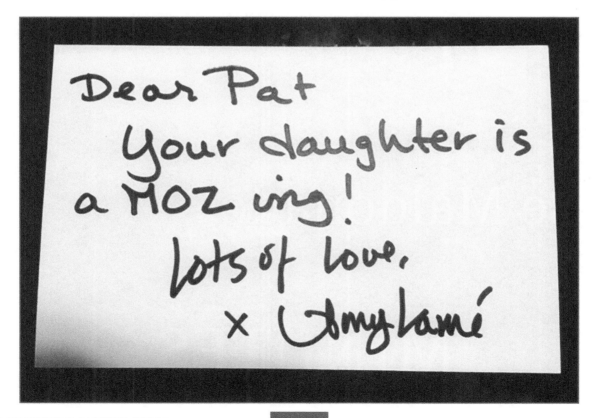

Jose Maldonado

'The Mexican Morrissey'

Image by Gina Vadnais

15 MINUTES WITH YOU

WHAT do you do if you are an impersonator, and the person you are impersonating impersonates you right back? This is what happened to Mexican Morrissey Jose Maldonado, lead singer with the Sweet and Tender Hooligans, as he stood in the crowd at the Wiltern Theatre in 2004 and heard Morrissey announce to raucous applause: 'We are the Sweet and Tender Hooligans ... I am Jose.'

'The Mexican Morrissey' has been paying tribute to his idol for over twenty years. A Latino phenomenon, Mexi-Moz has thousands of devoted fans that have spent years going to concerts trying to grab his hand or tear his shirt apart. His band have sold out concerts in Los Angeles, Orange County, San Francisco, San Diego, Seattle, Boston, New York, Austin, El Paso, Monterrey, Tijuana, Mexico, London, Leeds, Manchester and Glasgow.

During the interview Jose grabs every opportunity to compliment Morrissey, and his devotion is paramount. He reminds me of that picture of Morrissey when he's looking up to Sandie Shaw with rosary beads; full of admiration: 'When all is said and done, it's he I love'.

He hosts a Smiths/Morrissey radio show on indie1031.com—two hours of Smiths/Morrissey requests, news, tour dates and facts. He has appeared in Morrissey's video for 'Irish Blood, English Heart.' He has met Morrissey six times, and at their third meeting, Morrissey suggested to Jose that he release 'Lost' as a single, having seen footage of his performance.

I met him in the Cosmopolitan Hotel, Las Vegas. It was hard for me to believe that this very sensible guy, neatly dressed in shorts, t-shirt, white socks and trainers (who spoke very politely with a tiny hint of a lisp while he ate my Polo mints) is the same man who induces crowd frenzy and hysterics with his uncanny impersonation of Morrissey. Grounded and earnest, he is grateful for the chance to live the dream with the Hooligans: *'Don't wake me up.'* When he's not whipping the microphone he's at home in Pasadena and his day job is as an LA lifeguard. He enjoys date nights with his wife, pineapple on his pizza and racing bikes home from school with his two sons.

JH: Please say your full name.

JM: Jose Raul Maldonado the II.

JH: You have three jobs—singer, DJ, lifeguard. Which do you like best?

JM: The job that has been the most financially and spiritually rewarding of all would be LA County Lifeguard. My other job is lead singer of a Morrissey/Smiths tribute band called The Sweet and Tender Hooligans. We've been doing our tribute band for twenty years and I'm also a DJ on Indie 1031.

JH: So which is your favourite?

JM: Each is rewarding in its own way. I have different reasons for each.

JH: See, I would have said my favourite is being a rock star.

JM: Um yeah, well I do love that, but I don't do that nearly as much as I'm a lifeguard.

JH: You have a nickname - 'The Mexican Morrissey'. Who gave you that nickname?

JM: A couple of years ago I did a show where we were on the bill with the Mexican Elvis (El Vez)

and I thought 'Oh, this is great, we could bill it as the Mexican Elvis meets the Mexican Morrissey', and from that point on it sorta stuck.

JH: Other than the Mexican Morrissey, how would you describe yourself in a sentence?

JM: Oh ... um ... gosh! Oh gosh, I don't know! Um, in no particular order I am a Los Angeles County lifeguard, marathon runner and the lead singer of Sweet and Tender Hooligans.

JH: What sets your band apart from the other tributes?

JM: Are there any other tributes?

JH: There are plenty in the UK, about five different groups.

JM: I'm pretty sure that we've been going the longest.

JH: You've been going the longest, and I also think that you may be the only tribute band that Morrissey has seen?

JM: Only to the degree that he acknowledged us. It is the highlight of my career that Morrissey introduced himself, as me, while I happened to be in the audience.

JH: Tell me about that.

JM: It was in 2004 at the Wiltern Theatre. He said, 'We are the Sweet and Tender Hooligans … I am Jose.' I stood there catatonic while everyone was beside me, nudging me, saying, 'Did you hear that?' I looked back and said, 'Please don't wake me up'.

JH: You've met Morrissey a few times, haven't you?

JM: Yes, six times. The first time was a very chance encounter. We had no idea we were going to meet him. It was while he was touring for *Your Arsenal*. We used to rehearse every Thursday then go to this pub in Pasadena. And there he was. Along with his bandmates. Everyone was mobbed around Boz Boorer actually, because there was a rockabilly band on, and that night it was Boz who was the celebrity and Morrissey was hanging out in the background not really being bothered by anyone. So I went back to my car and brought back a CD for him to sign so that I would have something to break the ice. I had always rehearsed what I was going to say to him—that was, 'Every day of my life is always that much better because your songs are always a part of it.'

JH: And what did he say?

JM: Something to the effect that the feeling was entirely mutual and his life was that much better because he knew that there were people enjoying his music. He asked who to make the autograph out to, and I said Jose. That is when he remarked that it seemed as though he had a lot of Latino fans in California.

JH: Is it true that when you met him he thought that your band should release 'Lost'?

JM: With Morrissey I can't tell if he's serious or he is just leading me on, being polite. At this time when I was going to meet him and I was in line and as I'm about ready to say hello, he looks right at me and says, 'Oh there you are!' And I said, 'Really … you know me?' and he says, 'Of course I know who you are. How was the show last Wednesday night?' I told him about the songs that we had played, including 'Lost', and he said, 'Oh, you've done that one before. A friend of mine brought me a VHS.' I was afraid to ask, but I did ask, 'What did you think?' and he said that he enjoyed it and that we should release 'Lost' as a single. I don't know if he was genuine or just being polite, but it was very sweet of him to say. Following this, I translated it into Spanish.

JH: So why don't you release it?

JM: We perform it, including it as one of our standards.

JH: But you could record 'Lost' as a single, couldn't you, with Morrissey's permission?

JM: I guess in the iTunes era anything is possible. We have talked about it, but the song I'm most pleased with is 'Let Me Kiss You', which translates really well. We also perform 'There Is a Light That Never Goes Out' in Spanish. The fans love it and we love performing it for them.

JH: Is it true that some of your fans are so devout that they follow you with the same devotion as they would do Morrissey?

JM: We do have loyal followers, yes.

JH: Do you have plans to come back to London?

JM: We want to go back to the UK at least three or four more times before we decide to hang it up.

JH: I have a new type of question for you.

JM: Oh gosh, what now? I know about your crazy hypothetical scenarios.

JH: Morrissey is on stage, and he sees you in the crowd. Actually, before I ask, this happened as well, didn't it?

JM: Yes, I saw him last year and he pointed to me and said, 'Well, what a surprise.'

JH: That's incredible. So Morrissey is on stage, he sees you in the crowd, he says, 'Hey you, the other Mexican one, come up here and do a duet with me! And you're like, looking around going 'Who, me?' like the winner of a beauty contest. And you climb up onto the stage to huge applause and Morrissey whispers in your ear the song you're going to perform. What does he say? What's the song?

JM: Wow. Um. It has to be 'Speedway'. Or 'Lifeguard on Duty'.

JH: Who would sing first?

JM: Can we pretend that I summon Christina Hendricks?

JH: I'm afraid not. Not in this dream. Let's just say that she couldn't get a concert ticket.

JM: Ah, gee, all right.

JH: If you *were* on stage with Morrissey, would you kind of start to elbow him over a bit, you know, subtly and gradually, accidental-like, so that you were in the middle of Boz and the boys and he was at the curtains?

JM: No! I've got my own band!

JH: If Morrissey came into this bar right now, and walked over and said, 'All right, Jose?' What would you say?

JM: I'd say 'Hey! Let's have a drink! Let's talk about Vegas, Elvis, old records!' I'd love to ask him what's the one artist or group that he'd be embarrassed for others to know that he liked.

JH: Ah! His guilty pleasure.

JM: We all have that artist or band that would blow our street cred.

JH: What's yours?

JM: Why, it's the Bee Gees, of course, just for 'How Can You Mend A Broken Heart'.
[Jose's phone rings—his ringtone is 'Ain't Talkin' About Love' by Van Halen]

JH: I think yours is Van Halen.

JM: I couldn't possibly comment on that.

JH: If Morrissey came to your house, what snacks would you put out for him?

JM: Maybe some cheese and crackers? When we saw him for the first time he was drinking a Corona, which is great because my fridge is always well stocked with Coronas!

JH: What do you make of The Smiths reunion discussion?

JM: Morrissey has made it clear that it will never happen. Throughout the years I've seen the Sex Pistols, The Police reunite. Even Van Halen patched up a very serious rift and reunited with David Lee Roth. The Pixies, The Eagles, Pulp, Blur, so I understand that it's more complicated and there are certainly a lot of hurt feelings, but the future hasn't been written yet. It wouldn't break my heart if they didn't get back together, because when all is said and done, I'm a fan of Morrissey.

JH: Was that a little bit of a lyric there?

JM: Yes! When all is said and done, it's he I love. Morrissey and Johnny were—undeniably—a beautiful combination, but he has since done so much and I love it all.

JH: What's your favourite drink?

JM: Coca-Cola. If I ever needed blood they'd have to put some Coke in there.

JH: Sandwich?

JM: My famous breakfast sandwich. Toast two sandwich thins—the ones I have are wholegrain—then scramble the egg in the microwave for exactly 57 seconds ... and at that very moment the microwave stops, the thin is popping up out of the toaster. I then take the sandwich thin out of the toaster, rest the egg on top of it, put a slice of cheese on that and rest the whole masterpiece on top of my toaster so that the cheese will melt.

JH: What's your favourite pudding?

JM: Banana cream pie.

JH: Film?

JM: *Pulp Fiction*.

JH: TV show?

JM: *Mad Men*.

JH: Favourite Morrissey phase?

JM: *Vauxhall and I*. 'Gentleman Morrissey.' 'LA Morrissey!' 'Hollywood Morrissey!'

JH: Favourite Morrissey single?

JM: 'Let Me Kiss You'.

JH: What's your favourite pizza topping?

JM: Pineapple.

JH: Can you write a note to my mum?

JM: Sure!

JH: Thank you so much, Jose. It was lovely to meet you.

JM: You too, Julie!

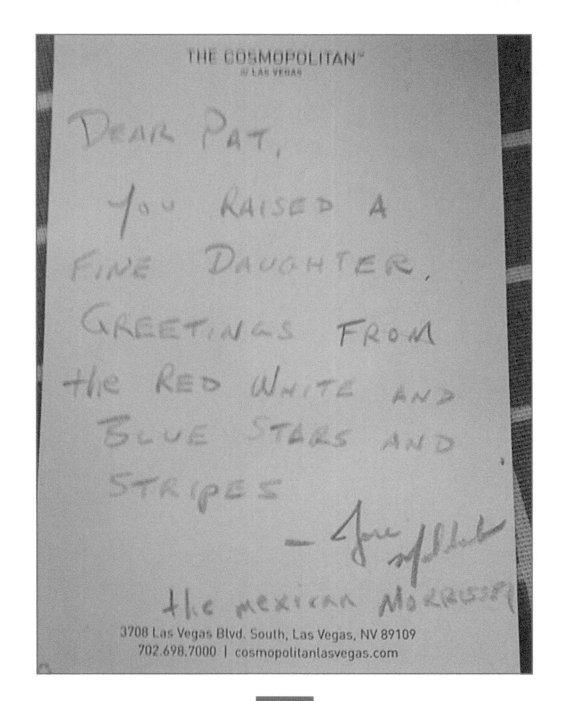

Kevin Armstrong

Guitarist and co-writer on Bona Drag.

Image by Gaz De Vere 2014

15 MINUTES
WITH YOU

GUITARIST Kevin Armstrong has had a golden musical career to date, working with everyone he admires—David Bowie, Iggy Pop, Thomas Dolby, Sinead O'Connor, Prefab Sprout, Sandie Shaw, Paul McCartney, Mick Jagger, Robert Plant, Elvis Costello, Rick Wakeman, Brian Eno, and of course, Morrissey. Before we met I had a quick flick through my record collection and was delighted to find an abundance of Armstrong in there, whether it be as writer, guitarist or producer, so I had lots for us to talk about (and plenty for him to sign).

I sat with him in his kitchen in north-west London to talk about working with Morrissey during the *Bona Drag* sessions, including playing on some of Morrissey's best known hits: 'Ouija Board, Ouija Board', 'Piccadilly Palare', and 'November Spawned A Monster'.

'I made these lovely baroque guitar pieces to: 'He Knows I'd Love To See Him' was one and 'Piccadilly Palare' was another, and I gave them as guitar demos and he just went for it.'

We took a tour of his recording studio and I admired his collection of guitars, including a beautiful vintage Fender Telecaster from 1954. He played two of the new tracks he's been working on for a new album, the latter of which I could have easily started a decent pogo to.

He likes salt and vinegar crisps, his favourite drink is a Mojito and he once hovered over the Live Aid crowd in a helicopter beside David Bowie. He was a fan of The Smiths before working with Morrissey.

'I wouldn't describe myself as a 'rabid' fan of anyone, but sometimes I have little crushes on artists and I did follow The Smiths for a while.'

J: Please say your full name.

K: Kevin Alexander Armstrong.

J: Can you describe yourself in a sentence?

K: I'm still a child.

J: Were you a Smiths fan before you worked with Morrissey?

K: Yes—oh yes, I was. I bought 'This Charming Man' right after I heard it on the radio. I fell in love with it immediately, the bubbly African guitars and Morrissey's lugubrious delivery over it—superb. Straight away, I loved it.

J: Did you continue buying Smiths records throughout their career?

K: Yes, I bought *Meat Is Murder* and *The Queen Is Dead*. I was hooked. I used to listen to the John Peel sessions. I wouldn't describe myself as a 'rabid' fan of anyone, but sometimes I have little crushes on artists and I did follow The Smiths for a while. On hearing something like 'How Soon is now?' I just thought I could do something like that and retire happy.

J: What was it like co-writing and playing guitar with Morrissey?

K: Well, I didn't know him before. I knew Clive Langer [producer of *Kill Uncle*] quite well, and had done lots of records with Clive. I worked on 'Absolute Beginners' with Bowie and 'Dancing in the Street' with Bowie and Jagger. Then I did Sandie Shaw stuff, and I was a regular session dude with Clive. I knew he [Morrissey] was looking for songs. On knowing Smiths stuff really well, and admiring Johnny's work, I figured that musically it sounded to me that often Johnny would present a completed guitar piece, which stood alone as a piece of music, and give it to Morrissey and then Morrissey would do these 'five notes' over the top and suddenly magic was born. He's a very private guy and I'm not really accustomed to sitting round a table passing ideas backwards and forwards. So I made these lovely baroque guitar pieces, 'He knows I'd love to see him' was one and 'Piccadilly Palare' was another, and I gave them as guitar demos and he just went for it.

J: I like the way you described it. 'Putting the five notes on top'. I've always seen the shape of Smiths Morrissey/Johnny music criss-crossing and weaving like a DNA structure.

K: Absolutely. That's what is so striking about the Smiths—Morrissey would ride on the musical patterns of Johnny.

J: How did Morrissey find you?

K: I have no idea. I think maybe he noticed that at that time I was playing with people like Iggy Pop and Bowie.

J: 'Ouija Board, Ouija Board' is a great record. I watched Morrissey perform it at Hop Farm in 2011 and you could have heard a pin drop. Beautiful.

K: We put a lot of work into that record. We all loved it. So did Clive Langer, he loved it. And then to have it dismissed by the press was upsetting for us and obviously Morrissey. But I believe that if work has a timeless quality, or a real quality, it will surface in the end.

J: Which of the songs you co-wrote or played on with Morrissey is your favourite?

K: 'Yes I Am Blind', which is an Andy Rourke song. I really like that song, it's lovely and moving.

J: Did you ever get a chance to perform live together?

K: No, we never did a gig together.

J: Tell me about your day-to-day relationship/ conversations with Morrissey when you were working together.

K: He's one of those creatures that one works with that are so feted for what they do. Because he's famous, people want things from him, so there's always a slight distance kept. I did meet him briefly backstage at a gig he did with Boz, and we shook hands and said hello.

J: Have you heard from him since?

K: No. He doesn't keep in touch with me, I don't keep in touch with him, there was a minor communication to use some lyrics in a book somewhere where we both gave permission. I still get dribs and drabs of money from what we did together.

J: Do you keep in touch with Boz?

K: Weirdly enough one of my daughters is very friendly with one of his daughters, so I went to pick her up one day, opened the door and there was Boz, so we had a little chat.

J: You're friends with Mark Nevin too.

K: Yes. We worked with Sandie Shaw, and we have the Clive Langer connection, and I work with the drummer in Fairground sometimes, so Mark and I know each other. We send each other music sometimes, and I run into him in Café Rouge in Highgate.

J: That would be a collaboration I'm sure many people would be interested in hearing.

K: What? Me and Mark? It would, actually!

J: Yes! Let's make that happen. Put that band together.

M: Well, we'll remember it was your suggestion.

J: If Morrissey rang your doorbell now, and said 'All right, Kevin?' what would you say?

K: I'd say, 'Come in and have a cup of coffee!'

J: What kind of snacks would you put out for him?

K: Well, I know he's not averse to rich foods, because I remember at Hook End he had employed Princess Margaret's personal chef or something, who came and cooked. We thought, 'Oh, great, we'll have vegetarian healthy food,' and she cooked the richest food, with cream and pastry and all this stuff. It was nice, but rich and heavy. Everything was like a Sunday lunch— 'Everyday Was Like a Sunday Lunch!'

J: Did you sit and eat together?

K: Yes, we all ate meals together. It was really nice, good banter. One of the people who was there was Andrew Paresi, an old friend of mine; we worked with Sandie Shaw together. The mealtimes were interesting with Andrew and Morrissey there, as Andrew was a little bit in love with Morrissey, idolised him, and Andy Rourke was there too. I like Andy tremendously. Seen him once or twice with Primal Scream.

J: Are you a vegetarian?

K: No, I'm not, my wife is and she cooks vegetarian at home, but if I go out I'll eat meat.

J: Would you describe your guitar style as 'pop'?

K: Yes. Essentially I am a pop musician, although I have worked with some people on the very left side of pop, like Bowie and Iggy and Morrissey [points to my *Bona Drag*] who are not particularly mainstream acts. And Thomas [Dolby]—more slightly maverick artists. That's what I'm drawn to.

J: You have worked with an incredible amount of artists. Do you only work with people whose music you like?

K: Just by accident! I'm not trying to tell you that I handpicked everybody, it's just that's what's happened. And it's what they need from me too. I've just been on an American tour with Thomas Dolby, and recently with Sinead O'Connor, and I look back and think 'How have I achieved this consistency of quality people that I've worked with?'And the answer is: 'I don't know!'

J: Did you enjoy doing 'Dancing in the Street' with Mick Jagger and David Bowie?

K: Oh yes, massive thrill to work in the studio with these legends. That was in the same room as I did my stuff with Morrissey. Rick Wakeman and Julien Temple were in there. All sorts of great people were in those sessions.

J: You seem like you're not too 'affected' by your success—like you still enjoy and appreciate being in the company of the big names.

K: I still have a sense of wonder about it, and I wonder how all my life I've been 'allowed' to do it. But I don't think I'll ever lose the sense that, 'Isn't this fun, and aren't I lucky?'

J: Who would you like to work with that you haven't worked with before?

K: Well, I always thought I'd like to work with Van Morrison, from a musical point of view. But from what people tell me he sounds a bit scary, and I would have liked to work with Captain Beefheart or Frank Zappa or one of those geniuses. I don't think I would have been good enough in either of those instances. But I can honestly sit here and say that I've got to play with some greats; some amazing people, whether it be on a TV show for five minutes or in the studio.

J: Do you literally just get a phone call: 'Kevin, we need you to play with Superstar X today?'

K: Yes, that's what used to happen, especially in the 1980s after working with David Bowie on Live Aid—my one big lucky break that led to all the phone calls. I got a call from EMI saying,

'Take your guitar along and play a session with Mr X—you won't regret it, he'll be there at eleven o'clock.' That was David Bowie. Luckily, I managed to turn that opportunity into an on/off ten-year association. After Live Aid, everybody wanted to know.

J: How did Live Aid happen?

K: It was as a direct consequence of working on 'Absolute Beginners'. I helped him finish it in an Abbey Road session, and then on the same day we did 'Dancing in the Street', but between those sessions he called me and said 'I've been asked to do this charity gig, and it's going to be a big deal. Do you want to put a band together with me?'

J: Blimey.

K: I had no idea how big that would be until the morning of Live Aid. Thomas Dolby was involved in that too ... my old girlfriend Clare Hirst from The Belle Stars, and Neil Conti from Prefab Sprout. When the morning came, London was quiet.

J: What was it like, walking out on stage?

K: We were bouncing about like idiots. Beforehand, we had hovered over the stadium in a helicopter and that was really brilliant. I got a lot of offers after that.

J: Any that you turned down?

K: I turned down Level 42.

J: Would you sign my albums and answer questions about your favourite things?

K: Of course!

J: What's your favourite drink?

K: Mojito

J: Favourite guitar?

K: Fender Telecaster. I'm a huge Telecaster nut now.

J: Crisp flavour?

K: Salt and vinegar.

J: Smith?

K: Andy Rourke. I'm a fan of the accompanist. I worked with him and he's a nice guy.

J: Favourite childhood toy?

K: Airfix Slot car set. I loved it. They made racing tracks, really fiddly, had to put copper contacts together. The cars were great. I had enough to cover the garden in it.

J: Not Stretch Armstrong?

K: No.

J: Favourite biscuit?

K: I don't eat wheat, so all biscuits give me the chills.

J: Is that through choice or are you intolerant?

K: I find it best for my digestion. But I was a fan of chocolate Hobnobs.

J: So you don't have toast?

K: I don't. I sometimes have rye bread.

J: Favourite song of all time?

K: Jeff Buckley, 'Last Goodbye'. I sometimes play old Roy Orbison songs. My favourite is 'Song to the Siren' by Tim Buckley. Liz Fraser does a striking version. Very, very sad. Hopelessly romantic. I'm attracted to melancholic music.

J: Favourite gig that you played?

K: It has to be Live Aid. I enjoy Thomas Dolby

and Iggy Pop gigs as well.

J: Favourite pizza topping?

K: Pepperoni. Meat is lovely.

J: Could you write a note to my mum?

K: Okay then!

J: I'd love to have a listen to what you're working on now.

K: I'll play you some bits if you like.

J: Yes, please!

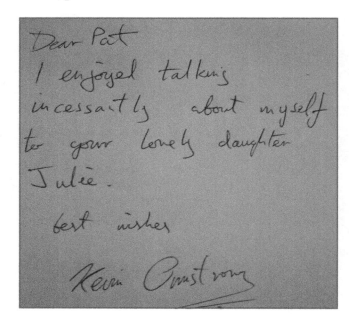

Dear Pat
I enjoyed talking incessantly about myself to your lonely daughter Julie.
best wishes
Kevin Armstrong

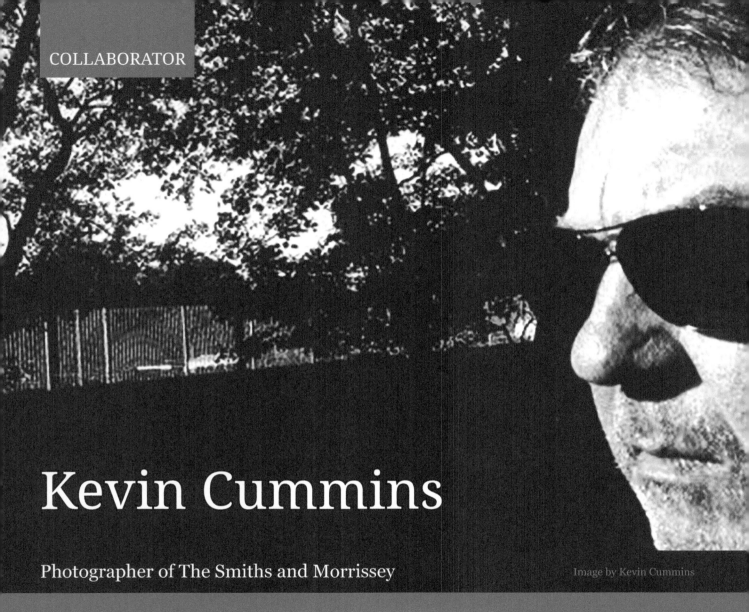

Kevin Cummins

Photographer of The Smiths and Morrissey

15 MINUTES
WITH YOU

AS Kevin Cummins—photography icon—arrives to meet me at The Regent pub in Balham, it suddenly strikes me how much he looks like one of his own shots: a dishevelled grey mane, a cool grey/black jacket and arty T-shirt, a square silver ring with 'love' and 'hate' on both sides, and a chunky bike chain bracelet hanging heavy on his wrist. It would be easy to mistake him for a rock star, or indeed a 19th century poet, as he *personifies* black and white, both in appearance and in his plain spoken, factual and fascinating delivery.

His work is instantly recognisable because it has that distinctive 'brand of Cummins'—black/white/grey, urban, with a nod to the rain clouds of Manchester. Sunny LA was too bright: *'I had to wait till about seven in the evening before the light was manageable for me. I was only used to working in dusk and greys.'* On taking pictures of 'Mr Morrissey' (as he calls him), he reveals that Morrissey is an exceptionally creative subject: *'He has lots of ideas, that's why he's good to work with'*; loves being photographed: *'he's happy to have his picture taken from dawn till dusk'* and has an *'element of tease'* to his character.

He showed me some shots from his 'Manchester: So Much to Answer For' collection, and each one has its own story that captures a crucial/poignant or humorous moment in time. There's a fantastic one of Andy Rourke with his head in his hands on hearing of a possible band split, another one of Johnny Marr and an old man passing by—showing the expression on Johnny's face as he wills the old man to 'hurry up'. There are several beauties of Morrissey—one that I love of him leaning out of a bus, smiling, which Kevin calls his 'Charles Hawtrey moment'.

Cummins has the initial air of someone who might be antisocial, a bit gruff and miserable; but in fact he is loveable, funny and strangely calming. I could have listened to his best-seller fireside celebrity storytelling all day … but his car was on a meter (and he didn't like the way I was holding onto his trouser leg).

He loves The Smiths, Corrie and Deirdre Barlow's chain belts, and his brother cheats at *Cluedo*. He drank Guinness when we met. Well, it's black and white, isn't it?

J: Please say your full name.

K: Kevin Cummins.

J: Have you got any middle names?

K: Not that I use.

J: Can you describe yourself in a sentence?

K: Professionally? Photographer and Man City fan.

J: You talk about Man City a lot on Twitter.

K: It's because I don't tend to like talking about personal stuff too much, and it's a great forum for talking to people about football, and I don't live in Manchester, so it's my way of dealing with it instead of going to the local pub. Whenever I try and talk about photography people say 'Oh shut up, talk about football instead.'

J: Were you a fan of The Smiths before you started working with them?

K: Oh yeah. I find it difficult working with bands I don't like. It becomes a job if you do that. I had seen The Smiths a few times and thought they were great.

J: How did you end up working with them?

K: Well. I guess when I studied photography I went to a lot of gigs. I fell into it really, I never thought working with musicians would make me a living. It was just something I did because I wanted to go to gigs free when I was a student. I used to take the empty college camera case to the gig, and after I got in a couple of times I thought 'Well, I'll put a camera in it.' In those days they didn't have backstage passes, so I turned up and got let in because they thought I was from the *Manchester Evening News* or something.

J: Which bands did you photograph at those gigs?

K: Most of the Factory bands. I worked for Factory - without being paid – just like most people who worked for Factory. Then I was asked to photograph The Smiths for an *NME* cover. Most of my stuff is quite urban, I felt it important to locate people within a city, but with The Smiths, because it was a softer sound, I didn't see the point in putting them against brick walls and steel and all the elements of the industrial town, so we went out to a park. There's a lovely shot of Morrissey lying with his hands out, and I wanted that to be the cover, and when they were looking through the shots, the features editor wasn't a big fan of The Smiths and he decided at the last minute that they were not going to be big enough to put on the cover of the *NME* and he put Big Country on instead.

J: Oh no! Did you ever shoot Big Country?

K: Yes I did, only one proper session in Belfast, and it was absolutely hurling it down. Any time and anywhere it rained on shoots I was always blamed, being from Manchester. I shot them under an umbrella.

J: What do you do in that situation? Presumably a great picture needs 'amazing light'?

K: Not at all! If you needed amazing light, you'd never get a good picture in Manchester. You have to work with what's there. The first time I went to LA to do a shoot I couldn't cope with the light—it was far too bright. I had to wait till about seven in the evening before the light was manageable for me. I was only used to working in dusk and greys.

J: What's your style of working with musicians?

K: I don't tend to impose myself on people too much, I let them do what they want and then I start to work around them. I'm always interested to see what they want and how they respond to each other at first. So rather than say 'Right,

I've got this great idea, I want you all to do this' I'll just say, 'Right, what do you all want to do?' Bands tend not to have ideas. Morrissey has lots of ideas, that's why he's good to work with, because you can channel that in different ways. And he does like having his picture taken—from dawn til dusk—so you can get a lot of variety out of the session.

J: Can you describe the working relationship inside The Smiths? What were they like, as four lads together?

K: I think they were still finding their way; it was very raw and fresh. It was interesting the way they lined up, exactly as they would onstage, with Morrissey right in the centre, Mike behind him and Andy and Johnny either side, so that's how they think. I moved them around a bit and did single shots.

J: Morrissey seems really happy when you take his picture, there's a certain smile in a lot of your shots.

K: There is a connection, an element of tease when you work with Morrissey.

J: Yes, 'tease'—that's it—a look, a glint, a slight smile. How do you get him to do that, or does he just do it himself?

K: I get people to connect with me rather than the camera. It's quite hard breaking down that barrier. But if you do get time with somebody they start responding to you and not the camera. We used to go away on *NME* trips and go to the States for four or five days with a band, and you really don't need to be photographing all that time. So the first couple of days I'd just observe them to see what the dynamic was, and for them to get used to me being part of that group. And once you bring the camera out, there's no intimidation there, and they still respond to you as part of that group. When you look at Morrissey in those pictures he's looking at you— and that's because he's looking at me rather than at the lens.

J: What's your relationship like with him?

K: Morrissey has the reputation of being difficult to work with and I think that's because he's very single-minded and he knows what he wants, but so do I and so do a lot of people. I'm not interested in going along and taking a photograph and have everything set up for me; you may as well take your own photos. I like the picture to be how I want to craft it. There's

no point in asking me or another photographer who has a strong style to do it. Having said that, Morrissey has lots of ideas and you can say, 'I don't think that's going to work,' and show it to him later. When I did my *Manchester* book, the Faber book, I got a very nice note from Morrissey and he was on the cover.

J: What did the note say?

K: He told me how much he enjoyed it, and as he was writing his book, he had been able to check a couple of dates in my book!

J: What is the most unusual idea that you've composed with Morrissey?

K: There are accidents that happen when you take pictures. He wanted me to do some pictures while we were in Cologne. He was lying on the steps of this railway bridge, and while he's lying there in quite a contorted position this little kid walks past and just looks at him, really puzzled, wondering if he's dead. And I got a before and after, and I did a similar thing with Johnny.

J: Is it Johnny with the old man?

K: Yes! We were doing pictures around locations where The Smiths had been photographed, a big piece for the *NME* about the aftermath of the break-up, a two-parter. I was photographing him outside Albert Finney's dad's bookies in Salford and I had one frame left in the camera as this old guy was walking towards us, so I thought, well, I won't shoot until he's gone. But he was taking so *long* to walk towards us I thought it would make a really good shot, so I waited for the perfect moment, and Johnny looked at the guy as if to say 'Will you *please* hurry up?' and as I was looking at Johnny I didn't see the expression of the old guy, but it was perfect.

J: It is a wonderful shot.

K: We thought he was going to die before he got to the edge of the frame. He had no idea he was part of a lovely image.

J: How do you, as the photographer, deal with it when bands fall out?

K: I never become the band's best friend and always maintain a working relationship. I've never invited myself round for Sunday lunch; I just carry on and get on with it.

J: I love your ring. Who designed it? [Shows me his square ring that says 'Love' and 'Hate' on it.]

K: Stephen Webster.

J: It's fantastic. Better take it back before I slip it in my pocket. Did you ever eat dinner with The Smiths?

K: I ate with Morrissey in Japan. He just got them to make him egg and chips every day.

J: Fried egg?

K: I think a range of eggs, actually.

J: Was it a runny yolk or a hard yolk?

K: No idea. I couldn't have sat there if it was that runny. I'm not a fan of runny eggs. I suspect it wasn't too runny. I'm not sure Japanese eggs lend themselves to runny yolks anyway.

J: When was the last time you photographed Morrissey?

K: Probably about 1995, and Johnny Marr probably a year or so ago in some pictures when he was in The Cribs, then some pictures of his hands as well. I'm doing guitarists' hands.

J: I love the sound of that. Will it be an exhibition?

K: Yeah, I hope so, but no magazines like it, they don't understand it.

J: They are clearly idiots. I'd like to see it if you feel like sharing it.

K: I'll show it to you.
[Kevin shows me the collection of photographs at the end of the interview. I am struck by how inelegant guitarists' hands are. Quite stubby and often tattooed fingers. However, I now know that Johnny Marr bites his nails and wears blue nail polish.]

J: So you don't keep in touch with Morrissey now?

K: I sent him a book, and he sent me a bag of Morrissey CDs, some limited editions as well.

J: If Morrissey walked into this pub right now and said, 'All right, Kevin?' what would you say?

K: I'd say, 'It's your round.'

J: What if he came round your house—what snacks would you put out for him?

K: I probably wouldn't let him in.

J: You must! It's raining outside. He's banging on the window: 'Kevin! Are you in? Kevin?'

K: He'd probably prefer to stay in the rain.

J: He has a key. He gets in. What snacks do you put out for him?

K: I wouldn't make any special effort, he'd have to just root and see what's in the cupboards. Nobody comes round my house. I don't invite them. I don't like having people round.

J: Were there ever any football conversations on the split in the band re: Man U vs Man City?

K: No, not back in The Smiths days. I do talk to Johnny quite a bit about football.

J: Do you still see Johnny?

K: Yeah. I could have seen him recently—he was up at City but I didn't have time. We bump into each other occasionally, email and things.

J: You've got an amazing collection of work with artists on your website portfolio – the Happy Mondays, David Bowie, Joy Division … Aside from Morrissey, I love the shots of Bjork and John Lydon. Have you got any personal favourites?

K: A lot, actually—it's difficult to single one picture out. I've got one photograph of my own at home. I swap pictures with other photographers. I have one picture of mine in the house, a picture of Richey Edwards covered in Marilyn Monroe stamps.

J: You have a book coming out about the Manic Street Preachers.

K: Yeah, it's very limited edition, 250 copies. I've interviewed James Dean Bradfield for it. It's about the iconography of the band.

J: Did you talk about Richey?

K: Not really, a little bit about how they felt. I wanted to talk more specifically about why they used that kind of graphics, quotes, cut-outs. There's a broad range of pictures in there.

J: Is there anybody you'd like to shoot but you haven't yet?

K: I'd like to photograph Rufus Wainwright. I really like him, I think he's really interesting.

J: Can you just get in touch with them and say 'I'm Kevin Cummins and I'd like to take your picture?'

K: It's never that easy, really; you'd think it would be. I mean, you can do that with some people, but it's all a bit too controlled these days, not like it was in the late 80s, when I had more time with people. A lot of bands take their own pictures now, on their iPhones, so they don't think they need anybody there, but they do. That's the difference between photographs and pictures. A photograph is well crafted, has a certain learning behind it, you know. We could both take a picture in here and it would be very different. We'd see things differently.

J: Shall we do it?

K: Nah.

J: We could have a competition?

K: Nah.

J: Righto.

K: The working title for my book *Looking for the Light in the Pouring Rain* was *My big book of my favourite pictures*. The thing is, photographs are like my diaries, really, I look at those and I can remember how I was feeling. There are a lot of people I've photographed who died very young; it just reminds me of good and bad times. There are pictures that resonate for different reasons. The picture I've had to talk about most of all recently is the Stone Roses covered in paint. I'm living with it at the moment.

J: I noticed your pictures of Courtney Love. She seems like an interesting character.

K: Yeah, I liked her a lot. Very complex. She was very happy to have her picture taken as well. We got on well, and we got a lot of pictures in a short burst. I arranged to meet her at 4 p.m. and it was 2 a.m. when she eventually turned up. You can't have a strop and walk off; if you work with musicians you have to work to their time. They're not being disrespectful … I think that's the nature of the job, really, sitting waiting and reading.

J: What do you read?

K: My favourite author when I was at school was Graham Greene. I like Paul Auster.

J: Any favourite Smiths and Morrissey singles?

K: Yes, lots, but all the remastered stuff that came out recently was really great. There's a Morrissey and Vini Reilly outtake of 'I Know Very Well How I Got My Name' and they just crack up halfway through and it's called 'I Know Very Well How I Got My Note Wrong', I love that. 'Everyday is Like Sunday' will always be a cracking record. I like most of The Smiths, I always change my mind. I love 'How Soon is Now?' but it's usually 'Heaven Knows I'm Miserable Now' especially after a football match. I've also been listening to Spanish cover versions, which are astonishing. I listened to it for three hours in the car. It was hard going, but worth it for the version of 'Some Girls Are Bigger Than Others' where at the end the singer just goes: 'Oh, who cares!'

J: What's your favourite song of all time?

K: 'True Faith' by New Order. When we have to do compilations for the car or are off to a football match it's always on there. That track always stands out. 'Come By Sunday', by Diana Dors, is also a great song.

J: Is that the song you would play if you were at a party and you needed to get it going?

K: Depends on the party; you'd have to tailor it to the crowd.

J: You'd have to let them in your house first, as well.

K: I wouldn't have a party at home. No.

J: What's your favourite childhood toy?

K: I was never very fond of toys. I always wanted books; my mum taught me to read before I went to school. The first thing I remember being bought that wasn't a book was a camera. My dad bought me a camera for my sixth birthday. He was a keen amateur photographer with a darkroom/cupboard under the stairs. I loved the smell of all the chemistry. I took my own pictures on a trip to London then processed and printed them myself. I liked board games. I'm really boring, aren't I?

J: No! My favourite toy was *Monopoly*.

K: That's not really a toy though, is it?

J: You'd find it in a toy shop.

K: You would find it in a toy shop, but you'd also find a bloke behind the counter with a cat.

J: Yes, but he's not for sale. Or is he? Unless he's a cuddly toy cat. How about *Scrabble*?

K: I don't really like 'showing off' games.

J: *Mousetrap*?

K: Didn't like that. I liked *Monopoly* and *Cluedo*.

J: Yes I can see you with *Cluedo*.

K: Yeah. My board has a dent and a tear in the middle of it where I smacked my brother over the head because he was cheating.

J: Did he look in the envelope?

K: He just cheated! There's no need to cheat at board games, or there's no point in playing.

J: Is he younger or older than you?

K: Younger.

J: Favourite crisp flavour?

K: Again, I don't really like crisps. They're a bit greasy, but, if you forced me to eat a bag I'd have salt and vinegar.

J: I just can't wait to hear what your favourite biscuit is.

K: [long pause]. Now this is going to sound pretentious, but Waitrose do these fantastic biscuits that are an accompaniment to wine and they have four flavours, one for red, white, rose and champagne.

J: They sound great. What are they called, 'Winos biscuits'?

K: Mondovino or something ludicrous.

J: Favourite pizza topping?

K: Margarita with half the amount of cheese ... Napoli-style with Tabasco on.

J: Red or green Tabasco?

K: Red. Not the green junior one! I don't really eat wheat anymore, but sometimes I'll have the biscuits, but then if you have the biscuits you've got to have the wine. If I get a pizza to watch the football, occasionally I'll cut some tomatoes and some chilli and put that on as well. Pimpin' my pizza.

J: So what colour wine do you buy to go with the biscuits?

K: I like white burgundy, Merlot, wine from anywhere in France. And champagne.

J: Your house sounds magic! Wine, biscuits, pizza. I don't know why you don't let people in. What's your favourite holiday destination?

K: Oh, um, Mexico City. If it was closer. I like cities rather than beaches. I like the south of France and most of Spain. Two hours is far enough to go.

J: Did you ever visit Morrissey when he was in LA?

K: No. We went to Rome to see him once; that was nice.

J: Have you seen him live recently?

K: I saw him at The Palladium (2011).

J: I was there too. I wasn't happy with the bouncers.

K: No, that was terrible, brutal. It's odd. Maybe they were being protective of *The Wizard of Oz* set or something.

J: The Wizard of Moz! Favourite TV show?

K: *Coronation Street*. I only Sky Plus two things, that's Corrie and *Match of the Day*.

J: Who's your favourite Corrie character?

K: Varies.

J: Mine is Norris.

K: I hate Norris.

J: Oh.

K: I photographed Coronation Street for the cover of the *NME* on their 25th birthday. I spent a day there and photographed Deirdre, Elsie, Ken … We interviewed Pat Phoenix, she was great. I went to Manchester recently and had my picture taken with Deirdre. It was a highlight, actually.

J: I like Deirdre's belts.

K: I commented on her belts, actually.

J: Your bracelet would make a good belt design for Deirdre.

K: I did say to her, 'I'm really disappointed you're not wearing your chain belt,' and she said, 'Oh, it's just the character that wears that.' I said, 'We want to interview in character,' and she said, 'My brother's in a band and I've brought you a cassette to listen to.'

J: Favourite film?

K: *King of Comedy*.

J: Favourite actor?

K: Nick Sidi. He's in the next series of *DCI Banks*. He's very good. Normally plays perverts, but this time he's playing a DC. He's usually got sandals with socks when he plays theatrical roles. At his request.

J: Does he pull the socks right up or fold them over?

K: Pulled up, and beige. Socks and sandals is a good look.

J: Favourite Smith?

K: ALL of them.

J: Can you write a note to my mum?

K: Yeah, what's her name?

J: Pat.

K: Does she like football?

J: She likes Celtic. And *Coronation Street*.

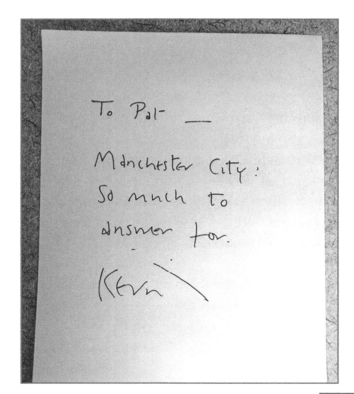

This is my favourite Morrissey shot. What I like about it is that it has elements of Northern-ness and it could be a still from *Room at the Top* or of any period. The cobbles, the Iron Bridge, and Morrissey in silhouette. It could only be Morrissey. He is so distinctive and so rare. It's like a brand for Manchester. It's iconic.

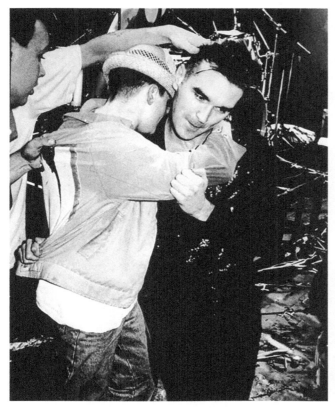

This is my favourite live shot from the first solo gig at Wolverhampton. I just like the way they are holding onto each other. There are two stewards trying to separate them without it looking aggressive or anything. It's just a very tender moment, I think. Also, when you shoot live, being on the stage is quite a privilege because you get to feel what they are feeling when you see thousands of fans just screaming. And it was special because it was the first gig they had done. It was really a Smiths gig without Johnny.

Morrissey's hands—that was the shot for the first *NME* cover. As a photograph it works perfectly, I like the slant, the angle, the whole framing of it, it would have made a brilliant *NME* cover to launch the band.

Dickie Felton

Author of *The Day I Met Morrissey* and *Morrissey International Airport*

15 MINUTES WITH YOU

WHAT would you say to Morrissey if you got the chance to meet him? How about this:

'Er, Morrissey, er, how's it going?'

Morrissey: 'Oh, it's not too bad.'

Dickie Felton is one of the fortunate fans who have had a chance to meet Morrissey—six times—and he has written a book about others who have done the same. *The Day I Met Morrissey* 'contains real-life accounts from fans who for a split second found themselves in the right place at the right time' (Dickie Felton, 2009). Fan encounters include a chance meeting at the pic'n'mix at Woolworths, seeing Morrissey dragging a suitcase at a train station, and parents putting their child on stage in Atlanta (Morrissey picked her up and hugged her).

I went to the St Pancras Hotel in London to chat to Dickie, and he gave me one of his books. After we parted, I read it cover to cover in an afternoon. It's part 'Louis Theroux investigates' and part 'Smash Hits! I met my hero!' and being an avid fan of both I found I just couldn't put the book down. I was fascinated by the stories. It's a vicarious read, because these are ordinary people that managed to meet Morrissey and talk to him. Who hasn't wondered what *they'd* say to Morrissey, given the chance? There aren't many books about the fans. Dickie's book is different, because it's *us*. This genuinely lovely, big-hearted Scouser does an amazing job of celebrating the unique and devoted Morrissey fan in his book, and of course gives great insight into what Morrissey is really like during those chance encounters.

His new book *Morrissey International Airport* (2012) focuses on the people who have travelled extensively to follow Morrissey around a series of twelve dates in the UK, Europe and America. *'So many people travel through airports, B & Bs, trains … It's the travels of a pop star and his people.'* He recognises that the community of Morrissey fans are very special: *'A lot of people go [to concerts] on their own … I don't know any other band where you could do that;'* and very warm: *'I have met so many nice people over the years, who have gone on to be really close friends.'*

Felton is a man of no frills. He likes plain crisps, *Rich Tea* biscuits and a pint of *Sam Adams*.

J: Please say your full name.

D: Richard Philip Felton, and I'm not sure if it's one 'l' or two 'l's in Philip. On my passport it's one l but on my birth certificate its spelt with two l's. God knows, I'll get confirmation off my parents. Only this week my mum revealed that she called me Philip after Prince Philip! I was devastated!

J: Please describe yourself in a sentence, Dickie.

D: Father to Frankie, husband to Jen, vegetarian, Moz fan, runner and PR guy.

J: Is that your job?

D: Yes. I am the Communications Manager at National Museums Liverpool. My background is PR.

J: How did you get into The Smiths/Morrissey?

D: It was 1988, and I was living in North Liverpool in a semi-detached house. The girl next door used to have her windows open and the music would be blaring out. It was The Smiths and Morrissey—'Ask', 'Suedehead'. So I just went round, knocked on her door and said, 'What on earth is that music?' She said, 'its The Smiths, but they've only just split up'. I was gutted. I borrowed all of her records and bought *Viva Hate*. I have always been a much bigger fan of Morrissey solo than I have been of The Smiths. I was there the very day all the singles came out, I love the solo stuff.

J: How would you describe Morrissey fandom?

D: It's like following a football team. You can go watch Liverpool or Celtic, week in week out, or you can go watch Morrissey. It's exactly the same. And you don't know what you'll get during a match, like a Morrissey gig.

J: Tell me what happened when you met Morrissey.

D: He has always been very nice to me. But the first time was at a 1994 signing session for Vauxhall and I, I made a complete fool of myself. In fact, every time I've met Moz I've said the wrong things.

D: In 1994 I said, 'Hi Morrissey, how are you doing?' and then I gave him a Liverpool Football Club badge and he looked at me rather bizarrely and said, 'Oh, thanks.' The next time was at the Lowry Hotel in Manchester, the night before his appearance at Manchester Move festival. Somebody spotted him by the lift and I just ran over.

J: What was he wearing?

D: He was wearing a red shirt and a really nice jacket and jeans. I said to him, 'The tour is so amazing, it's a fantastic tour,' and he said: 'It's not that good, Dickie.' I then said, 'We love 'Let me kiss you" and again he said, 'It's not that good, Dickie.' And then I said, 'We can't wait until Sunday night. It's going to be amazing.' And he said, 'It's not going to be that good, Dickie.' Then in 2007 outside the concert hall in the Royal Oak, Michigan, he was getting off a tour bus pre-gig and I said, 'Hi, Moz—it's Dickie from Liverpool. Will you sign my arm for a tattoo?' and he did. Then in 2009 on the pier in Great Yarmouth. I had *The Day I Met Morrissey* book with me—it had just come out. I handed it to him. He flicked through it as we walked and he signed my copy, which was great. During the gig he said something like, 'Where's Dickie Felton?' He passed me the microphone during that night's gig and we had a bit of a chat.

J: What did you say into the mic?

D: It wasn't long after the Hillsborough anniversary, so I said 'Justice for the 96.' I also asked him what he thought of the book. He said, 'I think it's very attractive.' I was so made up after that. I have vowed that if I see him again I won't approach him, because it's like ... what else is there to say?

J: I like that you have taken the angle of devotees for your book. Why did you do that?

D: I have always been fascinated by Morrissey fans. I have been going to Morrissey gigs since 1991. I love the culture of what they wear, how they dress ... just always fascinating, seeing these stylish vegetarians. I have met so many nice people over the years, who have gone on to be really close friends. I only started chatting to a lad on my first day at university because he was wearing a Moz T-shirt - twenty years later he was one of the best men at my wedding.

J: Have you ever met anyone who is associated with Morrissey? Boz? Johnny, Mike?

D: I have met Boz Boorer. I think everybody has had a couple of pints with Boz. I ended up back in a hotel with him once after a Moz gig. We had a couple of pints, me and a few other fans at The Silver Birch hotel in Omagh. They had been to a special kind of Moz night in the town centre called 'Top of the Town'. Boz Boorer and his friend Kevin Kelly and Jessie Tobias and a load of fans. They had guitars out, singing songs, all joining in. It was one of these magical nights that nobody wanted to end. Amazingly, Morrissey was a few yards away—sound asleep on the tour bus!

J: What were they drinking?

D: Just drinking lagers, I think. There was this little waiter who kept disappearing and bringing out all these beers because the bar was shut. We stayed up till four or five in the morning. The next day was on to see another Moz gig in Belfast. I had to get up and get a bus. I felt horrendous. But I went and did it all again. I went on my own to those gigs, but I'd never go and see any other band on my own, just Morrissey. Loads of people go on their own. You always meet people who are going from place to place. I like to see who I bump into. I have met loads of crazy people, too. I went to Inverness on my own, met a lad on the 9.21 am. train from Inverness to Dunoon, he was also doing the tour. So I went with him again to see Morrissey in Texas. I don't know any other band that you could go and see and do that.

J: How many gigs have you been to?

D: I've kinda lost count now, but it's in the seventies.

J: Tell me about *Morrissey International Airport*.

D: In the new book—*Morrissey International Airport*—fandom reaches the next level, exploring those who give up their jobs to make following Morrissey their life. I met one girl in Inverness by the stage door and she was from California. She was in Britain for a fortnight just following the Morrissey tour. I was like, 'You must be looking forward to seeing some sights of the UK,' but she was only interested in the tour; she said, 'All I'm going to do in the next two weeks is get to the venue and wait outside, get down the front rail to get a handshake. And if I get one handshake, it will be worth it.' I really look up to people who queue up for all that time.

J: What has been your favourite gig of all?

D: Great Yarmouth in 2009 I mentioned was amazing, because he said, 'Where's Dickie Felton?' And I managed to get on stage during the last song and get a handshake very briefly, to 'First of the Gang to Die'. That was special, but one of the best gigs was at Dublin Castle in 2004 at an open air gig, small venue, it was nice weather and it was a great gig. There have been so many.

J: Any unusual fan stories in the new book?

D: I met Jamie Skelton, the lad from Leeds, in Inverness. I was having a drink with Jamie at the bar in Inverness and we saw these girls with Morrissey T-shirts on. We beckoned them over and started chatting about Morrissey, and found out that they were on a hen do! And the hen do was the Morrissey tour! The T-shirts on the back were like: 'Hen party on Tour/Morrissey'. They had done two stages of a hen party, one of them was somewhere else and the second part was the Morrissey tour. Only two of them had remained for the gigs. That was the first hen do I've met at a Morrissey gig. There was also a fan—Tom— who I met on the Texas dates in November; he'd customised his car especially for the tour.

J: What's your favourite Smiths and Morrissey song?

D: Smiths is 'Stop Me If You Think You've Heard This One Before' and Morrissey is 'Suedehead'. That's my favourite song of all time.

J: What was the first song at your wedding?

D: We played six songs at the wedding, one of which was 'Please Please Please Let Me Get What I Want'.

J: Ah!

D: It was nice for Morrissey to be involved. What about yourself?

J: 'William, It Was Really Nothing' was ours. We hand-picked the first ten songs. It's one of the early Smiths songs that got me hooked, and it has always been a most uplifting song for me. If I ever feel down, it picks me right up. Literally, as soon as it begins, it's like a breath of fresh air every time. If Morrissey was to walk in here right now, to this hotel, and say, 'All right, Dickie?' what would you say to him?

D: I'd probably run a mile.

J: You would not! You have spoken to him before.

D: I know, but it would just be terrible, I'd be like, 'Great weather we're having, Moz.' Terrible banter. I'd probably talk about the new Liverpool FC manager and watch his eyes roll up to the sky and be like, 'Is that all you can ask me?' Thing is that I've got a million things that I'd love to ask him, from vinyls, to sleeves ...

J: Well, now's your chance.

D: I'd probably ask him about the tough times, through not having managers or record deals or being attacked by the media. There must have been times where he felt pretty low—I'd love to know how he bounces back, every time, like the phoenix from the flames. I think there's a great story there for anybody who has been through the mill in whatever form. I'd like to know how he manages to carry on, when it might have been easier to hide away.

J: That's a great question. If you and Jen were to have him round your house, what snacks would you put out for him?

D: Plain crisps. Olives. Hummus and pita, carrot sticks. Glass of champagne. Some veggie scouse!

J: Sounds perfect! Would you sign my copy of your book?

D: Of course. My other book, *Morrissey International Airport* is really a travel book based around a dozen Morrissey dates. So many people travel through airports, B & Bs, trains to follow him ... It's the travels of a pop star and his people.

J: What's your favourite drink?

D: I like beer. Sam Adams. I like tea, but I'll go with Sam Adams.

J: Favourite pudding?

D: I'm not really a dessert man. But I like ice cream.

J: What flavour?

D: Vanilla.

J: Plain crisps and vanilla? You're a riot!

D: I have very simple tastes in food!

J: What's your favourite thing your mum says?

D: When she calls me Richard! I know I'm in trouble. When she talks to my dad, 'Tony! Tony! Tony! Look what he's done now! Tony!' My dad is the most mellow guy on earth. He'd be like, 'He can do what he wants, he's forty!'

J: What's the best thing about being a dad?

D: Lots of things. It's just a joy these days. Every Saturday morning we go down the bus stop, and we wait for a double-decker. We get on the double-decker and sit down the front, get an all-day pass and go anywhere. Frankie likes 'double buses' and single-deckers. It'll be fun now because we'll get the train back to Liverpool. Transport with him is fantastic.

J: Favourite spread for toast?

D: Newly discovered honey—reasonably good for you, as well.

J: Favourite childhood toy?

D: A teddy bear called Sebastian.

J: Did you give him that name, or did he come with that name on a label?

D: My mother probably gave him that name.

J: He's a posh teddy bear.

D: My mother was going to call me Rupert! 'Rupert Felton' until my dad stepped in and said no way.

J: Here's Rupert, and his teddy, Sebastian …

D … In Liverpool! Can you imagine, in Liverpool? I would have got battered!

J: Your favourite lyric?

D: 'The sanest days are mad, why don't you find out for yourself?' I love that song.

J: Pizza topping?

D: Very boring. Cheese and onion.

J: Crisp flavour … Is it … Ready Salted?

D: Yes, plain.

J: TV show?

D: *Match of the Day.*

J: Biscuit?

D: I don't really like biscuits.

J: What is there not to like about biscuits?

D: I just don't really do 'em.

J: No biscuit? Nothing with your tea? Not even a Bourbon?

D: No. I'd maybe just have a plain Rich Tea.

J: Will you write a note to my mum?

D: That's fine. She supports Celtic as well, doesn't she? Is it Pat?

J: It is! Well done!

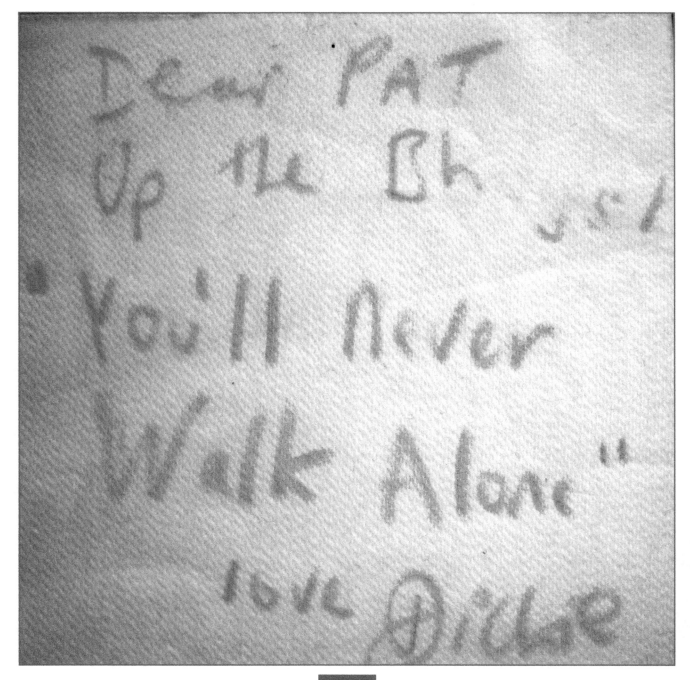

Shaun Keaveny

BBC6 Music DJ and Morrissey fan

15 MINUTES
WITH YOU

**I** FIRST met Shaun Keaveny at '6Fest' in 2010—an event held to celebrate the end of the news that BBC 6 Music station might be taken off the air. Shaun had put together his own band to perform (amongst other songs) 'There Is a Light' by The Smiths. It went down roaringly well, amongst some singalong, sympathy and laughter.

Shaun was in merry form throughout the evening. After the performance we chatted about music, his job and kids. After a good half hour it was getting late and I had to leave, so we bid our goodbyes and he shouted after me, 'Cheers, Julie! See you at work tomorrow, yeah?'

I waved back with a nervous smile, wondering if I should correct him, or if I should carry walking up the stairs. I didn't know whether to be happy that he thought I could be a cool person from 6 Music, or sad that he had no idea who I was. In true Keaveny style, on the tube home I imagined retelling this story, as a future guest on his show, and how we'd both laugh! (To date, this has not happened).

Four years on, his radio show is more popular than ever, with a great number of listeners. The listeners are completely involved with the show, and on most days they can dictate, distract and direct his agenda. Part of his brilliance is to make himself and the show out to be quite tragic, hopeless and useless, and to look for the listeners to save him: *'It's either genius broadcasting, which I doubt, or it's a deep-seated lack of confidence … half of what comes out of my mouth is what listeners have come up with.'* Through his interaction with the audience and his own tales of failed bike wheelies and middle-aged shout-outs, he has made himself one of the most unique broadcasters on the radio, as he chats through the airwaves like he's sitting beside you on the couch, unafraid to make a fool of himself, perfectly open and at home with who he is.

He man-cries at *DIY SOS* and his favourite crisp flavour is salt and vinegar. He likes coffee and walnut cake; he's a bit in love with Johnny Marr and early on he described our interview as 'a small death'.

J: Please say your full name.

S: I am Shaun William Keaveny.

J: Please describe yourself in a sentence.

S: I'm an incomplete person seeking completion.

J: And you're nearly forty.

S: At the time of going to press, I am six days short of forty.

J: Are you excited?

S: Excited is an interesting ... um ... I wouldn't say I'm 'excited', I'd say that I'm resigned to it, as the only alternative is death, so I might as well just roll with it. But I have it on good authority from people older than me that it's not all *that* bad.

J: It's not. I was forty in December. Do you feel better now?

S: How was it? I had you pegged for years off that.

J: The run up to it is actually worse than the turning. It's a bit like ripping off a plaster. Once you get to forty there's nothing you can do about it. The worst part is knowing that the next year you'll be forty-one, headed to fifty.

S: It sounds a lot older than forty, doesn't it? 'Fortyone.' Some ages are like that. Somebody else said that it's quite good because then you are in your 'early somethings' again for a while. The other one I enjoy is when you get told that you can't double it, so fifty—well, I'm not going to make a hundred, really, so at forty we can pretend that we're just at the halfway mark. I have been panicking about dying since I was five.

J: Oh. Have you put a lot of thought to dying, then?

S: I've been thinking about it, yes, and I'm thinking about it now. And I'll be thinking about it again, soon.

J: Is this because I'm interviewing you?

S: Yes. This interview is like a small death! I am quite a macabre person. If you worry about death a lot, it means you're enjoying your life. You don't want it to stop.

J: You enjoy your two boys, don't you, Arthur and Wilf?

S: Yeah! Arthur and Wilf. Wilfie. He's Wilfred, but for some reason it comes out as Wilfie, like Wolfie; we don't know why. Incredible things, children, aren't they? They put a spring in your step, stop you being too introspective.

J: Yes! And I know it's a cliché, but they do say the funniest things …

S: God, yeah, funnier than any adult human could ever be. The sad thing about being around kids is that you realise what life robs from children. Your ability to think like a kid is just taken from you slowly as you are expected to assume responsibility.

J: You've managed to keep a hold of your childish qualities, though.

S: What are you saying? I know, yeah, you're right, that's a great gift given to me by the cosmos.

J: Underneath your silliness you're really quite bright, aren't you? How many O levels have you got?

S: I'm not *that* old. It's GCSEs, actually. I was in the first year of GCSEs! I inhabit a weird world. I am not that kind of brash, filthily intellectual broadcaster (I won't name any names). On our station you've got your Gideon Coes, and your Lamacqs … you know, who are distinctly more cerebral.

J: Yes, I think they are musically intellectual though, aren't they? Lamacq in particular, he's, well … the 'Lamacq-apedia'

S: Oh yes, that's a good one. Write that down. I have his book somewhere. I realised recently that the reason I have *any* popularity is because I'm fallible.

J: Fallible?

S: Laughable, but fallible.

J: Lafallible.

S: I'm lafallible. It's annoying. It's a rod for my back as well as being a great thing.

J: But you have encouraged 'lafallibility' very much. You put yourself out there—'I apologise, the show is terrible today, keep up the work'—and you wholeheartedly encourage listeners to slag you off. It is very, very funny, but why do you do it?

S: It's difficult to know. It's either genius broadcasting, which I doubt, or it's a deep-seated lack of confidence, and that's why I do it. If I attack myself first, then nobody can hurt me after that ... I've noticed a lot of comedians do it. Maybe take their worst critic's quotes and put them out there. You are taking the weapon away from somebody. There's nothing more hurtful, no matter how long you've been doing your radio show, to come into work, at s*** o'clock to get some horrible email or text from somebody saying, 'You are a ...'

J: Do you still get that?

S: Yes! I've been doing this show for five years now.

J: I know. I enjoyed the celebratory Bowie.

S: Aww! Yeah! I can't wait to do that again in five years time ... Oh no, wait! That won't work ... 'Ten Years Gone', Led Zeppelin we'll play.

J: Your style of DJing is to lift the listeners up and celebrate the little things, like the positivity of seeing an orange car. If you come to work feeling a bit rotten or down, how does your mood affect the show?

S: The good thing about doing our kind of programme is that we are very open about everything. If we're all feeling low or tired, we usually try and make it part of the show in some weird way, try to get the listeners on board, hope that maybe some of you feel like that. You guys are brilliant at coming back with stuff, in fact you're all genius at it, so we can make an entire show that includes all your feedback.

J: You have straplines ... 'Keep up the work ...'

S: ... all created by the listeners. That's Woganerian. He is one of my life gurus. We've had him on the show once or twice. He'd come down and bring me a sandwich and sit and chat. People like him are the real benchmarks. People like (adopts Ken Bruce voice) 'Ken Bruce! Ken Bruce! Popmaster!'

J: Your impressions are very funny. Is it possible for you to say someone's name without doing their voice?

S: It is when I can't do an impression of them.

J: Your Samantha Jones is top. It's the whispery/sultry male-doing-female voice.

S: It's so wrong, isn't it? I am acutely aware of the fact that it pisses some people off that I have become inhabited by different characters. I know people who say 'Shut up, just play the music.' It's quite boring when you spend a lot of time on your own. Me, the microphone, texts and emails. I'm just mixing it up a bit. I enjoy it. I'm never going to do anything that I don't enjoy, because I'm forty.

J: Brian Cox features on your show every week ...

S: ... Taught him everything he knows.

J: Could you beat him in a pub quiz?

S: Yeah. Unless it was a pub quiz about physics.

J: No, it would be general—news round, sports round, music round, etc.

S: I think I would beat him. He's good on music and science. He's got two strong areas.

J: Is his music strong, really?

S: I suppose D:Ream weakens his position a bit.

J: Can you do an impression of him?

S: (adopts Cox voice) 'Yessss.' I texted him this morning. He texted back saying (does wispy voice), 'I'm in Madagascar. Trillions and trillions of degrees hot. Give me a call in an hour.' Then sent this massively long landline phone number. One of the things I love about the show—if you do it for long enough—is that you just get left to do stuff, and be terrible, and carry on being terrible until you're good. The BBC don't like change—in a good way. It's because of this that we have people who constantly crop up. Having Brian on the show now is like having Tom Cruise on the show, and he still loves it.

J: Do you think he is aware that he talks like that/smiles all the time?

S: Have you seen the spoof on YouTube? That is so funny. He is acutely aware of how parodied he is. I think he can laugh at it.

J: It's good that he has still got his feet on the ground ... while reaching for the stars...

S: ... Thanks to gravity.

J: Has Twitter changed the way that you work on the radio?

S: When I started it was just email. Before the technology existed I guess people just had: 'I've got letter here, from Marjorie …' We used to call people when I was at XFM. I did the X-List from 1-2 p.m. and took requests. I remember when texts came in, that was mind-blowing. We got texts all the time. The interactive element has revolutionised what we do, because our show is basically your show. Half of what comes out of my mouth is what listeners have come up with.

J: Do you enjoy Twitter?

S: When you get a minute it's nice to go in and have a look at the feed, because you always find some video or piece of music that you wouldn't have come across otherwise. I feel terrible when I don't get through the big stack of emails and tweets that we get. I carry that guilt.

J: Who's the genius that put 'Two Tribes' behind the features?

S: That was me.

J: It instantly improves any feature, no matter how bad. Can you bring back 'What's in your lunchbox'?

S: All these things are in an orbit. They come back around like Halley's Comet. It doesn't really matter what you call the feature, because the feature probably should be called 'Let's get a listener on and chat for a bit', because that's all it is. We dress it up with a name, but it's the same every time.

J: Let's talk about The Smiths.

S: Is this the reason we're here?

J: I know that you're a Smiths fan.

S: How do you know that?

J: I saw you murder 'There Is a Light' after twenty pints four years ago.

S: I am embarrassed to talk about The Smiths in your company and I was the same with Amy Lamé. You two are proper fans. I do love The Smiths. I love Morrissey and Marr in particular, and Joyce and Rourke. And I love the work, but I consider myself a dabbler compared to you.

J: A dabbler how? How did you get into them?

S: I would say it was about 1988. My uncle Martin, who is only two years older than me—my gran had him late—got me into all kinds of stuff. He bought a couple of albums. That was all we did, really. Before he discovered the pub we used to just sit and listen to records. Led Zeppelin, Thin Lizzy, all the dad rock stuff I'm into now.

J: Have you got a favourite Smiths song?

S: I do love 'Cemetery Gates' because it reminds of my old music producer Nic Philips, who left the show two years ago to work with heroin addicts in Hong Kong. He's that kind of a guy. He always wanted to hear that song. I love the obvious ones as well—I love 'There Is a Light'. I love murdering that. I love 'Heaven Knows I'm Miserable Now.' But I'm not as obsessive about them as *some* people. But they were such an important band. And Johnny Marr is such a brilliant person. I'm a bit in love with him. I've met him a couple of times. I just think he's The Don when it comes to guitars. He's so inspirational. I need to get Johnny into my life. We've kind of agreed that he'll bring his guitar in and accompany me on my song 'Cheddar Cheese'. I want to get him on it. All the money will go to charity, of course.

J: Cheese charities. Help the Cheese-ed.

S: Air dropping cheese to the starving cheese deprived.

J: Have you ever met Morrissey?

S: No. I was thinking about this the other day. Who have I not met/chatted to that I'd like to? I'd be very interested to meet Morrissey, but I've got a feeling that he'd terrify me in equal measure. I'd love to chat to him, he's deeply fascinating.

J: What if Morrissey was to walk into this cafe right now ...
[Shaun sticks his chin out].

J: Is that meant to be Morrissey?

S: This is how I imagine him.

J: If he was to walk in here right now and say, 'All right, Shaun?' what would you say?

S: I'd be so chuffed. I have these chats with my mate Kev. I'd probably say something awful like, 'Thank you for the music.' To which he'd reply, 'This is why I don't enjoy meeting the public.' And then walk out. Get back in his car. What do you say to somebody like that? You're always trying to impress singers like that. Whereas Marr, Joyce or Rourke you can be a bit more relaxed because they are more down to earth.

J: You were a singer in that band doing 'There Is a Light' though.

S: Yeah, but I'm a singer/*guitarist*. I can also play the drums and bass. I'm multi-talented and therefore 'down-to-earth'.

J: You're a 'musical handyman'.

S: Yeah. Jack of no trades, master of none.

J: Man of a thousand voices, all of them the same. So Morrissey is coming round to your house. What snacks would you put out for him?

S: If Morrissey was coming round, Lucy would call the cleaner. Because we do live in north-west London, so we have a cleaner. That's my MASO [Middle Aged Shout Out].

J: You say MASO? I say it like 'MAISO'.

S: That's fascinating.

J: You could do a whole show on that.

S: 'MAISO OR MASO, which is it? 6-4-0-4-6.' That would be funny, because they'd *write* it the same. It's a *visual* joke, on the radio.

J: You could put 'Two Tribes' under it and there you go. Instant national panic about how it's pronounced.

S: Just on that, I've never felt so excited in my life than when Holly Johnson was tweeting me during *DIY SOS*. I was like, 'This is it now—Holly just tweeted me.'

J: You just need to RELAX ... What snacks would you put out for Morrissey?

S: I'd play it safe. Those vegetable crisps. Some hummus, carrots, celery. I don't like taramasalata, so we wouldn't have that anyway.

J: He wouldn't eat it. It's cod roe.

S: He'd throw that against the wall.

J: Leave your house, never go back. I wouldn't blame him.

S: Maybe a sun-dried tomato paté.

J: Do you make that yourself?

S: No. Maybe when I'm older—retired. I've got better f***in' things to do with my life at the moment than make paté, Julie. Jesus.

J: All right! What if Holly found out and he came too?

S: I think Holly is a lot more laid-back than Morrissey. He's deliciously camp and Morrissey is more private. My aim would be to get Holly drunk very early on, and come on to him in a dress.

J: Who's your favourite DJ?

S: Danny Baker.

J: TV show?

S: *DIY SOS* and *Blackadder III*

J: Favourite cake?

S: Coffee and walnut.

J: Favourite biscuit?

S: Belgian chocolate shortbread.

J: Favourite sandwich?

S: New York pastrami with pickle on rye bread.

J: Lyric or song of all time?

S: It changes all the time but, really, the most regular answer would be 'Daydream Believer' by the Monkees.

J: Favourite pizza topping?

S: Something hot, pepperoni with loads of fresh chilli, black pepper. Oh yeah.

J: Are you hungry? Do you want to order something?

S: No, no, thank you. I've got to hold out for a dinner party.

J: Who's coming?

S: Becky and Sam.

J: Favourite thing your mum says?

S: 'Don't eat that apple on your own—you might choke.'

J: Favourite concert?

S: Stevie Wonder at Hyde Park. I cried three times.

J: Childhood toy?

S: Evel Knievel wind up. I used to whizz him into the wall until he broke all his plastic limbs, like in real life.

J: Smiths/Morrissey song?

S: 'Heaven Knows I'm Miserable Now' now and 'Suedehead'.

J: Favourite person to interview?

S: I think I would have to say the holy trinity of Jimmy Page, Nile Rodgers and Jessica Hynes.

J: Favourite soap character?

S: It would have to be Norris Cole.

J: He's mine!

S: Forget soaps—he's the best thing on TV.

J: I agree. Would you write a note to my mum?

S: Of course.

(In the voice of Mike Read from Eastenders) PAT! PAAT!!

Thanks so much for listening to our daft show. You have raised a lovely daughter!

Rock on

Shaun

Sean Hughes

Comedian and Morrissey fan

15 MINUTES WITH YOU

WHEN I was twenty-one, I thought *Sean's Show* was the funniest programme on the telly. At the centre it featured this awkward, fumbly, fantastic floppy-haired boy-man, Sean Hughes, who wore cardigans and cords, talked to a spider named Elvis and loved The Smiths. His childlike humour, vulnerability and insecurity he shared so comfortably on screen and in stand-up resulted in him being the youngest person ever to win the Perrier Award and secured his place as the comedy crush of every other daughter, granny and mother in the UK. Post *Sean's Show*, he went on to have a consistent and successful career as a multi faceted artist: actor, panelist, DJ, author, poet and stand up; rooting him as one of the UK's most respected and loved TV personalities.

During his stand-up show I watched at Udderbelly, this forty-six-year-old gentleman with the light-as-a-feather Irish lilt offered cuddles to the front row and ginger nuts to the seniors while talking about the significance of his *Six Million Dollar Man* doll. There were a few 'fecks' in there for expression and delivery: *'I do that Irish swearing. It's like punctuation.'*

After three hours of walking his dogs, a chat on a bench then eating vinegared chips while drinking cold coffee, I could see that he hasn't changed in twenty years. He's curious and whimsical like he has butterflies up there instead of neurons. His 'la-la-la-la' love of life—which skips from the profound and poignant one minute to the surreal and hilarious the next—still reigns. Sean lives his life being gently and happily distracted by, well, stuff people do: [to me] *'What do you mainly eat?'*

Sean had plenty to say about my mum: *'Are you trying to set me up with your mother?'* and stew recipes: *'It's pretty much like boil-a-load-of-sh*t-up-together.'*

Whilst he no longer sings 'It's Seany's Show! La-la-la-la' in the bath he still has a lovely singing voice, but he would definitely not let Morrissey come and live in his house to hear it. Impressively, he can drink up to ten cups of peppermint tea a day, he loves his dogs, Sweep and Betty, and yes, he does know how 'Jeane' goes.

J: Please say your full name.

S: So this is a court of law now? It's all of a sudden got very formal! Erm, I'm Sean Patrick Hughes.

J: Oh, there is a Patrick in there? Same as himself?

S: Oh, I must tell you—one of the last times I saw Morrissey I was in Dublin at a gig and I said, 'All right, Morrissey?' and he went, 'All right, Hughes?' So I was like, 'Do I start calling you Steven from now on, then?'

J: You did an interview with Morrissey on GLR where you sound so excited. He was really nice to you.

S: I *was* excited! It was a live interview, so it couldn't be edited. It was the first time I've really been nervous about something in a while. I don't think it was a great interview, because every time I was saying something I was like: 'Morrissey is sitting beside me!' He wanted to go to HMV to buy some black and white movies. I had to give him a lift, and my car was full of dog hair, and he doesn't like dogs.

J: That's nonsense! He does like dogs! He loves all animals.

S: You know they did that 'The Importance of being Morrissey?' There was a leather chair and he said something like: 'I don't want to be seen near this chair.'

J: Quite right, too.

S: Morrissey is trapped in his own personality.

J: What?

S: I think I'll say that about myself: '*Sean is trapped in his own personality*'.

J: You're a Scorpio, is that right?

S: Yeah. You don't want to live with a Scorpio.

J: My mother is one.

S: What is her actual birthday?

J: November 18th. She's mad about you in 'The Last Detective.'

S: I went to America last month and I got recognised four times—all from 'The Last Detective.' I had women hugging me, I was like, 'Get off me, Mrs.'

J: People are very fond of you.

S: Unless they get to know me, then it all changes. Your mum is proper Scorpio. My brother is the 5th and he's not Scorpio at all.

J: What is he, then?

S: He has no traits of it.

J: What are Scorpio traits?

S: The old sting in the tail. We feel quite set upon most of the time. We're intense in the sense that we're very loving, but when you let us down, oh Jesus you won't know the end of it. I try not to bear grudges. I watched that one-woman show by Carrie Fisher and there's one line in it at the end where she says, 'Living a revengeful life is like drinking poison while waiting for the other person to die.' Scorpios always feel let down, we expect too much from people. The lesson I've learnt from my life is to lower your expectations.

J: Are you still a vegetarian?

S: Morrissey once told me that the one thing he hated people asking him was, 'Are you STILL a vegetarian?'

J: I'll scrub that out.

S: I prefer people who eat meat to people who 'used' to be vegetarians. Are you vegetarian?

J: I am.

S: Is it because of Morrissey?

J: He did play a large part in it, yes.

S: Yeah, he did with me as well. I hate to admit it.

J: I never liked the taste of meat, though. Maybe it was my mum's gammon steaks.

S: You were fairly working class, then?

J: Potatoes were on the menu a lot.

S: Tatties!

J: I love potatoes.

S: I still have potatoes a lot. What do you mainly eat?

J: Potatoes.

S: I like a lot of that fake meat.

J: I like the thin Quorn deli 'ham' slices.

S: Nah. I mean when you put it in stews.

J: You make stews?

S: Yeah. The Swedish fake meatballs are great.

J: Where do you get them—Ikea?

S: No—get them in Tescos, the big Tescos in the frozen foods. Do you not do stews?

J: No, what's your stew recipe?

S: Whatever you want it to be. It's pretty much like boil-a-load-of-sh*t-up-together. Parboil the potatoes. Bear in mind some things will be harder than others, so you've got to time it right. Put whatever spices and herbs you like in. I can't stand carrots, so I put mushrooms, potatoes, a bit of onion ...

J: I don't think mushrooms go with potatoes, though, do they?

S: They do in my world! I'll have to go home now and be like [to mushrooms]: 'Well YOU'RE out apparently! Can't see you two together again!'

J: I thought that you didn't like talking about yourself? I haven't even got to question two yet.

S: It's your fault for getting me talking about recipes! Once you get me onto recipes there's no stopping me.

J: Could you describe yourself in a sentence?

S: Do you watch that show, *Mad Men*?

J: Yes, I love it.

S: I was trying to put my finger on why it's so good. I think it's because I cannot describe one of those characters in a sentence. Can you?

J: Well, let's try: Roger Sterling: Lothario, joker. Don Draper: Dapper...

S: See, I'm not even going to let you away with the first one, because you say that and you know that Roger doesn't like that high life. When he did that LSD trip he realised that. I just got to the bit where Don is turning off The Beatles from the record player.

J: It's about to get a whole lot better. One word: Lane. I'll say no more.

S: Did you know he's Richard Harris' son?

J: Is he? No, I didn't know. My mum probably knew that, though. Your dogs are so cute. How old are they?

S: Sweep is sixteen, Betty is eight.

J: So can you describe yourself in a sentence? Maybe something about stews?

S: I'm the type of person who can't be described in one sentence. I hope.

J: Right then ...

S: You won't get that answer ever again, will you?

J: I don't know.

[Sweep growls at two passing dogs. Sean: 'Sweepie! Which one do you not like?']

J: Are the dogs your special ones in your life?

S: They're not even that special.

J: Do you call yourself 'daddy' to them?

S: No! I just say their names. I don't say, 'Come to daddy!' It's really weird, because ... I refer to them both as boys. I say, 'Come on, boys.' Do you do that with your kids?

J: Sometimes we'll say, 'Away the lads' to both of them. Look at Betty. She needs some sheep. [Betty lies down and wags her tail, waiting for Sean to throw the ball.]

S: It's in her DNA. I have a cat as well. She's lovely. She's even older than Sweep.

J: Did you like the pictures of Morrissey with a cat on his head? The Jake Walters ones?

S: I'm sure I've seen them. Was the cat in his arms?

J: No, you're thinking of the baby.

S: A cat and a baby?

J: No. Fanny the cat. On his head.

S: Oh!

J: I am a big fan of how you used The Smiths in *Sean's Show*.

S: Were you into The Smiths then?

J: Yes, very much. There was nothing like your show on TV when you came along ...

S: OR SINCE!

J: You were quite childlike, innocent and vulnerable. Clean and sweet. None of that swearing you do now ...

S: I do that Irish swearing. I forget. It's like punctuation. When I listen back I just go 'Oh my God.'

J: Is it your age?

S: Well, rather than mellowing I do get a bit more perplexed by life, but I will always question things. You always worry that you will become Chris Rea, 'Here's another very bland song.'

J: Were you aware of how unique *Sean's Show* was?

S: I think that the only way you can be different is by not being fake. I think that's why Morrissey is a success, because he's not fake. You get your natural performers and those people who try very hard. I'm natural on stage. I enjoy it. I don't then go off stage and throw a hissy fit.

J: What is your favourite joke?

S: Jokes come and go, but I still laugh at them. The last thing I laughed at was in *Mad Men*, when Roger brought Pete Campbell into the office to collect two sets of skis. And he went out with them really clumsily and Roger went, 'Well, I'm glad I saw that.' The recent Carrie Fisher thing made me laugh as well.

J: Why did you get rid of your armchair in the live shows?

S: I never really thought it through. Everything evolves. I have a 'pint' of ginger nuts now and the box feels like a pint. You've really just got to move onto the next chair, haven't you?

J: You do talk about your mid 40s and being old on stage, I just thought that you'd have a more comfortable chair than a hard stool.

S: If I sit in a sofa there's a good chance I won't be able to get up, without it really having good purchase. I can't take those risks.

J: Do you still sit in the bubble bath and sing 'It's Seany's show, la-la-la-la'?

S: Well, what do you think? I thought you were going to be a serious interviewer?

J: This is a very serious question.

S: Did you really want an answer?

J: I do.

S: No, I don't. No.

J: Do you ever sing it?

S: Erm, well, I wrote it. Every day on Twitter somebody does a *Sean's Show* reference, which I like. It was over twenty-five years ago! Channel 4 is doing a top 30 sitcoms and it's not in it.

J: You're joking!

S: Not even in the top 30. I'm not going to kick up a fuss.

J: Tell me who I need to write to?

S: Not write, Julie. The days of writing are finished. We need shooters now. We should just kill. It's time for the killing to start.

J: Why did you leave *Never Mind The Buzzcocks*?

S: I didn't want to be known for just that. I did ten series. It was a long time.

J: You've done *Sean's Show, Sean's Shorts, Buzzcocks*, but what I really want to hear about is Corrie's Eileen Grimshaw.

S: I tried to get rid of that memory ... I still keep in touch with Sue. She's a lovely woman; I really like her a lot.

[Sweep sees another dog he doesn't like and goes for it. Sean: 'SWEEP! Why don't you chill out, yeah? Live and let live, yeah?' Sweep grumbles and lies down under the bench.]

S: When they [*Coronation Street*] phone to say, 'You're going to have a love interest with one of the characters', I assumed it would be, like, Tina O'Brien or someone. They were like, 'Nah, it's big Eileen from the cab office.' I'm like 'Wha'?' *Coronation Street* made me realise that I was getting on a bit.

J: Tina O'Brien?

S: We live deluded lives.

J: But you took the part.

S: Yeah, because my mum loves *Coronation Street*! I rang up to get some background information on the character. I asked, 'What does he sell?' They said 'Oh, you've got me there.' He never had a briefcase. He must have sold really tiny sh*t [goes into inside pocket]: 'Here—I'm Pat the salesman. You want to buy some of that?'

J: What was it like being in Corrie?

S: There was no fanfare or anything. They were like: 'You've got the job.' At ten past nine on Monday I was in The Rovers Return doing my first bit and Craig Charles was like: 'By the way, that door doesn't work.' The regulars don't like doing scenes in The Rovers because there are loads of extras around. I realised I was over my panic attacks from my younger days when I could just stand that and be like, 'A pint, please.'

J: Do you get a proper pint in there?

S: They put a tiny bit of real beer in there. I don't drink anymore, but I remember with lager, I don't like the gas; this was a problem in *The Last Detective*. Too much build-up in my stomach.

J: That couldn't have been nice for your co-stars. Did you ever get to try on Deirdre's belts?

S: No, they keep them locked up. Bill Roache [Ken Barlow] is nice. He came up to me and said, 'I'm so happy that you're in the show.' I thought, what a sweet man.

J: Aww.

S: One of my favourite Morrissey lyrics is: 'It takes guts to be gentle and kind', because it does, it does take guts to be gentle and kind. I remember at some do I was at during *Sean's Show,* Richard Stilgoe was there. He came up to me and said, 'It's really nice to meet you; I'm a big fan. It's really nice to see the younger generation coming up.' When he walked away I was like: 'W*nker!'

J: Yes, but you were twenty-five. It was probably nerves.

S: I know, but I just feel really bad. I really regret saying things like that. This is Sir Richard Stilgoe.

J: I don't think you can give yourself a hard time about it. You were young.

S: Yeah, I guess, but I still think there's no excuse.
[Betty paws my foot. Sean: 'That's her way of getting your attention. She wants the ball.' I throw the ball for her. She's back in seconds, dropping the ball at my feet again.]

J: She's sprightly.

S: She's very clever. Is your mum very active?

J: Her dog, Sally, keeps her fit. Would your mum get a dog?

S: No. She could do with one. She says,'Oh, I'm away too much', but she goes nowhere. The original storyline in Corrie was that I was to get Eileen pregnant. But Sue didn't want that, because if you get pregnant on a soap you don't get a storyline for two years cos you're lumbered with a baby. It would have been too confusing for my mum anyway, to see her grandchild living in Manchester.

J: Any more TV planned?

S: No. I'm doing the two shows in Edinburgh and that's enough. If all the stars were aligned, I'd possibly re-think of doing *Sean's Show*, but I'm worried that it would ruin the legacy, unless it seemed absolutely right.

J: That might be a bit like The Smiths reforming. What would Sean be doing now?

S: I'd love to know what the character is up to now. But it would be a huge costly thing and I wouldn't do it unless everything is in place.

J: Would you play him? Sean as an older man?

S: Well, yeah, I'd have to! It would be an absolute joy to see what he's up to now. I'm not going to do a panel show or anything like that now. But it means less people come see the show. It's diminishing returns when you're not on TV. It's a fact of life and you've got to deal with it.
[Sweep digs. Sean: 'Have you found the body, Sweep? Is the body down there, yeah? Good boy!']

J: How was BBC6 Music?

S: It was great, I loved it. I had a contract for a year, doing Sundays, and they said, 'Would you please play three tracks off the playlist every hour?' And I said, 'No.' and they said, 'Well we're not renewing your contract then unless you do that.' That wasn't me being an a*rse, that was just about the music. I said, 'I'd rather not do it if one of the tracks I have to play is Stereophonics.' If I had been doing it every day, of course I would have done it, but not when it's a Sunday special show. The last song I played was 'I Don't Mind If You Forget Me' by Morrissey, containing the lyrics: 'Rejection is one thing, but rejection from a fool is cruel.' Then the producer said that they cut it when they put it on the Internet, and so that song wasn't in there.

J: Tell me some of your favourite Smiths/Morrissey tracks.

S: It's a weird one, cos if you put Morrissey's solo career up against The Smiths, Morrissey solo wins now. If you're going to pick your best ten Smiths songs versus your best ten Morrissey songs, Morrissey would win.

J: How did you get into The Smiths?

S: I was a real johnny-come-lately. My mate got there first. But it became an addiction, really. I wasn't as obsessed as the guy from *Sean's Show*.

J: Really?

S: I was really thrilled when Morrissey asked if he could use one of my quotes from the show. I said: 'Sometimes I feel like Morrissey. I feel like a man trapped in a man's body.' So that's in some book somewhere.

[Sweep growls. Sean: 'All right, Sweep, are you in cranky mood today, are ya? You got the stick? You showing him who's the boss, yeah? With your little twig.' Sean addresses the passing dog: 'He's the master! He's not an old man! He's got the big stick!']

S: Morrissey was a big influence on the way I was. When I was nineteen I shared a dressing room with The Smiths on a TV show in Ireland. It was quite intense. Have you ever noticed how Morrissey looks like George Best? It's in the eyes.

J: I haven't ever noticed that, no. I'll have a closer look.

S: He does, he really does, look in the eyes!

J: Can you tell us about the interview with Morrissey on GLR?

S: I think he is a very beautiful-looking man as well. Morrissey intrigues me. I remember the first time I met him was in Camden, he was with Stephen Street. We had never met but we were both aware of each other, so we stopped. I said to him, one of my favourite songs is 'Speedway' from the album *Vauxhall and I*. But you know that 'Why don't you find out for yourself'? that lyric 'Bad scenes come and go', I said to him, 'I always thought it was 'bad seeds', *which* is a much better line. [sings] 'Bad seeds come and go, for which you must allow!'

J: You have a lovely singing voice.

S: I can sing quite well. This is the question that you should ask every Morrissey fan: Would you let Morrissey come and live in your house?

J: Would you?

S: No.

J: I have written a short fictional/comedy story about when Morrissey came to my house. Perhaps you'd like to read it?

S: I do have to get on with my own life as well, Julie. I'm now reading plays of yours, short stories, I've got two shows to prepare for, I can't be reading all your stuff all the time …
 [Betty searches for her ball and can't find it. Sean: 'Betty! Over there! Your ball is over there! Over there!' Betty goes and finds the ball.]

J: If Morrissey came into this park and walked up to you right now and said, 'All right, Sean?' what would you say?

S: I'd be perfectly happy to go for a coffee with him or something. When I met him and he said, 'All right, Hughes?' I thought that was cantankerous.

J: You're not over that? I think it's quite affectionate!

S: I will always have an endearing love for Morrissey.

J: So if he was coming to your house, what snacks would you put out for him?

S: Whatever's in the fridge. I wouldn't make a fuss.

J: What's in the fridge?

S: Mushrooms, potatoes ... No, you know I had an allergy test that says mushrooms don't agree with me.

J: That's all the stews.

S: I don't know what he eats. What does he eat?

J: He doesn't like spicy food; from what I know he used to be fond of eggs. And chips. But I very much suspect he likes more than that, these days.

S: I suppose he could share my stew.

J: We'll do your favourite things then go get a coffee.

S: Yeah, I'll buy you a coffee. Did you see me do the 'Morrissey mic' on the show?
['Morrissey mic' = flick the wire up]

J: I did!

S: [sings] 'And when you SLAM (pretends to flick mic) down the hammer ...'

J: We thoroughly enjoyed your show the other night.

S: Thanks. If you see it again, it'll be slightly different. When I do the ginger nuts bit I'm going to get some marshmallows and hand them like out shots. But they're marshmallows. Let's do shots!

J: I like it when you lose your thread through the show then just spend five minutes talking to an audience member.

S: In Edinburgh I can only do an hour. I leave out a different section every night. It's such an important part of the show, that chatting with the audience bit, I need to keep that.

J: What's your favourite breed of dog?

S: Ah, it would have to be a Heinz Beans, really. All my dogs have been from Battersea. Even though this one (Betty) was pissin' on my kitchen floor this morning. She gets excited; I don't think she knows she's doing it.

J: You might want to let her out every now and then ...

S: She did it when the door was open! That's what annoyed me.

[Betty paces around Sweep. Sean: 'Sweepie! You know you're sittin' on the ball, don't you?']

S: Do you like the Brotherhood of Man?

J: I can't remember their songs.

S: 'Save All Your Kisses For Me', was one ...

J: Oh yes, I do.

S: They had one about Fernando, I think ...

J: Wasn't that Abba?

S: No, it wasn't 'Can you hear the drums, Fernando' it was more like: 'There was something in the air that night ...'

J: That's the same song. What's your favourite thing your mum says?

S: She says, 'Do you understand?' at the end of every sentence.

J: And do you?

S: Only too well.

J: Favourite pizza topping?

S: I don't eat pizza anymore. I'm allergic to cheese. With any cheese I just sweat here (points to his cheeks) for a minute.

J: You get the cheese sweats.

S: Yeah. But I like cheese. I guess the best pizza is a DEAD PIZZA.

J: Favourite biscuit?

S: Anything involving ginger. Ginger blueberry biscuits. Marks and Spencer do some really nice ones.

J: My mum loves ginger.

S: Are you trying to set me up with your mum? What would your dad say? 'All right Mister? I'm just taking Sally and Pat out for a walk!'

J: What's your favourite thing to do on a Friday night?

S: It certainly isn't going out. I catch up on my Sky Plus stuff. Last Friday I watched the Bowie night. I'm a bit of a Maltesers person in front of the telly.

J: Box or bag?

S: Sainsbury's have been doing the bag quite cheaply lately. PART-EH!!!

J: What would you drink with that?

S: Peppermint tea.

J: I love that.

S: How many cups do you drink?

J: I could easily drink four or five cups.

S: I drink ten a day.

J: I drink twenty.

S: I think I have an addictive personality. I like ginger tea as well.

J: My sister taught me how to make fresh ginger tea. Do you do that?

S: No, I have the tea bags.

J: Peel and chop fresh ginger. Add hot water. Delicious.

S: I love a bit of ginger. How do you boil eggs now, Julie? Can you explain that to me? I have a lovely Japanese teapot. Maybe I could put the ginger in the thing and do that.

J: Favourite childhood toy?

S: *Six Million Dollar Man* doll.

J: Favourite trousers?

S: Cords. I don't like jeans. I've never liked jeans. They're a bit hard on my knees.

J: Were you not wearing those cords on Sunday?

S: Yeah, I was—you can get a good 4-5 days out of cords before you need to wash them.

J: What's your favourite crisp flavour?

S: Salt and Vinegar. Why? What did you have me down for?

J: Something a bit more exotic—a pickled onion or Worcester sauce, maybe.

S: I try not to eat crisps. I think everything about them is bad for you.

J: And they clash with Maltesers.

S: Exactly. Put 'balsamic', obviously.

J: Favourite Morrissey song?

S: I went to The Forum to see him and I told him that 'The Ordinary Boys' was my highlight. The next night I went and he played it as the encore!

J: See? He does listen to you! Favourite Smiths song?

S: 'Jeane'. [Sings] 'All the alcoholic afternoons ...'

J: 'These Things Take Time'?

S: Hmm?

J: You were just singing 'These Things Take Time'.

S: That wasn't 'Jeane'? Am I actually having a stroke? [sings] 'That had more worth ... than any ...' Actually, put 'Meat Is Murder.'

J: Will you write a note to my mum?

S: I will. Tell her that Peter Davison is a really lovely fella. What's the name of her dog?

J: Sally. Do you know how 'Jeane' goes?

S: Yeah, like this: [sings] 'All the alcoholic afternoons ...'

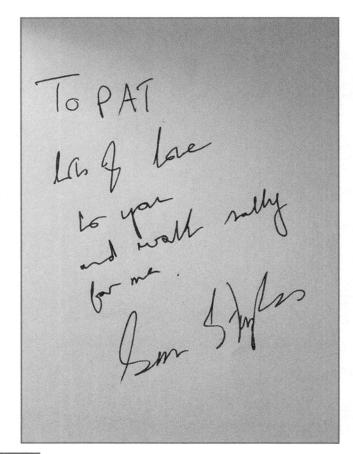

Jonny Bridgwood

Bass player with Morrissey (1990, 1993-1997)

15 MINUTES
WITH YOU

EIGHTEEN-year-old rockabilly Jonny B walked into Suttons music shop in Norwich to try out the double bass. He had never played an instrument before; he just knew from a very young age that he wanted to be in a band. Like Arthur and Excalibur, as soon as he touched the strings, a magical connection was made. Jonny could *already* play—he had no lessons—he learned just from listening to Elvis. This natural talent and musical 'ear' went on to shape his future, and eventually led him to create the bass lines of Morrissey's most critically acclaimed album, *Vauxhall and I*.

Selling his pushbike to buy strings, Jonny's passion for the bass knew no boundaries. He worked his way through difficult times through sheer hard work, practice and determination to meet his dream: *'I got to do what I wanted to do, which was largely by not knowing what I was doing, single-mindedness and rejecting everything else.'*

As we talked, Jonnny shared the importance of his family, and how working with Morrissey touched one member in particular—his daughter Harriet. Harriet was born three months premature and had a brain haemorrhage which left her with hydrocephalus, a condition of fluid in the brain that caused severe brain damage. Sadly, her twin sister Florence did not make it. Harriet is now twenty and enjoys listening and singing along to Morrissey (sometimes at 3 a.m.). Tenderly, she only sings the songs that Jonny is on, knowing the presence and talent of her daddy. Jonny's bass is self-taught and technically brilliant: *'Now when I play I just hear it, it just comes. I deconstruct records. It's dimensional. It's separate but it goes together.'* He defends and understands Morrissey's nature: *'Morrissey is pretty much a generally nice person surrounded by idiots',* and he has a warm and fun family life: *'You watched me do it!' is a stock phrase in our house.'*

He likes cherry and coconut cake and knows a lot about tea: *'Peppermint tea in the evening, Earl Grey in the morning and maybe a spiced blend in the afternoon.'*

I left Jonny feeling like I'd had a sort of spiritual experience. Yes, we talked about Morrissey, the songs, the shows, the tea, the pub. But behind the ambition, talent, history and fame, Jonny reveals himself to be a gentle soul and a calming influence; a person with no hard edges or harsh words.

JH: Please say your full name.

JB: Jonny Bridgwood. I have no middle names. My name is as it is.

JH: Did your parents call you 'Jonny' straight away?

JB: Jon.

JH: Who lengthened it?

JB: Probably an auntie, my dad had the same name. When I was at school people used to call me Jonny and I preferred it. It's somehow cooler, even though I had no idea what was cool and what wasn't.

JH: Please describe yourself in a sentence.

JB: Very nice!

JH: Very good! How's life for you at the moment, what are you doing?

JB: I've always got fingers in pies. Yesterday I was doing a Cerys Matthews session with Tom Paley, an American legend who knew Woody Guthrie, who would have been one hundred years old on Saturday (July 14, 1912). All these people were a huge influence on Bob Dylan.

Tom used to be in a band called New Lost City Ramblers, who were ahead of the folk revival and who Dylan went to see. I also play with a really good singer/songwriter called Alex Highton. He's really good. You'd probably like him, you should check him out.

JH: What music were you listening to in your youth?

JB: When I was a kid I was into two things, football and music - Manchester United. In 1966 a song called 'Bend It' came out, which I loved, aged three. I thought it was called 'Brenda', because my older sister had a friend called Brenda. I used to sing the song like that: 'Brenda! Brenda!' It was years later I discovered my mistake. I was also aware of The Beatles, 'Penny Lane', stuff like that. I used to love to watch *Top of the Pops* in the early seventies during the glam rock era. In my teens it was Gene Vincent, Eddie Cochran, Buddy Holly, and of course early Elvis.

JH: Have you got a favourite bass line?

JB: With Morrissey, it's probably something like 'Nobody Loves Us'.

JH: How did you get into playing bass?

JB: I had played a lot of double bass, but on the first tour with Morrissey I actually borrowed a bass guitar from Alain, because I never really had one. When we did *Vauxhall and I*, I hired one and then I bought it. I first got into the double bass when I heard 'That's Alright, Mama' by Elvis. I was intrigued by that, so I borrowed an Elvis record from a friend and was like: 'What's this?' I also played all my friend's dad's records, which all had double bass on; that's how I really became aware of it. After that I got into rockabilly revival, Stray Cats, etc. I met some like-minded kids at school, we all started growing quiffs. We discovered there was a rock'n'roll club and went to that. That was when our gang became a band. We didn't have any instruments but we were a band. Then my friend got a guitar. When he went to buy new strings he said, 'There's a double bass for sale!' So I went down to the shop and it was like a great moment, because when I picked it up I discovered I could actually play a little bit. It was amazing. There was a huge gang with us and it was like I was actually over there, watching me with them. It was a really surreal experience. I could feel it in my whole body. Quite magical. I had to have this instrument. It was £180. I had been working and was made redundant but had a little bit of money—£60. I was in that shop every day for a fortnight. I borrowed £60 and they let me take it, owing £60. They just said, 'Come in when you've got it.' Once a fortnight I would go in with my dole money. I kept a pound for myself. Fifty pence to get into the rock'n'roll club and a bit for a couple of pints. I sold my records and clothes, apart from some essentials, and I just paid it off. I played until my fingers bled. Then when the pain subsided I'd play some more. It was the only thing I had.

To begin with, I played a lot on one string. I remember the A string breaking, so I moved over onto the D string and it broke. I had a pushbike which I managed to sell and I went into the shop where I got the bass and said: 'I need some strings.' The cheapest set they had was £35. I only had £25, and had sold my bike to get that, and they said, 'You can take them.'

JH: That's a great story; clearly you were fated to play bass, and that shop had a big hand in it.

JB: The shop was called Suttons. It's not there anymore, but I found the receipt the other day. By then we had formed a band, buying a cheap microphone and a snare drum, and the singer would hold the mic in one hand and play the snare in the other.

JH: Still no name at this point?

JB: Initially we called ourselves Trio Three. We were kind of like the rock'n'roll Ramones, because we tried to do records and couldn't do them, so started doing our own stuff. We bought drums and another guitar and we were a five piece. So then we were called Fireball XL5 after the Gerry Anderson show. We didn't last that long, but a year in we did our first gigs then a record. By the time I was twenty-one I was down here in London, then at twenty-two I was touring with The Cramps all round England on a thirty-day tour.

JH: What were The Cramps like?

JB: Incredibly nice people. Our band was named The Sting-Rays. Their agent tried to get a buy-on, but we said, 'We're not doing it.' We felt it was wrong. But The Cramps really wanted us, so then we did it and they paid for our catering and everything. They fed us and helped us. We even had free beer—it was rude not to drink it!

JH: Did you like to have a few beers before going onstage?

JB: Well I remember being really drunk and falling off a really low stage, and the singer falling over the guitar amp during an early gig.

Later I got seriously hammered during an all night gig in Berlin, and I looked at my fingers and thought, 'Why are you not doing what you're supposed to do?' At the time I thought, 'Well I'm never doing that again,' so invariably I don't drink now.

JH: What did your family think of your success at the time?

JB: Well, I got kicked out of home when I was seventeen. My father was an abusive alcoholic and I don't keep in touch with my mother. My father is dead now.

JH: I'm sorry to hear that. I think some parents can teach you how not to be a parent.

JB: Yes, definitely. I think all families are mad to a degree, but there's good-mad and just insane.

JH: So where did you go after The Sting-Rays?

JB: I was heavily into The Beatles, and I wanted to do different music. So I set about forming a band with the guitarist from my first band, but it didn't work out, so I went freelance.

JH: Your bass playing was all self taught?

JB: Yes, I just copied records. I copied an Elvis record, 'That's Alright, Mama' lifting the needle back to the beginning over and over. Ten years after I started playing I had a few classical lessons for bow technique and I taught myself to read music. I followed this with a few jazz lessons. Now when I play I just hear it, it just comes. I deconstruct records. It's dimensional. It's separate, but it goes together.

JH: I think that what you are saying completely applies to The Smiths, all separate talents coming together.

JB: Yes, definitely, they are all individual voices, which is what a good band should be. If you listen to a really good record like 'Day Tripper' by The Beatles, you can hear all the different layers together.

JH: How did your involvement with Morrissey come about?

JB: I went back to Norwich. I took a bit of time out to see where I was going, having gone from band to band. I really seriously started practising my bass in a more technical way that I hadn't done before, listening to jazz and understanding how all that worked. It's at this time I decided to become freelance. Morrissey was my first major session. I had been friendly with Boz, we had done a little band together Boz and The Bozmen. Via Carl out of Madness [Cathal], Clive Langer said to Boz, 'Do you know any people that play rockabilly?' So Boz had a meeting and they asked him to bring a bass player. So he asked me and I said, 'Yeah, I'll do it.' The actual message (via a friend, as I was of no fixed abode at the time) was: did I want to do a session with Van Morrison? I was like, how did that come about?

JH: Did you know of Morrissey's previous work with The Smiths?

JB: No, because I wasn't a Smiths fan. I was aware of him, I knew he was around, but no. We set up to play. Richard Hawley was there, auditioning for the band.

JH: What? No way!

JB: Yes, he auditioned but didn't get in!

JH: He's fantastic.

JB: Yes, he is. Would have been a different journey.

JH: So you got to work on 'Pregnant for the Last Time.'

JB: Yes, that's when I met Mark Nevin, who I also gig with these days, but I wasn't on the *Top of the Pops* appearance. I got a call from EMI, saying, 'We need you to give permission for somebody to mime your part (Gary).' I was going to get paid anyway, so I said yes. I remember hearing the demo of 'You're Gonna Need Someone On Your Side', which I was supposed to play on, and I did a song called 'Born To Hang.'

JH: You just kind of morphed into the band, didn't you?

JB: Yes. From 1992 I had a very complicated personal life. We lost a baby at six and a half months [a twin]; my wife, Helen, nearly died. We were just visiting hospital every day. We had a very ill, small child and we had to survive. When I got to 1993 I just thought, 'What am I going to do now?' Then Boz called me up and asked if I'd play bass on a new Morrissey album. So we had a meeting in Shepherd's Bush—Woodie Taylor was there—and I vaguely knew Woodie, and we just played, working on 'Billy Budd'. I didn't realise Morrissey had come into the room and was sitting on the sofa watching us. He said something like: 'That's really good,'

and told me that I hadn't aged. So I told him that I had a portrait in the loft.

JH: It is documented that during the recording of *Vauxhall and I* you all played football.

JB: Yeah! Morrissey is good! I was on his team, we won—he scored and I scored. Then we went to the pub and had pints of beer.

JH: How many pints?

JB: Oh, at least twelve! We didn't get pissed, we'd just have a couple of beers. Hook End Manor is in the middle of nowhere, surrounded by trees. We'd just go on walks and find a pub.

JH: Working remotely with Morrissey, playing football, having dinner, going for a pint ... such a small group of you together in that remote location ... Did you connect?

JB: No, not at all. Morrissey keeps a distance, he's just like that. He was like that before he was famous and when he was in The Smiths. Fame exacerbates certain traits, but that's just him. Morrissey is pretty much a generally nice person surrounded by idiots. People have a preconceived idea: 'Oh it's Morrissey and I've got to behave in a certain way.' He can't relate to a person that's not being themselves. So you won't get to know him like that, he'll just think they're a bit … weird.

JH: Was it you with the lads and then Morrissey separate?

JB: Yes, to a degree and certainly later. When you're doing something for a long time there has to be a level of social bonding. It was 'Go for a drink', but it wasn't really personal. There were no personal conversations.

JH: So when you went to the pub, were you talking 'music'?

JB: It was quite light-hearted. I remember going past this deserted country pub and Alain went, 'Look! It's the Nobody Inn!' We thought that was really funny. We also went to a really smelly, dingy pub, and dubbed it The Stench Inn. We quickly drank and left. There was lots of humour. I remember at Hook End I had boiled the kettle and said to Morrissey, 'I've made some Earl Grey. Would you like some tea?' and he said, 'That's not tea.' I said, 'Well, what's tea then?' and he said: 'Assam.'

JH: Morrissey seems to be very witty and sharp.

JB: He is. The funniest thing he ever said to me was at the start of *Vauxhall*. He asked me about playing bass, what bass players I liked. I said lots of jazz players, you know, Paul McCartney, his Beatles work. Then he said, 'Bass isn't something you want to start playing at the age of five, is it? It's not like a guitar or drums.' I said, 'Well it's a very integral part of a band. Name a really good band without a bass player.' I instantly thought of the The Cramps, but never mentioned it. I thought that was really funny. Musically there was a pecking order: guitar, drums, bass.

JH: Who was your 'pal' in the band?

JB: Alain and I really were quite close, but he lives in America now. He's the only one I have contact with. I had some brief contact with Spencer, we exchanged messages but I don't know where he is.

JH: You and Spencer left the band at the same time.

JB: Yeah. We had been on a fifty-date tour of America and it was 'Morrissey and the band'. I had just suddenly felt lost it with it. When you're doing something useful it's so intense like a marriage, but if you hit the wall …

JH: What happened?

JB: To go out on stage and play the songs without deviation ... I just didn't want to play the same bass part every night, and it was all rather predictable. I had another weird moment on stage looking at Morrissey, the band, the five thousand people, and I thought: 'They're all at the same party, I'm not there.' I could see myself playing, but it was like somebody was pulling the strings. I decided halfway through a gig—during 'Maladjusted', that was it. We were largely doing *Vauxhall and I* towards the end of that tour anyway.

JH: Do you listen to *Vauxhall* much now?

JB: My daughter does. My oldest daughter Harriet—who has special needs—loves Morrissey. She was born prematurely at six months, weighing 1 lb 6 oz. Her sister, Florence, weighed 1 lb 8 oz. Tiny ... you know. Delivered by C-section because Helen had pre-eclampsia. They had taken her in. I got a call at 5am. I jumped into my clothes and Helen was really quite unwell. They were trying to control it as best they could, but there was a danger of her organs ceasing to function. We had only just found out that she was having twins. All of this was like bombs going off ... Harriet had severe brain damage. She has hydrocephalus,

which fortunately became arrested, otherwise things could have been worse. She's much like a toddler, but she's five foot and twenty. And she loves Morrissey. She met him several times, once at the Drury Lane gig. She was there in her silk pyjamas in a royal box. He would always ask, 'How's Harriet, how's Helen ...' Helen got on with him well, probably better than I did. Maybe it's because she's not a musician. Sometimes singers feel intimidated by musicians.

JH: Is Harriet a fan of The Smiths?

JB: I played The Smiths for her recently. If she likes a song she will repeat some of it, and she doesn't sing some of those ones.

JH: Maybe she knows her daddy isn't on there.

JB: She sings 'Now My Heart Is Full'. She sings quite often at 3 a.m., which isn't always enthusiastically received. Well, one of us will be like, 'Did you hear Harriet last night?' and the other one will say, 'No, I was exhausted, I slept!'

JH: I think that's really sweet.

JB: She has a beautiful voice.

JH: Isn't it wonderful that she uses her singing voice in this way?

JB: Oh, yes. She can't really communicate, she has severe learning difficulties. She has no problem, however, asking for chocolate, crisps, cocoa and Morrissey!

JH: It must be a difficult thing to see your other two children grow up around her.

JB: It is. She went to the local nursery. There was a gap in development, but it wasn't so wide. Whereas now these kids at twenty meet up, go out, do things that young people do, boyfriends … you know. My daughter is happy, she doesn't know about all that kind of stuff. She's a princess, all of her needs are catered for. She loves music, YouTube, Morrissey. But then … we do have respite care, we get to go out together. Harriet also has epilepsy, so our sitter is trained to deal with any problems that arise, although her medication keeps it under wraps. This is one of the reasons why I stopped drinking, really, because if something happens, you can't not be 'with it'. You have to be responsible. There was one time, though, where Helen and I had an anniversary and we got a bottle of fizz, and we got a tiny bit tipsy and we were dancing around and the kids were going, 'This is great! Get some more!'

JH: I wonder if Morrissey knows the extent of Harriet's enjoyment.

JB: Sometimes I feel bad about leaving the band, because I'm sure she'd love to go to a gig.

JH: Oh, I'm sure if you contacted him again he'd be only to happy to have you guys along.

JB: Yes, but how would that be? If I've worked with somebody so intensely then I don't want to go and see them play. I caught a bit of 'Alma Matters' at Glastonbury and just thought it didn't sound right.

JH: Is there anything that he's done lately that you would have liked to be a part of?

JB: To be honest, I haven't listened. I got a copy of *You Are The Quarry* for Harriet and she didn't like it! I just thought she's a much better judge than me. I like some of his songs better than others.

JH: Did you ever have any 'this is amazing' moments with Morrissey?

JB: When we played Glasgow Barrowlands, that was great, because I had played there before with The Cramps and just got gobbed on!

JH: Morrissey got gobbed on loads in 1985 in the Barras. I remember he stopped the concert at one point and said, 'No, no, no—don't spit!' but the Barras was a filthy hole. A brilliant filthy hole. I think it was a show of appreciation.

JB: We tried that, it didn't work. We threw beer on everybody. With Morrissey it was a really good gig. Very intense. We went on to play Motherwell. We did the encore, 'Shoplifters' and everybody stormed the stage. Suddenly, I realised that I was the only person left on the stage, I couldn't see any of the others ... The production manager grabbed me by the jacket and all of us ran down the corridor to get on the bus. I was like: 'Wow! This is great! Like being in The Beatles!' We also did Central Park, New York, on stage as the sun went down, to two thousand people.

JH: What does Morrissey eat/drink?

JB: In those days it was lots of cream, pastry, eggs. Tea.

JH: How does he take his tea?

JB: With milk. I don't think he has sugar.

JH: If Morrissey was to walk in here right now and say, 'All right, Jonny?' what would you say?

JB: I'd say, 'Would you join me for an Earl Grey?' and he'd say, 'No. Assam, please!'

JH: What if he was coming round for dinner? What snacks would you put out?

JB: What snacks? This is highly unlikely. I don't know. Tea and toast, with butter. I'm sure he's a butter man, but he should be on the marge, the sunflower spread.

JH: I wonder if he'd do a butter ad.

JB: He could replace John Lydon. Or maybe a coffee advert?

JH: Like Clooney?

JB: No, Assam, Twinings!

JH: Yes, tea, great idea. In a suit— distinguished gentleman Morrissey with cup and saucer.

JB: I'd also put out some fruit. Maybe some grapes. He ate some grapes once.

JH: Red or green?

JB: Red ones. Seedless. Push the boat out. He might say, 'These aren't grapes!'

JH: What's your favourite crisp flavour?

JB: Ready salted. The Kettle Crisps. I like the black pepper and chilli ones too.

JH: Favourite cake?

JB: Home-made. Helen does very good cakes—cherry and coconut.

JH: Favourite Smiths song?

JB: I used to like playing 'Shoplifters', but I'll probably say 'There Is a Light'. It's very touching and also very humorous. Sums Morrissey up. Very funny imagery.

JH: Favourite Morrissey song?

JB: 'Suedehead', and I really did like it but never played it—'Everyday Is Like Sunday'.

JH: Favourite gig?

JB: Central Park. It was unique, perfect, couldn't be planned.

JH: Favourite song to perform live?

JB: 'Billy Budd, 'Speedway'. I remember once performing that and somebody threw loads of daffodils on the stage. It was so slippy I fell over, like on a banana skin. People offstage were saying, 'Wow, you're really getting into it there!' and I was like, 'I just fell over!'

JH: Favourite tea?

JB: Peppermint tea in the evening, Earl Grey in the morning and maybe a spiced blend in the afternoon.

JH: Maybe you should be doing the tea advert ... Favourite biscuit?

JB: Digestive. Good for dunking. And also Malted Milk.

JH: Favourite sandwich?

JB: Tomato.

JH: Just tomato?

JB: On wholemeal, or seeded, with a little bit of black pepper.

JH: Tomatoes that you've grown yourself?

JB: In my head I live the good life, but like most people I get them from the supermarket.

JH: Just tomatoes? No salt?

JB: No, I don't take salt on anything.

JH: Do you ache for a bit of cheese?

JB: No, I'm virtually vegan.

JH: What's your veggie weakness?

JB: Honey. I like to put some honey in the apple crumble. The children like that.

JH: Ah yeah ... 'The children ...'

JB: Blame them.

JH: Favourite book?

JB: Gandhi's autobiography. I like Gandhi, he's a good guy.

JH: Favourite movie?

JB: Something with Peter Sellers in.

JH: Favourite thing that Helen says?

JB: 'You watched me do it!' Like, 'Have you made that tea?' 'You watched me do it!' It's a stock phrase in our house.

JH: Favourite thing about being a dad?

JB: Gems of wisdom. My son said, 'So Dad, do you think I should have a wife when I'm older? Or are they just nothing but bother?'

JH: What are you most proud of?

JB: That I got to do what I wanted to do, which was largely by not knowing what I was doing, singlemindedness and rejecting everything else. Maybe it'll work out, maybe it won't, but I am committed to it.

JH: I think it has worked out. You have a lot to show for it. Congratulations.

JB: Yes, my proudest achievement is that I still practice, every day, except on weekends.

JH: Jonny ...

JB: Yes?

JH: You're right. You are very nice.

JB: Thanks.

JH: Please could you write a note to my mum?

JB: Of course.

To Pat.

Hi I'm a bass player and sometimes I play with Mark "Perfect" Nevin and most of the time with lots of other people. Mostly though I play with my kids!

I hope you're well.

My best to you.

Jonny Bridgwood.

xx

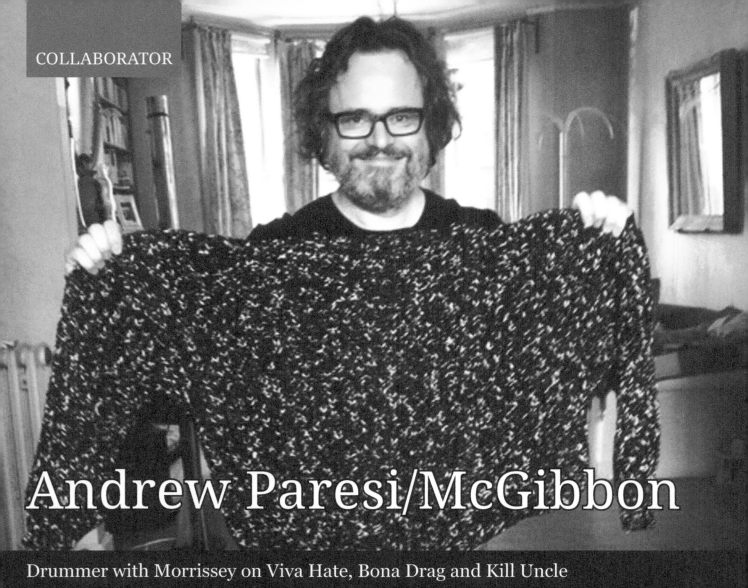

Andrew Paresi/McGibbon

Drummer with Morrissey on Viva Hate, Bona Drag and Kill Uncle

15 MINUTES
WITH YOU

CURLYHAIRED, bright-eyed and beaming, Andrew Paresi grandly beckons me through the wide front door of his West London home. We settle at the kitchen table and straight away he's looking after me, like an uncle. Up and stirring coffee by the Aga, he's smiley and chatty, busying himself around the cups and milk. I feel like he's going to ask me if I have enough money for lunch, check my bag for letters and reassure me that thirteen out of twenty is good enough for spelling, so it is with a fond and quiet smile that I politely decline his very kind offer of coins for the parking meter.

As I unpack my notebook, I notice a plate of oatcakes laid out on the table.

'Oh, do have one if you like!' He laughs heartily, curls bouncing.

Mr Paresi/McGibbon uses two names. One is for drumming—Paresi, and one for writing—McGibbon. It could be argued that he needs two hundred names, as his CV stretches across everything that encompasses the arts. He is theatrical, wildly enthusiastic about music (with an encyclopedic knowledge of drumming) and is a very entertaining and respected comedy writer/director. But above all, he's a performer.

As we talk, performances and mimicry ebb and flow from him as he smoothly delivers deadly accurate impressions. Blink and he's Billy Connolly … Blink again and he's Morrissey. It's like they're all *in there*, waiting for their turn.

He has never halted his passions of drumming and writing comedy since parting with Morrissey, and is currently recording a new comedy TV pilot for the BBC with his production company Curtains for Radio. His latest drumming work can be found on the Franc Cinelli album *Good Times*. His comedy writing of 'Eric The Gardener'/'Gripper' stories in the 1990s for Radio One has amassed a cult following and is to be released on iTunes in the coming weeks.

His time as Morrissey's drummer is well documented in a book and radio show: *I was Morrissey's Drummer*. It includes hilarious excerpts from Stephen Street, Suggs, Clive Langer and Andy Rourke, and Andrew still had plenty of stories to add about Morrissey, drumming, influences, acting, music … and Jaffa cakes.

Renowned as a constant source of laughter for Morrissey, it's not difficult to see why he was chosen as Morrissey's first solo drummer. In addition to his precise and powerful drumming on tracks like 'Disappointed' and 'Everyday Is Like Sunday', it's clear that Andrew must have been like smelling salts for the singer during a period of raw Smiths-grief.

During our interview he revealed what it felt like to make a record with Morrissey: '*It was agape really. Having that voice in your head while you were drumming was mind-blowing*'; he describes his style of drumming on the albums as hard-hitting: '*I played the nuts off everything I did*'; and when he heard the finished *Viva Hate*: '*It sounded fresh, disturbing and beautiful … a serious body of work.*'

He doesn't eat pizza, but if he did, his favourite topping would be quattro formaggi. His favourite drum is a snare (on top of a snare …) he loves a bit of *Brass Eye* and his favourite Smith is Morrissey. (Well, it was agape, really).

J: Please say your full name.

A: Andrew Paresi. My family name is Andrew Stuart McGibbon.

J: Why the change?

A: In the mid-seventies there was a song by The Goodies called 'Funky Gibbon' and it just got to me at a deep point and I thought, I can do without that. I thought that nobody would take the name seriously, so I took a decision aged eighteen or nineteen to change my name to Paresi, because my girlfriend at the time was doing an Italian degree and she thought that 'Andrew Heart Attack' would sound cool.

J: 'Paresi' does sound exotic.

A: … and it stuck. I thought it sounded interesting in a mock-electro kind of way. I've gone back to McGibbon for writing/producing/directing purposes, but Paresi is the drumming name.

J: So you drum under the name 'Paresi' and write under 'McGibbon'.

A: Yeah.

J: Is that in case Morrissey tries to find you?

A: Oh yeah!

J: Did he call you Andrew or Andy?

A: He called me Andrew. Most people do. Only people who are upset with me say, [Scottish accent]: 'Andy! You know what you have to do! You have to have a vocabulary of sounds!'

J: Can you do a Billy Connolly?

A: His voice is *down here*! He's a shipyard worker! My dad worked as a caulker in Port Glasgow shipyards on the River Clyde. He bashed hot rivets, without protective gear, into ship bolt-holes, as did my grandfather.

J: Did you want to go into that trade?

A: Well, my dad did very well and travelled down to London. He said that there was a shipyard Scottish comedy thing. There were a lot of examples of it—Chic Murray was another, born in Greenock like my dad—of people who were just very funny at telling stories. Scottish humour has a lovely, gentle view of life, and a cutting irony and ability to be classless ... Mind you, Frankie Boyle fans may disagree!

J: What are you working on now?

A: I just finished working on the Franc Cinelli album *Good Times,* produced by Danton Supple, who also produced Coldplay's *X&Y.* I also have a production company—Curtains for Radio and Curtains for Pictures. Our main production M.O. is comedy drama and we do film too.

J: Can you describe yourself in a sentence?

A: I'm an incredibly fascinati ... No ... I'm just battling to be the best I possibly can at whatever it is I am doing. After Morrissey I found it very hard trying to think of what to do at that point. Music was going in a different direction—all samples and ecstasy—so I shifted back to comedy and directing, which is what I wanted to do when I was fifteen. I'm passionate about what I'm doing. Oh God, I'm starting to sound like Tony Blair now ...

J: Things can only get better ...

A: [Juts out jaw, adopts terrifyingly accurate Morrissey voice]: 'Things can only get better ...'

J: That is a very good Morrissey, I've got the shivers.

A: Well, *is* it Morrissey or is it Professor whats-his-name?

J: No, I think the D:Ream prof is higherpitched.

A: [Adopts Prof Brian Cox voice]: 'Oh that's right, yes, it's a higher pitch, it's up here, with the sun, which rotates around, and can I have my knighthood ...'

J: I think your Morrissey impression might be the best I've ever heard. Have you ever done 'Morrissey' ... to Morrissey?

A: No, but we had some funny times.

J: It is reputed that you are one of the people that made Morrissey chuckle the most. What did you say or do to make him laugh?

A: We just used to muck about. I used to insert words into his songs and tell him jokes. We mucked about with titles and names. I did develop a Morrissey accent, but I was very cautious [adopts Morrissey voice]: 'Because it's fun to do because it's all so beautiful.' Only if you really love the guy can you do it with any real sense of humour.

J: I think it's clear that you really did love him, didn't you?

A: It was agape, really. Having that voice in your head while you were drumming was mind-blowing. You can feel so many emotions in yourself while you're playing with him. I felt like I was Dennis Davis playing with Bowie—this is it—if I'd had a heart attack—Paresi—while playing with him ... to me that would have been a kind of noble end.

J: Tell me more about what it was like to be the drummer in Morrissey's band.

A: I played the nuts off everything I did. The main attraction with him was that everything was completely unconventional. He was carving these beautiful poems and then attaching them to pieces of music. You're in that bizarre experimental laboratory when you're not really sure what a chorus or verse is yet. So you're playing, not knowing where everything is, and the chaos of that is just truly joyful! There's nothing like it. In *Bona Drag* and *Kill Uncle* there were moments —I remember with Mark [Nevin] and we were sitting at the back of the studio when we'd recorded 'Our Frank' and we were killing ourselves when we heard 'I'm gonna be sick all over your red pullover and see how the colours blend.' It was hilarious! The concept of songwriting was being reinvented by Morrissey. For me, it was just awesome.

J: It really must have been incredible, putting your stamp onto everything like that.

A: It *was* incredible, but the person who was under the most stress was Stephen Street. He was producing, playing bass and putting the songs together, and he was under the kind of astonishing pressure that probably comes once or twice in a lifetime.

J: How did you meet Stephen Street?

A: I was in a band called A Pair of Blue Eyes. We had been told that we were 'the thinking person's Curiosity Killed the Cat.' CBS asked Stephen Street to come in and mix the first single, 'You Used To Go To My Head.' He was going, 'where's the click? How is this drummer keeping in time?' And they were like: 'There is no click.' I think that impressed Stephen, particularly the power at which I hit the drums, which was not fashionable at the time.

J: How would you describe your style of drumming?

A: I was very American in my style, punky and funky. I hit the drums hard. I was influenced by early Motown; I love those grooves. I love Frank Zappa's various drummers, people who understand groove and are technically proficient, especially Steve Jordan and Travis Barker and W S Holland from Johnny Cash's band. Neil Conti [Prefab Sprout] is another drummer that hit hard at the time, but it wasn't the preferred style, if you like. It wasn't the 'drumming du jour!'

J: Did Morrissey know that you had played with Jim Diamond and Bucks Fizz?

A: No. Stephen [Street] was trying to keep everything in place. He knew that things could go awry from recording Smiths albums. He just wanted to know that the drumming thing was sealed and he didn't have to worry about it. As a producer he was cautiously removing issues that might be a problem before they even happened. So I had to do a Stalinist whitewash of my musical background there.

J: I know that Stephen gave you his denim jacket to wear when he first introduced you to Morrissey, but please tell me what you were wearing before!

A: Well, I had a different style, I was still in that 1982 Man at C&A era. I was wearing wacky jumpers. This one looked like a knackered television set—I've still got it in a bag somewhere

... Actually, hold fire there! [goes into hall, rummages in bag, returns to room] This was the jumper I was wearing when I recorded *Viva Hate*!

J: What? I really like that jumper! So Stephen said, 'No, you can't wear that'?

A: Only when we had to go out to a nightclub. He was just trying to prevent anything going wrong ... I think at that time the pressure was on and every nuance had to be managed in detail. Stephen is a consummate producer and is always aware of details. He is incredibly professional.

J: Did being surrounded by this creativity inspire you to write songs?

A: I did, but I wasn't a great keyboard player and I liked big juicy keyboardy ... dare I say it, postmodern jazz chords. Kevin [Armstrong] very helpfully decoded one that I had written into a guitar friendly version and played it and it came pretty close to getting a vocal on it, called 'Angie'. At the time of *Bona Drag* there were a lot of fantastic songwriters around. Clive had written 'Shipbuilding' for heaven's sake. It was brilliant to be involved as a drummer, but at that point in my musical cycle I really just was like the little boy trying to get a scribble in. I've composed plenty of music since then, however,

in *I Think I've Got a Problem,* starring Suggs, Bob Monkhouse and Bill Nighy, The Sinclair Singers and other music.

J: I love the drums on 'Disappointed.'

A: I'll play them for you. It's a challenging rhythm. I'll write it out for someone, someday. It's a left hand start, a tricky one, but once you get into the roll of it, it's a rhythm I was very proud of. It was like a steam train, like two bits of drumming going on at the same time.

J: Thank you. So you live here with your partner, Tanya?

A: Yes. I haven't got children, not to say that I'm not capable of making them! Tanya had kids already from a previous marriage—and now they have children too—so I'm a ready-made grandfather! [Adopts 'Victorian' persona]: I've instructed the children to call me 'Grandrew!' I'm not old enough to be Granddad.

J: Your time with Morrissey is very well documented in *I was Morrissey's Drummer*.

A: To me there was just a great comedy show to be made there.

J: It's very funny. Do you think he has ever heard it?

A: I don't know. There's no bitterness of any kind. How I saw things at the time. It's quite self-deprecating.

J: In the book/recording you describe yourself working with Morrissey as 'simply travelling with greatness and putting its cat out at night.'

A: The people who really strike you are the people who have an inner space, a force field, a buzz if you like, and you can feel your heart palpitating a bit more because there's something enormously special there. You have to give that part of your life to it. I don't think you can make a deep emotional commitment to any music at all unless there's love there.

J: You have described mealtimes with Morrissey as 'like dining with Jesus...

A: There's a specialness; a weird quality ... If you're going to be working with what we now know is one of the greatest English rock poets of the twentieth century that may be studied three hundred years from now, that won't always come with, 'Hey matey! Let's go down the pub'— though that did happen. Somebody like that will have a great deal of quietude. He would often get up before the rest of us and I remember once we had a chat, and he said something along the lines of: 'Andrew, most people are lucky to have one talent, and you have so many, where do you begin?' It was a thoughtful and supportive thing to say to me. Funnier if he'd said ' ... and you don't even have one ... so what are you going to do?' It was a brilliant experience and I left with good grace.

J: Did you hear from him afterwards?

A: Several times—quite recently, actually. He was going to come over and have Boxing Day dinner with us when we were in LA. It didn't happen for one reason or another.

J: How does he communicate with you?

A: The odd postcard ... now it's morse code. I have quite a few faxes that were flying around from the *Kill Uncle* days, but they are beginning to fade because of the paper. They are very funny, it's very witty stuff.

J: What's your favourite Morrissey track to drum on?

A: 'Disappointed' is something I'm very proud of, and 'Girl Least Likely To.' In terms of power, 'November Spawned a Monster.' And for just the inventiveness of it, 'Hairdresser on Fire' because of what he was singing, 'busy clippers'. But the track I'm most proud of is 'Late Night, Maudlin Street' because it changed a genre in a way. I was able to play very 'loopy' improvised drums towards the end of that. It's an incredible song.

J: What's your favourite album that you worked on?

A: It has to be *Viva Hate*, just for being asked to play on it. In the early stages I was coming down to play 2-3 tracks a day for a week at a time and it seemed that there was a real head of steam building between what Stephen was writing, what Vini and I were playing and what Morrissey was singing. Closely followed by elements of *Kill Uncle*. 'Mute Witness' is absolutely stunning. There was actually a song called 'Kill Uncle' that we did a backing track for and a vocal. It survived for a nanosecond! And *Bona Drag*— 'Striptease With a Difference', 'Oh Phoney'. I wish there had been a better reaction to 'Ouija Board', or 'November'. Radio One just couldn't cope with Mary Margaret O'Hara's middle vocal section. I remember Morrissey and I were in the car and Nicky Campbell cut it off just before and Morrissey was like: 'Oh. It's like having my lungs cut out of my body.' It was an epic song, but at a time when epic songs weren't popular with the powers that be.

J: So you didn't ever perform live with Morrissey?

A: I think from his perspective there just wasn't a band there for him. Stephen is a great bass player, and Vini is an outstanding artist too ... It's sort of ... I don't know why it didn't happen. Where he was headed he needed to have a band that looked how he felt. Although I was disappointed, I understood. He went back to work with Andy and Mike again, then we came back together. There was just that expectation ... people started arriving from the corporate rockabilly sector and that's what he wanted to do.

J: What emotions ran through you when you heard the finished *Viva Hate* album for the first time?

A: Incredible pride and satisfaction and a real sense that this was clearly a serious body of work. It sounded fresh, disturbing and beautiful. On a personal note, I was thrilled with how up in the mix my drumming was. This was a great validation for what I'd been working toward and was unusual. I am grateful to Stephen Street and Morrissey for recognising the drumming as a key forward-facing element in the album's sound.

J: Who was with you when you first heard *Viva Hate*?

A: Stephen, Morrissey, Vini, assistant engineer Steve Williams and I think Nick Gatfield from EMI, who continued to spot and develop great talent like Amy Winehouse.

J: What about when you saw 'Suedehead' and 'Everyday Is Like Sunday' climbing the charts?

A: Absolutely hyper-thrilled. This was drumming I was fantastically proud of, and to hear it on the radio prior to release and on the A-list at Radio One was just amazing. Nothing has come close to those moments. Especially after it went to number one. That was amazing. Around the time of the *Viva Hate* release I was in a smoky old pub in the Wandsworth/Battersea environs— before the yuppie plasmodia had a foothold in the area—and they were playing the album in the pub. Next to me were veteran drinkers and smokers, many unemployed in the area as a result of the dreadful recession. I was with a group of friends and one of them yelped out, 'Hey, it's Andrew drumming on this, everyone.' I'm quite modest and was calcified with embarrassment. I thought I was going to be lynched. This was a roll-out the barrel-Mrs Mills-Rockney pub. But to my surprise I got smiles, drinks raised and the guy behind the bar said,

'This is a great record, mate—have one on the house.'

J: What did you think of wonderful tracks like 'Bengali In Platforms' and 'Margaret on the Guillotine'?

A: 'Bengali' was the first of Stephen's backing tracks we recorded as a group. We did three takes. The third one had it. I'd worked out a drum rudiment fill for the end of each chorus section, except that I didn't know then what made the chorus or the verse. I recall Vini's lovely acoustic guitar playing and it came across as a very beautiful backing track. In my mind I'd started making up tunes that might fit round it and even thought of some words. Silly words I kept to myself, obviously. When I heard the finished version I recognised it as a paean, if you will, to double isolation. 'Margaret on the Guillotine' was a very passionately delivered end track. The sound effect at the end makes the proposition ruthlessly satirical. Music is one of the few non-judgmental, hurt-free, emotionally rewarding experiences left.

J: I love the drums on 'Break up the family.' Did Stephen create the percussion, or was that you?

A: This is one of my favourite tracks. Stephen Street had created a percussion loop made with AKAI 1000 samples of a cabasa, triangle and bongos. I asked for this backing loop, a click track, if you like, to be turned up loud in my headphones. I then played a tight rhythm on the kit to remain absolutely close with the loop by playing a steady, funk groove style BUT stripping it down so that I played the last 16th semi of the second beat bass drum note a grace to the third beat of each bar. So it went bs (b)b s with 8s on closed hi-hat over the whole thing. The only time I left this was to accent the end phrase of each chorus with four sixteenth note snare fills ahead of accenting 3 AND 4 in the last bar ('Wish me luck and say goodbye'). I went for the ride cymbal in the middle eight but kept the same 8s note pattern. Yes, one of my favourites and a chance to groove up in a low-key Brit funk way, but not too much!

J: Wow. Thanks for sharing that. I'm sure any keen drummers will be glad of it. What do you think of Morrissey's later work? Do you keep in touch with his music?

A: Yes. I love *Vauxhall*, 'The More You Ignore Me', 'Alma Matters', *Quarry, Ringleader* … they are all brilliant.

J: What does he think of your work now? Does he know what you're doing?

A: Yes, I think he may have followed it. There's a track called 'Melanie (Inject Yourself)' that I did with Radio One when I worked there writing music and bits of comedy for Eric the Gardner on the Clive Bull show. He may have heard it. Lyrics to 'Melanie (Inject Yourself)' a Morrissey parody composed by Andrew used on Radio One:
Oh Melanie, you say you really love me
You say that I'm the best thing that's ever happened to you
Oh Melanie, you keep telling me you love me
You say that I'm the best thing that's ever happened to you in this cruel world
Oh Melanie, honestly
If what you say is true, why do you continue to
Inject yourself, Inject yourself, Inject yourself
Ahh, the drug may have sex appeal, but I know what you feel isn't real
And I can't bear you when it wears off
Oh Melanie, you say really hate me now
You say that I'm the worst thing that's ever happened to you
Oh Melanie honestly
There's something really troubling me.
If what you say is true
I'd rather you continued to
Inject Yourself, Inject Yourself, Inject Yourself

Oh the drug may have sex appeal, and I know
what you feel isn't real
And I can't bear you when it wears off
I can't bear you when it wears off
Oh Melanie – (I wouldn't say no?)

J: Have you always done voices? Do you hear the voices first, then they become characters that you write about?

A: Definitely. I came from a school—Salesian College—that had a lot of funny people in it. Kevin Day and Catherine Tate went there. It's closed now but is currently being used to film 'Bad Education' with Jack Whitehall.

J: How did you come to write 'Eric The Gardner' and the other characters for Radio One?

A: Kevin Greening heard 'I Live In a Giant Mushroom' and then Matthew Bannister asked me to come in and do some bits for Radio One to do lots of characters. I made a deal with Kevin that all these characters—surreal, edgy ads, stories, sketches and stuff—would appear out of nowhere in between records then disappear again. He never back referenced them or me on his show. We were getting away with incredibly subversive stuff on a prime time breakfast show.

J: Were you able to influence the playlist when you were on the Radio One breakfast show?

A: 'The Boy Racer' was on the playlist, but it was only on B or C list and we were trying to bring it more attention. There was no way we could physically play this record more times, so I came up with this idea which was that Kevin would say, 'Coming up, we'll be playing the new Morrissey record' and then we'd play 'Melanie (Inject Yourself).' Kevin would never back-announce it, only forward-announce it, then afterwards say, 'And we look forward to hearing the new Morrissey record tomorrow.' This was a way that we could keep the single mentioned.

J: What a brilliant idea to keep fans listening.

A: All Morrissey and Smiths fans are very intelligent and enormously sensitive and vulnerable. They are the people who should be protected, loved and looked after.

J: That's very kind.

A: It flies in the face of how humanity normally works.

J: If Morrissey was to walk in here right now and say, 'All right, Andrew?' what would you say?

A: I'd drop everything, except my trousers. I'd be right there.

J: What if he was coming round to have snacks with you? What would you put out for him?

A: Well, it's Earl Grey tea for him, isn't it?

J: According to Jonny Bridgwood it's Assam.

A: Assam, okay, that shows a total lack of awareness on my part that I will have to correct straight away! I should know Morrissey's tea! Right ... well ... I'll put out a range of teas!

J: What would you put out to eat?

A: Well, my memory of him is that he enjoyed chocolate quite a lot. We used to raid the cupboards at Hook End Manor. It would be something like digestives or something very fattening, with no possible retreat from becoming fat. Morrissey would be like: 'I've found this!' Oh, now what was it he used to like ...?

J: Breakaways? Jaffa Cakes?

A: Jaffa Cakes and Maltesers in catering-sized packs. We weren't very rock and roll ...

J: What's your favourite biscuit?

A: Oatcakes.

J: The Nairn's chocolate oatcakes are delicious.

A: Oh, I haven't tried them.

J: What's your favourite Morrissey track?

A: 'Suedehead.' Everything just comes to life on that, but a close second is 'Everyday is like Sunday', and a close third is 'November Spawned a Monster.' Other Morrissey songs I love: 'The More You Ignore Me', 'We Hate It When Our Friends Become Successful' and 'He Knows I'd Love To See Him' (a very special and gentle song). And of course 'Girl Least Likely To' and The End Of The Family Line.'

J: Favourite Smiths track?

A: 'The Headmaster Ritual.' I love Johnny Marr's Rickenbacker playing, and his attitude. As a piece of work he just makes it sound like you're in the path of an express train and you can't get out of the way of it.

J: Favourite comedy?

A: Victor Lewis Smith's *Ad Nauseam* series, *The Day Today* or *Brass Eye*. I loved the show, because it had this combination of individuals, including Steve Coogan and Chris Morris, who all wanted to do their own thing. It was explosive, rather like a band on the edge of destruction with members like Lee and Herring, Armando Iannucci, Patrick Marber, David Quantick, Jane Bussmann—all heavily talented people. In that moment, they nailed it and pulled the rope ladder up behind them. It's a satire on the form of news, but also very funny and fantastically surreal.

J: Favourite set of clothes to wear?

A: I have a Comme des Garçons suit that I love; other than that, it's jeans and jumpers that look like broken down television sets.

J: Favourite member of Bucks Fizz?

A: I thought Jay Aston was very attractive and would make an ideal wife for someone.

J: Are you a vegetarian?

A: Yes, since before I played with Morrissey. I don't eat meat, eggs, wheat and various things because of allergies. I don't drink any more. I'm really boring.

J: Favourite pizza topping? Would you eat a pizza now that you don't eat wheat?

A: I don't, but if I did it would be Quattro Formaggi, although I don't eat so much cheese now.

J: Are you mostly vegan, then?

A: Pretty much, yes, but I still drink milk.

J: Favourite Smith?

A: I think they're all great. I know Andy because he did the show with me and he was wonderful. But it's Morrissey. It has to be.

J: Favourite restaurant?

A: The Ledbury on Ledbury Road, Notting Hill. It was raided in the riots. I made a lot of money that night. Did some time for it.

J: Who's your favourite showbiz pal?

A: Well, I keep myself to myself, but Suggs is one of the funniest people on this planet. He cracks me up. We had a lunch once with someone who was supposed to be representing a TV channel. During the lunch it became clear that she had no connection to the channel at all, and it was just because she wanted to meet Suggs. It was absolutely hilarious, he was very funny.

J: Madness videos are brilliant and funny.

A: Yes, the thing that's gone a bit is the mickey-taking, UK stuff. People being funny is one of our greatest exports, we got a hint of it at the Olympic ceremony opening, but I feel music is becoming stodgy with big agents controlling everything. Subversion is the meat of creativity and without that music can fall by the wayside.

J: Favourite song of all time?

A: 'How Soon Is Now?' is in there. Some Bowie—'Ashes to Ashes' is brilliant. I loved 'I Wanna Be Your Dog' by The Stooges and was bowled away by the beauty of a mid eighties Randy Newman song called 'Real Emotional Girl' (from *Trouble In Paradise*). 'Any Major Dude' by Steely Dan, anything by XTC and, strangely, going back to childhood with 'Ruby' by Kenny Rogers. 'Little Children' by Billy J Kramer. Other than that—a drummer's type of music is too esoteric to be known. I have a genuine love of The Band. Levon Helm was a hero. East Tennessee songwriters like Dolly Parton and the Porter Wagoner thing from the 60s and 70s. There is something very honest and beautiful about this period of American blues/country, pre-commercial Grand Old Opry, and the Gram Parsons thing that happened which we now know as Americana. Everything's got to have a label these days! Frank Zappa was the king of uniting great comedy, deep and subversion anarchy with mindblowing music. Anything from 'Freak Out!' onwards, especially 'The Black Page' from *Zappa in New York*.

J: What's your favourite drum?

A: The snare drum. I've invented this device where I have a snare drum and then a smaller one sitting on top of it. It's a tighter skin, so you can do more stuff on it. It has the depth and power of a big drum and it doesn't sound wimpy. It took me a while to get the groove.

I learnt drums playing with a big band every week at college. It took me away from academia, but I got to understand scores, percussion, and just playing in a wind band/orchestra setting rather than exclusively in a punk band gave me a different insight to drumming. I love drums. I'm 100% musician.

J: Could you write a note to my mum?

A: Of course I will.

> Dear Pat,
>   It was a pleasure to meet your daughter
>   We had a great afternoon and I really enjoyed the occasion.
>   Lots of love to you,
>   Andrew

Boyd Hilton

Reviews editor of Heat and Morrissey fan

15 **MINUTES WITH YOU**

I ARRIVED early to meet Boyd Hilton at *Heat Towers*, so I asked the receptionist if I could quickly nip to the ladies. She directed me through a set of double doors that led straight into an area of busy desks. I became slightly anxious that I was suddenly among the cool people, and wondered if I *shouldn't* have rejected the (as yet Gok-approved) 'double cord' look I had previously considered.

However, on second glance the *Heat* uniform appeared to be hoodies and Converse—a very informal, relaxed, laid-back environment—not the intimidating *Devil-Wears-Prada* fash-off I thought it was going to be.

As I make my way back to reception, I see the daddy of the laid-back. Boyd Hilton is wearing a green zipped hoodie, jeans and his trademark jaunty glasses.

'Hello Boyd!' I say, shaking his hand. *'So glad there's no pressure to dress 'cool' in the Heat office, what with all the celebrities and all ...'*

'Ha!' He laughs, 'Not at all! I'm always dressed like a chav!'

We head off to Costa Coffee and Boyd tells me about his day job, running what might be described as *Heat*'s 'arts corner'—reviews of books, movies, and TV shows, attending premieres, being on TV, [*Jews At Ten*] his radio work with Richard Bacon and his Arsenal podcast with other guest hosts such as Dermot O'Leary, Dan Baldwin and Ben Winston.

I'm fascinated by his Cilla-encrusted life, surrounded by stories of Chezza's new 'boyf' and latest vajazzles. He seems an unlikely Morrissey fan, but he's as ardent as any obsessive, claiming *Vauxhall and I* as the period in Morrissey's career when he was *'really on top of it'*. He does not conform to the *all-Morrissey-fans-must-just-like-indie'* belief, and has very catholic tastes in music.

He likes crime fiction and blackberries and his favourite Corrie character is the late Blanche. His drink of choice is Coors Light. Amongst all the movie premieres, concerts, events, parties and dinners, the best night out he ever had was Morrissey at The Palladium, 2006, 'when he wore the tux.'

His friend David Walliams introduced Boyd to Morrissey after the BBC Radio Theatre gig for *Years of Refusal*. When Boyd said he worked for *Heat*, Morrissey replied [something like]: '*It is what it is ...*'

J: Please say your full name.

B: Boyd Jonathon Hilton. My family originated from Eastern Europe, so my original name was Horovitz, then my grandfather changed it to 'Hilton' like a lot of anglicised Jews do.

J: Are you watching *Jewish Mum of the Year* on Channel 4 right now?

B: Yes, I am! I'm on the show that's on straight after, *Jews at Ten*.

J: That's a very funny show.

B: Yes. I make a few appearances throughout the series.

J: Please describe yourself in a sentence.

B: Hard core TV, film and music geek.

J: Can you give us a picture of your typical day at *Heat*?

B: I'm TV and Reviews Editor. I'm in charge of that section of the magazine, so one day I'm deciding what we're going to cover in terms of TV, music, books, films, DVDs, then the next day it's commissioning people to write about each one. I also write stuff myself, so it's then all a case of putting it together and delivering it, really. Equally, some days I might be interviewing someone, or doing my radio show with Richard Bacon on BBC Radio 5 Live, or going out to see a movie premiere, a launch, stuff like that.

J: There are lots of 'celebrity' magazines on the shelf now. What makes *Heat* different?

B: It's a celebrity gossip magazine, in the same market as about nine others. Most of the magazines that are in the same place have risen since we started. The element that makes us different is that although we cover all the same stuff in terms of *X-Factor*, etc., we also review films, TV, books and music, and the other magazines don't really bother with that.

J: Whose face sells the most magazines?

B: David Beckham, Victoria Beckham, just say The Beckhams. Cheryl Cole … The cover is all about a good story, really.

J: How often does *Heat* get in trouble for circulating rumours?

B: Very rarely.

J: Is it because you write it as speculation rather than fact?

B: Yeah. The stuff we write is harmless speculation, or stuff we've been told by people close to those people. We get access to the stars when they are available.

J: What's life like in the office?

B: It's great fun! I've been at *Heat* for thirteen years. It's a really nice place to work, we all work very hard … we listen to our iPods … it's very informal.

J: Do people heat their lunches in the microwave?

B: Yes, definitely, people do that all the time. I don't heat stuff up in the microwave, but it definitely happens. Newspapers are much more formal, you'd be encouraged to wear a suit and tie there. Not sure they'd have a microwave!

J: What type of celebrities do you enjoy interviewing/writing about?

B: It varies, really. I like comedians—Ricky Gervais, David Walliams, French and Saunders. I like TV comedy. Russell Brand, too.

J: Who's your favourite interviewee?

B: Probably Elton John. I spoke to him twice—once in Atlanta and once in Las Vegas. That was great and he is a brilliant interviewee. I've done Ricky Gervais about ten times, that's always a lot of fun, as is David Walliams. I've got another one with him due next week at the Literature Festival.

J: David is a big fan of Morrissey as well, isn't he?

B: Massive. Six foot five.

J: Did you ever want to work for other, more specialist magazines that reflect your taste in music?

B: Not really. I would have liked to work for *The Word* magazine maybe, but now that's closed, so I guess I'm lucky I didn't. Wouldn't mind doing a few interviews for *Rolling Stone*, though!

J: Do you find it a challenge when you have to review a Cheryl Cole/Elton John/N-Dubz album?

B: Well, I do also like Elton John. I give the big pop reviews to colleagues and I stick with Moz, Pet Shop Boys, etc. I like Elton's classic stuff going back to the early 70s ('Tiny Dancer' is one of the best songs ever). Not so much the Disney songs, though they do work with the films.

J: Have you ever met Morrissey? Did you ask him about *Heat*?

B: I did! I met him and asked him and he was fine with it. He said something like: 'It is what it is.'

J: When did you meet him?

B: I met him after the gig he did at the BBC Radio Theatre for *Years of Refusal* and I was just lucky enough to be introduced to him afterwards. I have been to lots of Morrissey gigs and the after-drinks that the journalists go to. At that particular time he actually came to the drinks in the basement of the BBC.

J: What did he have to drink?

B: A bottle of beer.

J: What was your conversation?

B: Well, I was with David [Walliams], so David introduced us and we talked about the scent he was wearing ... some kind of strong aftershave Morrissey was wearing ...

J: Did it smell like a church?

B: Yes! He was worried about going on *The One Show*. He was doing it because his mum watches it. We talked about what his mum watches on TV, and the soaps he watches, *Eastenders*, *Coronation Street* ... We talked about *Crossroads*! He thought the gig went really well, he was in a good mood; there was a good atmosphere and everyone was really excited. In general, he was really nice.

J: Have you ever featured him in *Heat*?

B: Yes! We did a whole page on him when his last album came out, we did five best Morrissey songs ... we've never interviewed him. (a) I think it would be a hard sell for me to do and (b) I don't think he would do it anyway.

J: In your magazine you have 'Spotted!' which has pictures of celebrities 'doing all the same stuff we do'. If you spotted Morrissey, what would you like to see him doing?

B: Oh God. Um ... It would be quite funny to see him buying a copy of *Heat*!

J: If Morrissey was to walk in here right now and say, 'All right, Boyd?' What would you say?

B: I'd say, 'Do you remember meeting me five years ago after that gig at Radio 2? You were very nice.' Although right now I'd probably ask him about that brilliant interview he did on *The Colbert Report*.

J: Great interview.

B: Yes, I thought Morrissey was really funny, got the whole thing, very jovial. I thought Stephen Colbert was brilliant. Some people seemed to think that he didn't get it, which I think is ridiculous, because he clearly did.

J: If Morrissey was coming to your house, what snacks would you put out for him?

B: I'd put out peanuts, a selection of nuts and fruit. I know he likes a beer; I'd get the best beer of the moment, Coors Light.

J: Is that your favourite drink?

B: Yes, I like Coors Light ... gin and tonic ... vodka and cranberry ... I'm easy!

J: As a fan through the years, what's your favourite Morrissey phase?

B: *Vauxhall and I* period, I'd say. I just thought he was really on top of it. Everything about that period was good. He looked good, the photos were great, he was free of controversies at the time. Or in between controversies! My two favourite albums are *Vauxhall and I* and *Strangeways*. For me, *Vauxhall and I* is as good as, if not better than, The Smiths albums.

J: Do you prefer Morrissey solo records to Smiths records?

B: It's interesting, really. Partly why he gets annoyed is because people don't talk about his solo work, and it's fantastic. *Speedway,* 'Now My Heart Is Full', that whole album is incredible … and off *Your Arsenal* there's 'Tomorrow', and I mean, 'National Front Disco' is a brilliant song. These albums stand out, and I do think that the songwriting, production and sound are as good as, if not better than, any Smiths album. I like the more recent albums too, but those are the best, for me.

J: What do you think of the recent reunion rumours?

B: All of those rumours are ridiculous. I am totally against a reunion. He wouldn't do it, he knows it would be cheesy and exploitative. It would be great if he did a gig or something with Johnny Marr. But all four members of The Smiths? Calling themselves The Smiths? No.

J: What books and magazines do you read?

B: I like crime fiction, American, Harlan Coben is one of my favourites, I like the Jack Reacher books by Lee Child—Tom Cruise is in the new film. I like literary books as well, like Michael Chabon, those kinds of things. I love magazines, I read *The New Yorker, Q, Mojo, Empire,* everything.

J: Did magazines play a part in your life when you were growing up? Did you remove and pin the posters to your wall?

B: Yes. The new romantic stuff was happening, Spandau Ballet, Duran Duran, but I also liked The Smiths, all the big Eighties bands, really.

J: How did you get into The Smiths?

B: I was about fifteen, sixteen when they came along. I remember a friend at school asked me if I'd heard 'Hand In Glove' and I think I was quite dismissive, actually! Of course, when I heard it I loved it immediately. I used to listen to John Peel as well, so I was hearing it there and on David Jensen, so every time The Smiths brought out a new song, I heard it there and I just liked it.

J: Did you ever get to see them live?

B: It's interesting; my memory is that I saw them at some kind of Anti-Apartheid festival in the early days. But I've since tried to track down what this gig was and I can't find it, so I may have imagined it. I may not have done.

J: Are you vegetarian?

B: I was for years. I went to a school that served horrible meat, and to get out of it I said I was vegetarian. Then I found myself in a situation where I had to eat meat (in hospital), and so now I eat fish and chicken. Morrissey would be horrified!

J: What's your favourite thing to cook?

B: I do a baked pasta with parmesan and leeks. Lots of vegetables.

J: I bet Morrissey would love that! Better than nuts.

B: Well, obviously I'd cook for him if he came round.

J: Favourite fruit?

B: Blackberries.

J: Favourite film?

B: *Manhattan*. I'm a huge Woody Allen fan.

J: Favourite soap character?

B: Someone from *Coronation Street*. Probably that one who died.

J: In the tram crash?

B: No, even before that ...

J: Mike Baldwin?

B: No, too far back.

J: Blanche? Deirdre's mum?

B: Blanche is the one! Blanche!

J: Favourite pizza topping?

B: Um, spinach and that egg one—fiorentina.

J: Favourite Smith?

B: Morrissey.

J: Favourite biscuit?

B: Custard Cream.

J: It's Friday, are you going to a Movie premiere?

B: Well ... yes ... tonight is the James Bond screening, but I always go to a gathering of friends on a Friday. I'd rather go out on a Friday than a Saturday.

J: What has been the best night out you've ever had?

B: The Morrissey gigs! The Palladium, 2006, when he wore the tux. The Royal Albert Hall after he'd been away for a while was also exciting.

J: Will you write a note to my mum?

B: Any kind of note? Anything?

J: Anything.

Hey Pat
keep enjoying Corrie!
love

Boyd xxx

Tony Fletcher

Author of *A Light That Never Goes Out: The Enduring Saga Of The Smiths*

15 MINUTES WITH YOU

TONY Fletcher's latest biography: *A Light That Never Goes Out:The Enduring Saga of The Smiths* looks big, thick and serious when it lands on my doormat. The front cover is a shot by Stephen Wright that features four serious Smith-faces staring out of the blackness, with the air of a whodunnit. As a self-confessed slow reader with a plodding pace, I was worried about getting through it in time for an interview with the author. It took me three weeks and four days to finish, after which I felt nourished, enlightened and excited to meet him.

It's true that Smiths and Morrissey books are well-trodden paths and that famous knock of Johnny on Morrissey's door has been thoroughly documented, but *A Light That Never Goes Out* is a bit like thinking that all the chocolate in the selection box is finished,then going on to find another untouched, unopened selection box behind the couch. The 'Mars Bar' chapter is in the second meeting of The Smiths, when Morrissey knocks on Johnny's door, climbing up to the attic passing pictures of *Coronation Street* heroes to reach Johnny's record-shop bedroom. Here, the book flips perspective to reflect a new view, and is in no small way due to Fletcher's in-depth interviews with Johnny Marr over the course of two years.

Glimpses into young Smiths' characters are revealed amidst the social and cultural backdrop of the seventies: Johnny and Andy as boys with guitars strumming along to *Peace, Perfect Peace* at Sunday mass; Morrissey leaving St Mary's at lunchtimes to go home to his mum for dinner; and Johnny getting egged after being sacked from The Co-op (then walking home in the snow like a 'frozen omelette'). It is this narrative of vivid 3D images that makes the book cinematic. The build up of the four individual paths coming together to rise, and fuse a chemistry of music and poetry that the world had never seen before—then end it all spectacularly, just short of the release of the final album.

Author Tony Fletcher has secured his own place in Smiths history. His nineteen-year-old self conducted Morrissey's first ever TV live interview at The Hacienda in 1984. Technical difficulties aside, he remembers the evening vividly, reflecting on how the four young Smiths were never apart: 'They were very closely huddled together, like the *South Park* kids ... I remember they would walk around together, cross the room together, go to the stage together ...'

Tony's lifelong relationship with music and literature began—incredibly—at fourteen, with an interview from Paul Weller for his school fanzine. On meeting Weller: *'I deliberately didn't put the school badge on my blazer, so that I could look like a mod.'*

We managed to cover most aspects of his life, including his other published biographies and his style of writing. We talked about The Hacienda (when he shared a dressing room with Madonna), and of course, his favourite sandwich filling. We even had a brief drift into the existentialist nature of The Smiths, but by this point, my mind had already been bombed by the fizz and excitement of Tony's tales, so we parted, and I floated home in the wrong direction.

J: Please say your full name.

T: Anthony John Fletcher. I don't know why my parents chose that name, I guess because it was popular at that time.

J: Please describe yourself in a sentence.

T: Doer.

J: What line of work were your parents in?

T: My mum was an English teacher and chorister. My dad was a professor of music, musician and author. If you think about it, it makes complete sense that I'm a music author; it was in the genes.

J: They must be very proud.

T: My mum has a shelf of my books. She even read my X-rated novel, *Hedonism*. I sent it to her because I wanted her to have every book of mine. I said to her, 'Just put this one on the shelf, you don't have to read it.' She got back to me later, saying, 'Oh, it's great! It's just like Irvine Welsh! Like *Trainspotting*!' I was like: 'Mum! You've read *Trainspotting*?!'

J: Who shortened your name to 'Tony'?

T: Paul Weller.

J: What? I wasn't expecting that answer …

T: I know! When I started, Paul Weller took me under his wing, to a large degree, and he always called me 'Tone' or 'Tony' and it was evident that 'Anthony' was just far too middle class. I was fourteen.

J: How did you know Paul Weller at fourteen?

T: I wrote to him after I started my fanzine at school. During the summer of '77 there was something going on in music. I was sitting in a maths lesson, reading *Sounds* under my desk and thought that starting a fanzine would be fun. We did four issues that were pretty crap, but I really enjoyed doing it. So about a year later I wanted to step it up and wrote to a bunch of people to get interviews. Paul Weller was one of them. He wrote back and said, 'Yeah, come up to the studio, we're making a new album'. It was *All Mod Cons*. I wore my new black school blazer, as we were moving up from third year to fourth year. I deliberately didn't put the school badge on, so that I could look like a mod. The first words he said were, 'Oh, all right, have you come straight from school then?'

J: Ah ... crushed! He was young himself then, too

T: He was around twenty. There was an interview he gave where he said that he couldn't write teenage anthems anymore because he was twenty.

J: You've had a lot of jobs: the *Jamming* fanzine, TV presenter; DJ, novelist, biographer ...

T: I have to say ... not one of those is actually a 'job'. They are all basically to do with avoiding having to do a job! The closest we ever got was at the end of *Jamming*, when it had an office, which I enjoyed, but it got too nine to five for me at that point with a PAYE scheme. But other than that, I've never had a job.

J: Because you've never wanted one?

T: Absolutely.

J: Which one of those areas of 'socio-cultural experience'—not job—did you enjoy most?

T: Well, there was a danger of me being like a jack of all trades, when I was younger. If you start out doing something and it takes off, you need to have incredible presence of mind to resist temptation to do other things. The weird thing is that I started the magazine because I thought it would be fun, but the truth is I thought I'd be in a band. We had a band at school.

J: What was the band's name?

T: The band was called Apocalypse, God-awful name, but we did release a couple of singles— Paul Weller produced one—we toured with The Jam, we were the last ever support group with The Jam. We did all right.

J: Were you the singer?

T: I was not. I've got an awful singing voice. I wrote part of the songs as guitarist, keyboardist, but part of the problem with the group was with two writers and there was competition for songs, as opposed to partnership. I didn't set out to be a writer until much later in life. I'm really glad I wrote books like the Bunnymen and the REM book and I had a busy career as a freelance journalist. When I moved to New York, I had a roommate who was waiter in the VIP room at The Limelight, so we started an alternative night there, where I was DJ, he was host. I mention that because it was too good to turn down. Eventually, when I got married, I came back from my honeymoon and packed in the club and decided to focus on my writing. I'm proud of all these things, but they are all very connected to music and media. I also worked for *Rapido* for a while, that was fun. In fact it was the most fun job I ever had because I worked remotely, with no boss. The first thing I did for them was with

Samantha Fox, and it went from that to Keith Richards and James Brown. I spent a day with James Brown where he called me 'Mr Fletcher', because it's the BBC. I couldn't believe I was getting paid for it.

J: Where do you live now?

T: The Catskills, NY. I lived in Manhattan first, then Brooklyn, then moved up to the mountains. It's a natural progression once you have kids. I knew when I got to New York it was where I wanted to be. So after living in Manhattan for a while we moved to Brooklyn. It was quite a rundown area at the time, but a very special block in Park Slope.

J: Park Slope is a very upmarket area now, isn't it?

T: Yes, but it wasn't at the time. There was gunfire at night and cocaine on the corner. Having said that, it was a multicultural block with stoops, and my older boy got to grow up in a culture where kids play on the street. When we moved we sold it to a banker couple, because that's what the place had changed into.

J: Why did you move from Brooklyn to the Catskills?

T: I wasn't moving forward, in my life and my relationship, in Brooklyn, so something needed to happen, and then our second kid came along and that was it. We already had a very small place in the Catskills to go to on the weekends, but we kept finding ourselves in that Sunday evening thing where we'd drive back to the city and were like: why are we doing this? We spoke to a few other couples that had settled up there and they recommended it. There are so many artistic people up there, musical, creative; it's a wonderful place to live.

J: Let's talk about your interview with Morrissey at The Hacienda for Channel 4's *The Tube*..

T: Okay …

J: When you look back at yourself, what do you think?

T: That is the one piece of my very short-lived on-camera career that I cannot bear to watch. I realise now, being older, how to handle a situation like that. It was just very tense. It was Morrissey's first interview. I had interviewed Wham and Elvis Costello live, so I was used to that, but this was the first ever live outside broadcast and it connected back to another live broadcast in Newcastle, so they were running two live shows at once. That might seem easy these days, but it was a real big deal then. In The Hacienda they had these Factory All Stars on stage and they were really cool members of New Order, A Certain Ratio and Section 25, doing something together to a backing track. The producer said to us, 'Right, you're up in the balcony; they're playing down there, when we count you in they'll kill the sound and you'll carry on with Morrissey.'

J: … and they didn't kill the sound …

T: That's why it's embarrassing, because they counted us in and I went to start talking and it was so noisy! The Hacienda had famously bad acoustics anyway, and Morrissey couldn't hear me! And I couldn't hear him. And he's tall! So I was, like, shouting up to him, but it's evident that he can't hear me so I made the mistake of looking to camera like: 'Are we on?' The face of the director next to the camera just dropped and they sent someone off to the soundboard. What could have been a really sharp two minutes, it was me just shouting at Morrissey and him shouting back at me.

J: It has a beauty all of its own … You're both young and awkward and it captures early Morrissey. I think it's lovely to watch how people develop.

T: That's interesting. From my perspective it was difficult, it was hard. It was great that people watched it, because it was his first TV interview.

J: I think you should forgive your nineteen year-old self.

T: I don't think I can forgive myself for that jacket! The Michael Jackson jacket! Having said that, it's a Johnson's jacket, so I'm assuming that Johnny Marr would approve.

J: How were all four of The Smiths that night?

T: They were new and they were very eager. I was talking to Johnny about this memory—that they did have that 'gang' mentality—despite what we now know about the financial set-up. All four of them were very closely huddled together, like the *South Park* kids. They all came in to give Morrissey their support and I remember they would walk around together, cross the rooms together, go to the stage together …

J: I love that image. The Hacienda was full of young talent that night. Madonna was there too, wasn't she?

T: Yes, Madonna was there, she shared our dressing room, and they gave her a little blind to change behind.

J: Madonna shared your dressing room?

T: I cannot think why, at nineteen, I needed a dressing room, but we needed somewhere to be in-between, like a green room, and Jools Holland was in Manchester, so he might have needed one.

J: How did you end up presenting *The Tube* at nineteen?

T: Because of doing the magazine. When *The Tube* started they did a story on *Jamming*, and put it out halfway through the series. Then they invited me up to be on live, which really was amazing. They said they were going to keep in touch, called me in the summer and did some testing.

J: How did you come to write the Echo and The Bunnymen book?

T: When my magazine packed up in 1986 and I was in debt, one of my really good friends told me that there were some problems with trying to get a Bunnymen book together. Barely a week passed between *Jamming* going under and me being in debt to be asked to write this Bunnymen book. It's never been so easy since, because I approached Echo and The Bunnymen and said, 'Are you interested in a book?' and they said, 'Yeah.'

J: Are you happy with your books?

T: The writing has got better over the years. The R.E.M. first edition just got a final update. I was rereading it and pretty happy with the writing, and thought it's okay, it's good, it's fine. The novel is great, but it was a hard sell. The Clash book doesn't really count in the sense that it's not a biography, but I really enjoyed doing it, just writing about the music for once. The book on the New York City music scene I'm really proud of.

J: What advice would you give to young writers?

T: Write every day. If you can't write everyday, then you're not a writer. That's how you'll answer that question, and in a way it will take over. I don't pick up my guitar everyday, but I do write. If I was meant to be a musician, I would be picking up my guitar everyday. You know what you are based on the fact that you can't live without it. I think writing is really hard as a creative endeavour because it's so solitary. If you're in a band, you get feedback from other musicians, and even if you're a solo musician with headphones on the music is feeding back to you, so you can stay up all night working on that. With writing, there's nobody out there to filter work. I've got nobody really that I could give half a book to, nobody I'd trust. If you have a piece of music, it's much easier to get a demo recording. The solitary aspect is a tough endeavour.

J: True, but I think what you said about the musician and the music feeding back to you rings true for writing, too. Reading over or enjoying writing about a character and their development can be rewarding and sort of 'the petrol' for the next bit.

T: You're talking about fiction now?

J: Yes, sorry.

T: I think with non-fiction, you get to the point that there's so much paperwork, and it's research all the time. It becomes work. I think it's harder, certainly for me.

J: And there's the pressure to be factually accurate all the time.

T: But I think when you're writing fiction and the characters go off and it's like you're watching them running around the room, it's really quite fun.

J: Was there a point in your life where you clicked and thought: 'That's it! I'm a writer'?

T: There's genuinely a part of me that still thinks, 'Hopefully one day I'll be a writer.' I read other people's books and think they're better than mine. But I also have people tell me I'm a good writer.

J: I think you need to have those insecurities to spur yourself on.

T: Absolutely. Michael Stipe has insecurities and he's a genius. The answer would probably be when the Keith Moon book came out. Barely a week goes by where I don't hear someone say it's a great music biography, and that blows me away. But at the same time, I'm like, well how

the hell do I follow that up?

J: You interviewed a lot of people for *A Light*, most significantly Johnny Marr.

T: I think Johnny was the most important interviewee for the book. If Johnny hadn't cooperated, it would have been hard. I did ask Morrissey—a few times—but I figured we wouldn't get him. Johnny holds the key to The Smiths legacy. The number of people I went to talk to who said, 'Does Johnny know about this?' and I had to tell them yes; then they were like: 'Okay, well, if Johnny's all right with it, then yeah, I'd love to be part of the book.'

J: Did you hear back from Morrissey?

T: His assistant assured me that he had received the letters. It would have been wonderful if he'd decided to write back with why not, but he didn't and that's that.

J: Before we get into the book, can we talk about the cover? It looks a bit like a murder mystery ... Morrissey is facing away from the other three, it's set on a black background, nobody is smiling ... Obviously I know what happens at the end, but if I didn't, I'd be expecting maybe a death ... or a prison sentence ...

T: That's great if that's what you thought. A few people have likened it to the cover of *With The Beatles*. We wanted something quite classic. The idea was that The Smiths didn't need an introduction, so we didn't put anything on the back cover either. It was just like, this is The Smiths, this is the book, these are the people. I hope that worked, I have a nightmare with covers.

J: It does. It has a very authoritative air. Is it an 'enduring saga' or a 'complete history'?

T: When I did the synopsis I just came up with 'enduring saga' and it stuck. I sold it as that title. The idea is that The Smiths are an ongoing fascination, and that's why it's enduring.

J: Within the introduction you talk about why you wrote it: to set The Smiths in a sociocultural and political context, with in-depth family background. Why did you approach it this way?

T: It's a pattern in all my books, it's massively important to set the cultural scene. My book about the New York City music scene has seventeen different chapters like that, all about the social, economic, immigration context and how that produced disco. I thought it was really important. That first chapter of *A Light*—about Manchester—took me more time to write than any other chapter in the book.

J: To me, *A Light* suggests a serious, authoritative and heavy read, but in fact the joy of reading it was in the many colourful demonstrations and glimpses into character.

T: I think details are important. Morrissey drops details into his lyrics, for example—a rented room in Whalley Range—it's all truth that adds colour. My favourite stories in there are the ones that I could identify with. I'm the same school year as Johnny and Andy and I went to a grammar school that became a comprehensive the same year as theirs did, so I felt I could identify with a lot of what they went through. Ivor Perry telling me that Morrissey was stopped for his lunch money on Kings Road intrigued me. They wouldn't beat him up; it was more of a tax, really. I was a weaker kid when I was younger and in those days it was accepted. It is what it is: 'Give us your lunch money, yep, fifty pee, now walk on.' I don't take any delight in reporting that, but I think a lot of us who grew up in England at that time will identify with this.

J: Please tell me what these symbols are at the start of some of the chapters, and what they signify—the first one is on page 20.

T: Ah! Well spotted. It's a spindle, the centre of a record.

J: Ah! Of course it is!

T: Do you want an exclusive?

J: Always!

T: That record, that says 'A Light That Never Goes Out' (p. 19). The idea was to have a 7" single. It's a tribute to what The Smiths always wanted when they started—an indie record with a classic punch out label. It's there partly to remind you that The Smiths were maybe one of the last great vinyl bands. They made 45s, and that's what this band is about. We scanned an actual rare Smiths record, that's the Rough Trade label, and we just put in 'A Light That Never Goes Out'. It's important to me that it was a Smiths record. That's the first time I've ever told anybody that.

J: Thank you. Is it your favourite Smiths record?

T: Those change day by day.

J: Every author/biographer/Smiths fan thinks that the story began when Johnny knocked on Morrissey's door. Do you think that is when the story began? Johnny and Andy were messing about and swapping guitars for years before that happened, developing sounds together.

T: Johnny developed The Smiths' riffs after that, though. And Morrissey had the poems ready, just waiting for someone to come along and accompany them. I think the answer is that it started at that door on Kings Road, when Johnny knocked on the door with Stephen Pomfret. It's that Patti Smith line: Morrissey looked at Johnny— 'The boy looked at Johnny' and said— 'You're the one I've been waiting for.'

J: I love that Morrissey was just waiting for something to happen, rather than going out and looking for it, almost as if he just knew there would be a knock on the door.

T: I think that's a very existential conversation, there's just no answer to this ... Morrissey is sitting indoors, waiting, just waiting ... and it happens. And it shouldn't! Because everything says 'Morrissey! You're wasting your life away, running out of opportunities ...'

J: He just knows it's going to happen.

T: There are no explanations for this. What would have happened if Johnny hadn't knocked on his door? Well, that's hypothetical, and he did, it happened. If you want to get conceptual and spiritual about it, you could say that Johnny was always going to knock on his door.

J: One of my favourite chapters in the book is when Morrissey goes round to Johnny's house for the first time, and again there are connections and commonalities, the landlady with the Corrie pictures ...

T: I took the description of the attic room from what Johnny and other people said, because everybody has always talked about when Johnny went to Morrissey's door, so I thought I'd flip it round. Johnny is four years younger, a real Jack the Lad, room full of records, I can imagine Morrissey might be intimidated the first time he walks into Johnny's room.

J: Were there any really challenging areas when you were writing the book, where you just thought, I need to persevere and get through this

T: I think sometimes ... there's a certain formula you try to avoid when writing about an album. I tried to make sure I wrote about each album in a different way. Trying to find a way to write about an album, do you talk about it song by song, or about the making of the album, or review the finished album as a complete entity? That's hard for a biographer.

J: Your opinions creep into the book quite a lot, particularly in the *Strangeways* chapter. I'm not sure you share the opinion with Morrissey and Johnny that it's their finest album ...

T: No, I don't. Do you?

J: I'm all about The Smiths' first album. I like the discovery. It's unpolished, fast, exciting, slightly harsh and wild in parts, gentle in others.

T: Some songs came out better than others ... 'The Hand That Rocks The Cradle' is one.

J: So if it's not *Strangeways* or *The Smiths*, what is your favourite Smiths album?

T: I think *Meat Is Murder* and *The Queen Is Dead* really stand up as albums, and will continue to do so. *The Queen Is Dead* is the stronger political statement. It's classic great lyricism, but it's not as much Queen Elizabeth as I had thought in 1986; it could be any queen, including a drag queen. *Meat Is Murder* is a great album, and knocked *Born In The USA* off number one. That was a massive achievement, and it stands up as Northern, indie. *The Queen Is Dead* is the conventional masterpiece that sounds better on American radio. *Strangeways* tarnishes the view, because you listen to it knowing that the band have broken up. R.E.M. were so smart, they knew they were breaking up, but the album came out six months before they did, so people were able to form their own opinions. Now the fact is, it's obvious that's their last album in retrospect. But people should be allowed to form their own opinion before knowing it's the last album. From my personal point of view there are great songs, but with the greatest of respect, you have to be wary that, just because somebody said 'Last Night I Dreamt That Somebody Loved Me' is the best production that it's the best song. If you asked somebody out in the street, they'd say 'This Charming Man' over 'Last Night.' It also reflects a band that's very much in the studio. Incredible production, but does it have the same impact as 'This Charming Man' or 'William'? I don't think so. I think it's a transitional album. I would have loved to know what they would have done next.

J: If they had continued, which direction do you think they would have gone in?

T: Well, again, in a way it's irrelevant, because it's back to existentialism. Having said that, there are lots of comparisons between The Smiths and R.E.M. The fifth album R.E.M. made was transitional, then they came off the road, and wrote *Out Of Time,* which was phenomenally successful. I think that's what The Smiths could have done.

J: Do you think that people listen to *Strangeways* differently, perhaps with a tinge of sadness because they know it's a break-up album, so as they're listening to it they have already formed their opinion sad, romantic, bittersweet ...?

T: Yes. It's very hard to listen to 'I Won't Share You' and pretending you didn't know the band were going to break up. I can't listen to that song without thinking, 'Surely there's a message going out there, surely...' Very hard to listen.

J: I have a question here from @vivahate72 on Twitter. He wants to know if your next book is going to be a Blur book, because you reference Blur at the end.

T: No, sorry! It will be the memoir, *Boy About Town*. It's fifty short stories that really recount being at school in the 1970s, dreaming of being a rock star, wrapped in a complete musical and social history of the era.

J: I can't wait.

T: It all weaves together, even though each story could be read on its own. I'm really excited about it.

J: Before we finish, is there anything else that you wanted to say about your current book that you haven't said so far?

T: Yes, there is. It's important to note that it's an international book. In the past biographers have written about The Smiths as the Manchester band, everyone else cut off. The Smiths don't just belong to Britain. The Smiths were massive in America. It lays out the American story too, the modern rock scene, so the Brits get their chapter a little earlier, then the Americans get their scene too. It's a big part of the story.

J: I notice that the American edition has a very bright and lively cover too! Is that reflective of the moods of each nation?

T: I don't know about covers. I do know that my British editor said, 'I don't really like that American cover' and the American editor said, 'I don't really like that British cover.' So you draw your own conclusions …

J: If Morrissey was to walk in here right now and say, 'All right, Tony' what would you say?

T: I'd say, 'Hi Morrissey, how are you?'

J: If he was coming to your house, what snacks would you put out?

T: Oh well, I'm vegan. I'm going to back up. I would say, 'Hi, Morrissey. Sit down.' He looked really good in Albany; he's lost weight. And the *Meat Is Murder* video is showing factory farming of hens. I read that he had finally given up eggs, which is great, but long overdue. So I'd sit him down and replicate all his dairy habits with vegan food, give him vegan cup cakes. So I'd like to talk to him about where his line is on vegetarianism is, and why he's always been such a strong proponent for vegetarianism, but continued to eat so much dairy and wear animal products. Because it makes sense to go the whole nine yards.

J: When was the last time you spoke to Morrissey?

T: Back in The Smiths days was the last time we spoke.

J: At The Hacienda?

T: We did a phone interview after that, but I won't pretend that I'm his personal friend.

J: What is your favourite record of all time?

T: *Ocean Rain* is a perfect album. Echo and the Bunnymen.

J: What's your favourite Johnny record or period since he left The Smiths?

T: The first Electronic record. They really caught that post-Madchester vibe. Johnny's input is quietly stated, but it's there all right.

J: What's your favourite drink?

T: I only drink beer and wine these days. It would have to be a good American IPA. I'm a runner. I strongly suspect that runners run so that they can have a pint at the end.

J: What's your favourite biscuit?

T: I don't really eat biscuits.

J: What's your favourite sandwich filling?

T: Peanut butter and banana.

J: Favourite movie?

T: *The Kids Are Alright* , The Who movie from 1979.

J: Favourite actor?

T: Albert Finney in *Saturday Night Sunday Morning* and Phil Daniels in *Quadrophenia*.

J: Favourite thing your mum says?

T: 'It's your beloved mother.'

J: Favourite Morrissey song?

T: I can't. There's not one. Changes all the time.

J: Favourite fruit?

T: Bananas.

J: Favourite discovery you made when writing your book?

T: Physical discoveries: the original Rough Trade contract and a number of personal letters from Morrissey to Tony Wilson, which I didn't reprint in full. Emotional discoveries, I think it was the importance of all four personalities in The Smiths. It wasn't just Morrissey, it wasn't just Marr, and it would not have been the same without Andy and Johnny. Especially Andy, who I think in many ways was the soul of the band and whose musical input has been underrated. Hopefully I got all of that across.

J: Can you write a note to my mum?

T: Yes! Do you have everybody that you interview write a note to your mum?

J: Yes. She keeps a folder.

Dear Pat,

I have just spent a really enjoyable two hours with your daughter. She is a writer, but you probably know that. Don't "panic": she isn't giving up her '15 minutes' just yet.

Love,

Tony Fletcher

Stephen Street

Smiths Producer and Morrissey co-writer/producer

15 MINUTES
WITH YOU

I DON'T like tea. But Stephen Street is standing in Miloco Studios kitchen, squeezing tea bags very tightly against the side of two mugs whilst asking me if I take sugar, 'No, just a spot of milk please,' I reply, thinking: there's no way I'm asking for coffee now, that's *Stephen Street's* tea, he's made it, and I'm going to drink it. He's dressed casually and yet impeccably neatly, wearing a grey wooly jumper with a high collar and a striped scarf around his neck that he doesn't remove. He is most charming in his manner, and listening carefully I am able to decipher a very slight rhotacism with the letter 'r' in his speech that, accompanied with a gentle smile, makes me warm to him instantly.

I follow him (with tea) as he walks quickly and purposefully through two huge soundproof doors, into the neat and tidy not-a-button-out-of-place studio he works in, producing magical albums.

As he settles in his chair behind the mixing desk, he describes how his time with The Smiths and Morrissey changed his life. At twenty-four, Stephen was a comfortable and natural extension of the band, on the same journey at the same age (one year younger than Morrissey) with the same level of experience and the same ambitious goal: to make the next Smiths album greater than the last: '*[The Smiths] is a very powerful album. By the time we got to Meat Is Murder we were using different techniques, sound effects, etc., so that was a step on. And we stepped on again for The Queen Is Dead, then on again for Strangeways. There's obviously great tracks from each album that I'm very proud of but overall the improvements are incremental.*'

Now, aged fifty-two, he is still excited about the work he did back then, and is engagingly youthful as he disappears back into the memories: '*You see this sometimes with bands; for whatever reason, all the stars just align and it's like a juggernaut that can't be stopped.*' Occasionally, he looks to the floor to find his answers, particularly when talking about the Smiths split: '*I can remember Mike [Joyce] sitting there, looking really down, and thinking, I'll look up in a minute and see Johnny come through the door.*'

Since parting company with Morrissey after *Viva Hate*, he has gone on to work with many successful bands such as The Cranberries, Blur and The Courteneers. His approach to producing albums is about capturing and delivering the 'brand' of the band at that time: *'When a person releases an album it's like a fashion house working on their collection for the season, it's how they feel they want to put themselves over at that point.'*

Described by Andy Rourke as 'very attentive [and loved] by everybody' and by Johnny Marr as 'totally partisan' [*A Light That Never Goes Out*, Tony Fletcher, p. 466], the appeal of Stephen Street is his inclusive approach: *'I try and make each member of the band feel important thoughtout certain key processes of the record. Everybody is very, very important, whether it be the drummer, the bass player or whoever.'*

His favourite Smiths song is 'This Charming Man', he's known to Blur as 'Streetie' and he cites the Smiths album *Strangeways* as his finest moment.

I give the tea five stars (engineered and produced by Stephen Street).

J: Please say your full name.

S: My name is Stephen Brian Street and I'm a record producer.

J: Where does the Brian come from?

S: My dad's name.

J: You've always had the name Street?

S: Yes, it is my real name. Some people have asked me that before in the past, have I made my name up to be 'cool'—but no.

J: Your name is very memorable. Did you find it helped you in your career?

S: Not really. When I was at school I was called 'Street' or 'Streetie'—which is what Blur called me later on in life—but no, I've never really thought that much about my name.

J: Can you describe yourself in a sentence?

S: Oh God, that would be … er …

J: You can come back to me on that later if you like.

S: Yes, it's very hard! I'm not very good with words, you see, Julie, that's the thing, it doesn't flow off the top of my head like that and I get … I'm not good at the one-liners!

J: Ah … I'm sure that's not true! When you were growing up, what music were you into?

S: The first time I was really conscious of really becoming interested in music was kind of the end of the 60s and 70s when Marc Bolan came through. My parents didn't have a record player, but there was a radio, and I remember hearing The Beatles and the Stones. Mum and Dad didn't get a record player until about 1970, one of those big long bits of radiogram furniture with a radio at one end and a turntable at the other. I think the first record to be bought were those awful *Top of the Pops* covers records. But I remember I wanted a record player in my room, so I got a flip-top single BSI player with the speaker at the front. The first records I bought were *Electric Warrior* by T-Rex and *Ziggy Stardust and The Spiders from Mars*. I had my black case from Woolworths that had my albums in and my smaller black case that had my singles in. They meant the world to me.

J: The cases with the briefcase clip on the front?

S: Yeah! I've still got all those singles and some went missing over the years. I've still got *Ziggy Stardust*, and the original *Electric Warrior* album. That means a lot to me. From there, I discovered that only nine months before Bowie had released *Hunky Dory*, and before that, *The Man Who Sold The World* and *Space Oddity*, so I threw myself into that, just loved it, this new guy who had suddenly arrived from the heavens with all this fantastic music. He was a huge inspiration.

J: What's your favourite Bowie track?

S: Hard to pick one out just like that, but I'm still a huge fan of the *Ziggy* album. I love 'Soul Love.' It wasn't a single or anything like that, it's just so Bowie.

J: I love the drum intro to 'Soul Love.'

S: Yes! [makes 'Tss-tss-t" intro] It's fantastic. I'm a huge believer that when a person has a good partner such as Johnny and Morrissey and Damon with Graham, it's worth its weight in gold. Mick Ronson was an incredible part of that sound.

J: Did Mick's work influence you?

S: Yes, definitely. Mick Ronson was a great arranger of Bowie's ideas. He took them to another level. When I was younger I used to look at album covers and see names like Tony Visconti, I was interested in the idea of finding out what they did. So I suppose even then I was interested in being a record producer. From reading record covers I got a schooling in record producing.

J: What do you think is the most important thing that a record producer can do for an artist?

S: To portray the image that the artist has got at that particular point in their career; that life. To put it over in the best possible way, without tarnishing it. When a person releases an album it's like a fashion house working on their collection for the season, it's how they feel they want to put themselves over at that point. 'These are the songs for 1975 or 2012.' The producer is the person who takes those songs and puts them into a package.

J: So you 'brand' the album.

S: Yes, at least as far as taking it to the point of release. Or putting it on the 'catwalk', if you like. It's a bit like being a film director as well. Got a great script, a great bunch of actors, with a good cameraman and sound engineer, just need to make it a good finished product.

J: You started as an assistant at Island. What was that like?

S: It was about '82 or '83. They were going through a refurbishment of the studio at the time and my first job was varnishing the wood that went up on the walls! It actually felt great, because I felt like I was part of the team. I had some experience recording, because I had been in a band, so I wasn't totally green to what went on. But I was always watching, asking questions, 'What does that button do?' So I got a good grip and understanding of some technical aspects and also just the etiquette side of things, like how to work without upsetting anyone. Within two years I was at the point I was able to start engineering sessions myself. I was at a really good place. There are places that you can go to where you end up being a tea boy for years. But the engineers there were very good and it was a good learning place.

J: And it was around this time you were introduced to The Smiths during the 'Heaven Knows' session?

S: Yes. My studio manager said to me, 'There's a band coming in at the weekend.' They were beginning to book outside acts into the studio to make it more of a commercial proposition, so that's why we were open that weekend to Rough Trade booking a band in. I said to the studio manager, 'Who's the band that's coming in?' He said, 'It's a band called The Smiths.' I was like 'Wow! Great!' because I had seen them literally two weeks before doing 'This Charming Man' on *Top of the Pops*. I think it's one of their best ever performances, people still refer to it these days. I was like, 'Yeah, I'll definitely be up for that.' So they came in on the Saturday when I was the in-house engineer. Obviously John Porter was there, as he was working with them on that. 'Girl Afraid' was mixed at Island, but John took away 'Heaven Knows' to mix elsewhere. I just strove to impress them as much as I could. I think they appreciated the fact that the engineer had turned up to the studio and heard about them, made it quite clear that I dug what they were doing and stuff. So at the end of the session Johnny and Morrissey thanked me and took my name, and indicated that they'd be in touch. So obviously, I was over the moon. The next thing they did was 'William', which was done by John too, elsewhere. I didn't get involved in that, but I didn't realise until years later that there is a thank you to me on that sleeve!

I kind of thought that was over and the end of it all, but then, thank God, a few months later Geoff Travis phoned me and said, 'The band want to make the next album, producing it themselves, and working with an engineer that they trust.' And that was the start of me working with The Smiths on their albums.

J: In Tony Fletcher's book, it is written that in your time with The Smiths you made each individual feel special, that their contribution was incredibly important.

S: I always try to do that, with any band I work with. I don't always focus just purely on the lead singer or guitarist. I try and make each member of the band feel important throughout certain key processes of the record. Everybody is very, very important, whether it be the drummer, the bass player or whoever.

J: How would you describe your connection with The Smiths?

S: Well it helped that I was just slightly younger than Morrissey, so we were all in the same age bracket. We shared lots of music that we all enjoyed. We just managed to click on a personal level. I was very aware that it was a professional relationship, but it was a good one. Very positive. I just loved working with them, and making *Meat Is Murder* was a huge challenge, because I had never worked outside of Island Records before, so to me it was my first job as a kind of freelance engineer working with a band that was much revered and that had so much attention. It was a bit of a steep learning curve.

J: You were all on the rise together.

S: Yes, it was just incredible.

J: Do you have any favourite memories of that time?

S: Travelling in that big white Mercedes! I think it was Dave Harper that was the driver. He drove us around between Manchester and Liverpool. Kirkby, in fact, which is where we started the session. Just being in this big white Mercedes was fun.

J: Where did you all sit? Who was up front?

S: If I remember rightly, there were two rows of seats facing each other like a cab, so I'd just be in the back with the rest of the band. I remember

sitting there once and Morrissey was showing round the artwork for *Hatful of Hollow*. I was so excited, I was like, even though we're working on this new album, there's this compilation coming out which everyone was going nuts about. You see this sometimes with bands; for whatever reason, all the stars just align and it's like a juggernaut that can't be stopped. It's exciting when it happens, because it doesn't happen that often.

J: Did you gravitate towards one person in particular as your 'pal'?

S: No, they were a gang. It was a working relationship. They were close-knit, I was very much a Londoner and they were Mancs. They were friendly towards me, but I don't think I'd ever be one of their best pals. I don't know if Mancunians are suspicious of cockneys! We got on great, we were friends and I warmed to all of them.

J: You have made many significant contributions to production of Smiths albums, most notably with *Strangeways*. Do you consider this to be your finest moment?

S: Yes. For me, it's my finest moment because I was on a learning curve. I had more skills as an engineer and mixer at that stage of my career than obviously two or three years beforehand. I was able to do things sonically that I couldn't do before.

J: It's quite a different album, much more polished than the others.

S: It was a conscious decision to do things a bit differently. We were all keen to do more work in the studio. You can see the graduation happen through the years. Look at *Meat Is Murder* compared to the first album. The first album is a kind of raw encapsulation of what they did live, which is great. It's a very powerful album. By the time we got to *Meat Is Murder* we were using different techniques, sound effects, etc., so that was a step on. And we stepped on again for *The Queen Is Dead*, then on again for *Strangeways*. There are great tracks from each album that I'm very proud of, but overall the improvements are incremental.

J: You were on a learning curve, you had brought the band to the peak of studio work, one album became better than the last, more experience was gained ... You end up with this epic finish that heightens every talent in the group ... Where are The Smiths headed next?

S: Well, I thought at the time they were going onwards and upwards. The next step to becoming a global touring band. It was there for the taking. America was going nuts over them, which I always found surprising, because British bands really struggle to break America, and it was interesting, why did The Smiths become so big in America, because they're not very ... American! At the time they were back to a four-piece again, which was making Johnny focus a bit more on his guitars, pushing himself without Craig. I sort of got the impression that this was it: make an album then go on a good solid eighteen months' touring. It was a machine gearing up to do things. There was talk of the EMI deal happening, the next big step, a multinational record deal, as opposed to Rough Trade. I got the impression that there was still an interesting bunch of chapters ahead.

J: So the platform was set for world domination?

S: Yes. That's why I was so surprised when the split happened, because I didn't see it coming. I could see the pressure that Johnny was under, but I didn't see it coming. I never thought that the band would split up permanently. I thought they'd make the album, take a bit of a breather then get back on the road after the summer and start touring.

J: Did you ever go on any of the tours?

S: No, I was never asked. They had a good sound man, Grant [Showbiz], so it wasn't necessary, really.

J: Did you go to see the band live?

S: Oh yes, I'd go and see them. I saw them play Oxford around the second album. Good show.

J: When the Smiths split up it was a tough time for the fans, because there was pressure to choose between Morrissey's voice and Johnny's music, to decide who to follow. Was it the same for you?

S: When they split up I just thought, well, they're going to get back together again. So when Geoff Travis phoned me to ask if I wanted to try a session with Ivor Perry [Easterhouse], I said yes. We did that session over a weekend, but it was obvious it wasn't going to work. Wasn't anyone's fault, just the chemistry wasn't right. I can remember Mike [Joyce] sitting there, looking really down, and thinking, I'll look up in a minute and see Johnny come through the door. I knew there was a desire to try and keep the ball rolling. I wasn't picking sides. If Johnny had phoned me straight away and said, 'I want you to come and engineer a session,' I would have done that.

I knew that we finished *Strangeways* and there was nothing left in the can. I had some ideas from my four-track demo at home. So I thought, you know, there's no harm in trying. So I wrote a little card: 'Forgive me for being presumptuous, but if there's any ideas on here that you feel would be useful for recording as B-sides, please let me know.'

J: What was on the four-track?

S: I think the original 'Everyday Is like Sunday' is on there. I think 'Angel' might have been on there, and maybe 'Suedehead'. There were a few works in progress.

J: Were these written on the guitar?

S: Guitar, bass, drum machine. A basic backing track. I sent them off in August then got married and went off to Paris for five days. When I came back there was a postcard from Morrissey that said, 'I want to make a solo album.'

J: How did that make you feel?

S: Very excited, but at the same time, full of trepidation, because I thought, this is a lot. I'm taking on a lot here. But I thought, well, if Morrissey feels that he can do it with me, then that's a big bonus. I don't think I ever thought

I was going to upset Johnny because I kind of still thought that Johnny and he would get back together. I really thought that's how it would play out, that Johnny would come back.

J: What did you do next?

S: I dropped everything and worked on that record. I just sat at home, writing and writing and sending cassettes of ideas to Morrissey. He came round one afternoon to the two-bedroom maisonette and sang down some ideas into a microphone. I can't remember which songs, I think one of them might have been 'I Know Very Well How I Got My Name.' We then discussed who we were going to use, and he wanted to make a clean break, so I knew Andrew [Paresi] was a good solid drummer, and I had worked with Vini Reilly as well. I also knew he came from Manchester, so he might click with Morrissey on a home level. His guitar style was also completely different to Johnny's—kind of ambient—but I though I could tailor it a bit, and it would be interesting to see if it would work. So I called Vini round to the flat, and he met Morrissey there, and it was like, okay, well, let's give it a go. So the studio was booked and we went in to do our first session together—Andrew, Vini, Morrissey and myself.

J: Would you say that you went above and beyond the call of duty to make *Viva Hate*?

S: Absolutely. It was August that we talked about it. By October we had the first session underway, where we recorded 'Suedehead' and I thought, we've got something here. I went home and wrote some more songs, out of which came 'Late Night, Maudlin Street' and 'Break Up the Family'. It was incredibly hard work, right up to the day before Christmas Eve. I made myself ill, I had a stomach ulcer, I couldn't get out of bed on the last day and I had to get the engineer to record the vocals for 'Break Up the family' and then I comped it later. We drove home the day before Christmas Eve, then I didn't hear from Morrissey for a good couple of months after that.

J: What's your favourite track on that album?

S: I still love 'Suedehead'. And 'Break Up the Family'. That was me trying to push it a little bit, make it funky. The percussion loop was influenced by Lionel Ritchie's 'All Night Long'.

J: I can hear it now!

S: I couldn't be Johnny Marr. I couldn't start with guitar lines. I was just trying to do things that were interesting in a production way. Like 'Alsatian Cousin' with its hard and dirty 'dun-un dun-un dun-un' at the beginning. I was just thinking, 'How can I make songs interesting, without having to rely on my guitar playing?'

J: 'Bengali in Platforms' has a lovely gentle sound.

S: I love that song. I know it got a lot of stick but I just love the middle eight section on that.

J: It always makes me want to do a little light tap dance.

S: It's great. Vini's guitar playing on it is really very nice as well. I remember Morrissey saying to me that he wanted a long, rambling kind of something that Patti [Smith] would do, something major that was different to anything else. So I was trying to make something interesting on 'Maudlin Street' before even the guitar playing started.

J: I don't think there's a bad song on there.

S: I think it's patchy in places, 'I Don't Mind If You Forget Me' could have gone missing for me. I do love the line '*Rejection is one thing ...*' but I'm not proud of what I did as a producer on that track, I think I could have made it better. I listen to that one and I go: 'Oh! Stephen, you could have done better with that ...'

J: Really? I love the pace of 'I Don't Mind'.

S: I love 'Ordinary Boys'. I don't know why Morrissey decided to take it off the reissue. It's great.

J: Going back to *Strangeways,*on 'I Started Something' there's the line: 'Okay Stephen, shall we do that one again?' Why did you keep this in?

S: Because normally when a track finishes, you hit the stop before people start talking; but for some reason, the tape was still rolling when he said it. I always remember talking to him about some Marc Bolan tracks where you hear Marc talking, and how, as a fan, you really kind of like that. So I said to Morrissey, 'Shall we keep it on there? People hear your singing voice but don't very often hear you talking.' It was kind of an in-joke too, because it's like me saying it to him too, or him referring to himself in the third person. I know he never called himself Steven, but we all know that's his first name. It wasn't an egotistical thing, it was a joke, him talking, who's he talking to ...?

J: Your work has a lot of little jolts and treats like that. Particularly with false fade out on 'That Joke Isn't Funny Anymore' and intro on 'Some Girls Are Bigger Than Others'.

S: True. That's something from the producer or engineer's point of view that's like a little surprise or jolt. Plus a little bit of Beatles' influence. There were always little treats for the ear.

J: Were there ever conversations regarding the Stephen/Steven similarity?

S: We never really referred to it. No one ever, ever called him Steven. We joked once about how my name is spelt wrong and his name is spelt correctly. I think he said, 'It's bad enough being called Steven with a v, let alone a ph.' Something like that.

J: Would you work with Morrissey again? If he knocked on this door and said, 'All right, Stephen?' what would you say?

S: Do you know, it's funny, because about two years ago I was lying in bed thinking, 'It's a real shame we haven't been in touch for many years.' So I wrote a really friendly letter and gave it to my manager and asked her to get it to Morrissey. We met up for dinner in London and had a really lovely evening. We got on great, exchanged emails and talked about remastering the *Viva Hate* reissue, which we went on to do.

J: Have you kept in touch with Johnny?

S: I saw him at the remastering of The Smiths stuff. He texted me and I hung out with him for a couple of days doing that. It was really nice.

J: Could there be something there, in the future?

S: I would like to work with Johnny again, but I think he has his own path, and his own engineer and studio that he uses. I really like his new single. I have a lot of professional respect for Johnny.

J: Did you follow Morrissey's career after you stopped working with him?

S: I did. Initially I followed it really closely, then I thought, 'Well, I've got to move on now really.' I tried to stop being so obsessed. I liked 'Irish Blood, English Heart'.

J: You must have been blown away when you found out that he was working with Mick Ronson and Tony Visconti.

S: I was. I love that album *Your Arsenal*. I really like that record.

J: If Morrissey came to your house, what snacks would you put out for him?

S: I think it would be a bowl of crisps. When we were making *Meat Is Murder* the band survived on crisps and chocolate bars. It was amazing. And eggs.

J: What's your favourite Smiths record?

S: 'This Charming Man'. It's just so exuberant; the whole thing is bursting with energy. You hear that guitar break and it explodes.

J: What about one that you produced ... 'Last Night', 'Death Of A Disco Dancer ...'

S: I love those tracks, but 'There Is A Light' is a track where all the components work together and make it beautiful.

J: Do you have a favourite Johnny record?

S: I liked what he did with The The. But I thought 'Get the Message' was a great single.

J: What's your favourite pizza topping?

S: I like fennel and salami. In Pizza Express. Check that one out.

J: Fennel and salami? Meat is not murder, then, for Mr Street?

S: I do eat meat, I'm afraid.

J: What's your favourite restaurant? Is it Pizza Express?

S: Ha ha! I do like it there, but there's a nice Italian in Putney called Enoteca Turi. It's got a great wine list. Fantastic.

J: Is wine your drink of choice, then?

S: Yes, I guess so!

J: Would you write a note to my mum?

S: Yes, I would.

J: Finally, if you could choose one word to sum up your time with The Smiths and Morrissey, what word would you choose?

S: That's a difficult one. I told you I'm not very good with words ... Erm ... it's two words: life-changing.

J: I think you are good with words.

S: Well, maybe those two.

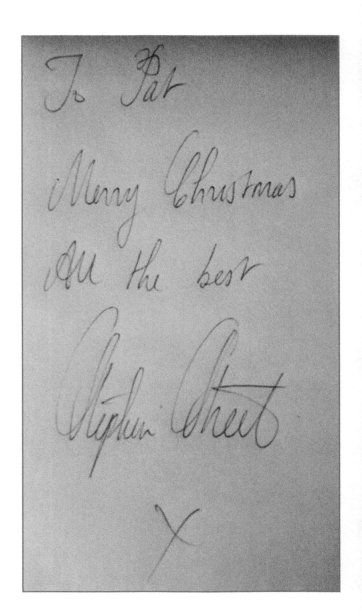

COLLABORATOR

Spencer Cobrin

Morrissey drummer/co-writer 1991-98

Photo from Spencer's archive

15 MINUTES
WITH YOU

WHEN I contacted Spencer Cobrin for a 'Fifteen minutes', I tried to persuade him that it would make for a better interview if we talked in some way, preferably face to face or on the phone, so that I could get to know him a bit better. He very politely turned me down, protesting shyness and Luddite tendencies towards Skype and telephones. I explained to him that I really only wanted to ask him his favourite ice cream flavour, to which he replied: *'Lobster-flavoured ice cream, licked, not bitten. LOL. See? This is why I do not give live interviews!'*

Although he drummed with Morrissey for most of the nineties, Spencer hasn't drummed in years, only on an odd session, and has turned his attention to, amongst other things, real estate and signing talent for music licensing company Muse IQ.

When we emailed back and forth (over the course of two months) about his time in Morrissey's band, he confessed to suffering from terrible stage fright before gigs. He revealed details about going back to a fan's house and witnessing a fight where Gary Day was thrown in the air, and explained how one of the most truly beautiful and much loved Morrissey songs came about: 'Lost'.

He classes his drumming style as *'emotional'* and this also may be true of his time with Morrissey. As he sensitively recalls his memories of drumming with the band, his emails become, at times, bittersweet, and his tone casts a small shadow over a what-was-once-special and fond experience, as he writes how he keeps in touch with *'sadly no one'* and describes himself as feeling *'jaded'*.

Spencer has closed his drumming chapter in the world of Morrissey, and, after much soul- searching, has moved on to a new and different life in music, and a happy home in Brooklyn with his girlfriend and their cat, Lion. On seeing Morrissey again, he says: *'I'd probably give him a hug.'*

J: Please say your full name.

S: Spencer James Cobrin. My name is anglicised, coming from a Jewish family. I was named after my deceased great-grandparents, Samuel and Jacob. My last name is from a village on the Polish/Ukranian border, Kobrin. If you want to get really fancy-pants, Cobrin in Japanese, Ko-Bu-Rin, translates loosely as Ko lonely Bu warrior (in the) Rin forest.

J: Can you describe yourself in a sentence?

S: I'm a tad shy and somewhat self-deprecating.

J: Why did you decide to do this interview on email?

S: I need to mull things over beforehand, I get self-conscious.

J: What are you doing now, and why did you decide to do it?

S: I am involved with a music-licensing agency called Muse IQ, based in Brooklyn, New York, where I live. They approached me a few years ago to see if I had any tracks I would want to include in their music production catalogue. I saw that they didn't have an artist component and they agreed that I would sign talent to the company for licensing purposes, so I picked up the A&R sticks. I do some work in real estate, give piano lessons and diligently practice aikido. I was recently sponsored by my dojo, Brooklyn Aikikai, to travel to Athens for a gruelling seminar, it felt like a three-month tour packed into three days.

J: How would you describe your style of drumming? Do you still drum these days?

S: My style would be emotional if you can call that a style; it's not technical, it's not flashy, it's simply from the guts. I haven't drummed in years apart from the odd session or sit-in. After I left Morrissey I turned my focus to writing, first for a band, then to film and advertising.

J: What was life like on the road with Morrissey? How did you guys prepare for the crowd reaction at some of the big venues that you played?

S: Life on the road was so many things; very exciting, totally exhausting, emotionally fraught plus I suffered terribly from stage fright. In regards to preparing I don't think it was ever a question of the size of venue, rehearsals were about knowing the songs inside out and then giving it all on stage wherever we played.

J: How did you deal with your stage fright? Did you have any methods?

S: There was nothing I could do to combat the stage fright, I just had to suck it up as best as I could. Initially it would occur an hour or two before we went on stage but then it progressed to where I would feel it coming on not long after waking up, so essentially I would suffer from it all day! I'd try to distract myself as best as I could but it was pretty hopeless.

J: Do you have any favourite gigs or tour stories?

S: There was the time after we had played on *The Johnny Carson Show*. Gary and Alain were hanging outside the hotel talking to fans, one fan invited us to a house party so about six or seven of us piled into a car, I had no idea where we were heading. We raced down the freeway for about an hour and ended up in a suburban district. There were some knuckleheads in the kitchen and I could see things were getting a bit tense. I went into the living room where everyone was watching our performance on *The Johnny Carson Show* we had taped a few hours earlier. The next thing I remember is looking over to the other side of the room and seeing Gary flying through the air with a pile of guys on top of him, it was a mess. The police showed up and arrested Gary. We bailed him out at 4

a.m. then packed as quickly as possible for the airport. This was just the start of the tour!

J: Which tracks did you look forward to performing?

S: On the *Kill Uncle* tour it would be 'Angel', 'Suedehead', 'November', 'Playboys', 'Everyday'. Later on, 'Glamorous', 'Fatty', 'Disco', 'Speedway', 'Shoplifters', 'Do Your Best'.

J: Did you socialise with the rest of the band outside of the studio?

S: Alain, Gary and myself played in various outfits and hung out at places like The Klub Foot, Dingwalls, upstairs at The Electric Ballroom and other North London rockabilly clubs. By the time we finished our first European and American tour with Morrissey I don't think we could stand to be around each other, we had been together so much.

J: Who do you keep in touch with now?

S: Sadly, no one.

J: Your cheeky appearance with a Cornetto in 'We Hate It When Our Friends Become Successful' is very funny. Whose initial idea was it, and why?

S: Ha, it wasn't anyone's idea really, I was just being a ham, I told you I was self-deprecating. It did cause a bit of a fuss between friends, roommates, even my family, I thought it was hysterical, some people take things so seriously, I just shook my head and quietly laughed back at them.

J: Was it your idea to make Morrissey laugh with the close-up tease?

S: I just put it close to his face. I guess he liked it.

J: Morrissey is quoted as describing your work on *Southpaw Grammar* as 'a great personal joy.' [Mozipedia by Simon Goddard, p. 76] how does that make you feel?

S: I never heard that from him, nice to know after all these years though. Maybe he could see how much I had grown under his wing and how much I contributed in spirit to the recordings.

J: Which single that you drum on do you feel most proud of?

S: It would have to be 'The Operation', I had worked and worked at trying to improve my drumming skills but I just couldn't make anything stick, I felt at a complete loss, I was also very hard on myself, but coming off the road and going straight into record that album [*Southpaw Grammar*] something shifted and clicked into gear unexpectedly and I immediately went up a huge notch, whereas I had been on a plateau for years.

J: Tell us how the beautiful 'Lost' happened. Did you ever try to persuade Morrissey to make it an A-side?

S: By the late nineties I was living in the East Village, New York between tours and I would get up early and sit at the keyboard to write. I wrote and wrote and that was how the demo for 'Lost' came to be. Morrissey was going to release it as an A-side but he changed his mind later after I left the band.

J: Did Morrissey ever come to your house? What snacks did you put out for him?

S: He came over to the apartment I was living in in the East Village (NY) and we had pizza.

J: Do you listen to the music that Morrissey makes now?

S: Not really, it doesn't inspire or fill me with emotion of any kind; as opposed to older material that gets the adrenalin going.

J: How would you feel if a chance encounter happened with Morrissey now? What would you say?

S: I'd probably give him a hug and be happy to see him again after all these years. I don't harbour any grudges, if you can open your heart you can conquer anything.

J: What is your favourite ice cream flavour?

S: Vanilla.

J: Childhood toy?

S: My father's air rifle.

J: Drum?

S: Ludwig Black Beauty snare.

J: Food?

S: Toasted cheese sarnie.

J: Pizza topping?

S: Olives, mushrooms and extra cheese please.

J: City in the world?

S: Undecided, still want to travel to many more.

J: Morrissey track?

S: 'Lost', ahem.

J: Smiths track?

S: 'There Is A Light ...'

J: Drink of choice?

S: Changes, right now it's Rhone Valley, 100% Syrah, any vineyard from the north or south region, still exploring, amazing stuff, pricey.

J: Movie?

S: *The Warriors.*

J: Time of day?

S: Zzzzzz.

J: Thing about New York?

S: My dojo.

J: Song in all the world?

S: How about, Billy Butler, 'The Right Track'.

J: Please could you type a note to my mum?

S: *Hi Pat,*

Greetings from Greenwood Heights, Brooklyn, New York! It seems that Julie is a tad sad with my answers to some of her interview questions, do you think you could you cheer her up with a cup of tea and a delicious cheese sandwich? :)

Hope you are well and enjoying your Sunday.

Very best,

Spencer

J: Thank you, Spencer. If you could choose one word to sum up your musical experience, what would it be?

S: Jaded.

J: Do you think that you will ever return to the UK?

S: Maybe, via Spain! Gracias.

Hi Pat,

Greetings from Greenwood Heights, Brooklyn, New York! It seems that Julie is a tad sad with my answers to some of her interview questions, do you think you could you cheer her up with a cup of tea and a delicious cheese sandwich? :)

Hope you are well and enjoying your Sunday.

Very best,

Spencer

FAN

Samuel Preston

Singer/guitarist/songwriter with The Ordinary Boys and fan of Morrissey

15 MINUTES
WITH YOU

FROM the day he received 'Boxers' from his brother on his twelfth birthday, Sam Preston has never shied away from evangelising that Morrissey has been, and still is, a significant influence on his music career. His band The Ordinary Boys took their name from a track on *Viva Hate*, and it was during their first interview for the NME that Sam began referring to himself as Preston. He has the signature quiff and glasses, tattoos of lyrics ('Come Armageddon, come' and 'Sweet and tender') and he describes Morrissey as his *'surrogate father figure.'*

In a later, extraordinary turn, Morrissey became a fan of Sam's band, choosing one of their songs, 'Little Bubble' to appear on a compilation album he put together for the *NME* in 2004. In the same year, both Morrissey and The Ordinary Boys performed on *Later ... with Jools Holland*, and Morrissey asked The Ordinary Boys to appear with him at Meltdown.

It could be argued that Sam's *'surrogate father figure'* helped him on his way, but the fact is that great writing was always in Sam's genes. His grandpa is a Professor Emeritus of English at Princeton University and his mother and brother are successful published authors. He has a remarkable family tree, branching back to his great-great-great-great-grandfather, The Right Honourable Earl Grey. Sam has chosen to spend his natural literary inheritance of songwriting on The Ordinary Boys, where his influences of Morrissey, The Specials, The Cure and Madness are all echoed in the cake mix of indie-pop-ska he plays.

On stage he is the irrepressible and resilient Preston, bouncing off his infinite energies to 'Boys will Be Boys', 'Talk Talk Talk', 'Lonely At The Top' and 'Run This Town', supported by the loyal fans in The Ordinary Army. Off stage he is a more reserved Sam, who, post gig, prefers to *'devour a Bolaño'* on the tour bus. It is this warm and bookish, sensitive Sam I meet, his boyish and innocent demeanor heightened only by a cuddly cream charity shop jumper.

Sam talks about his desire for fun and spontaneity in his life, and how he is fuelled by the nervous energy he has housed inside himself since he was a child: *'I never really think things through much further than one or two steps … it stops you doing things that would be fun adventures if you think too much.'* It is this impulsive energy that has pushed him to lead a life in fast forward, including three successful Ordinary Boys albums, several highly publicised television appearances, a 'Prestelle' marriage/divorce and, most importantly, a chance to meet his heroes, one of whom is Terry Hall, who appeared in the video for the Ordinary Boys single, 'Seaside'.

Recently, he has been enjoying working steadily as producer and writer for other artists. Unsurprisingly, he has the urge to return to the limelight once again, and he relishes the thought that another Ordinary Boys album may be against all odds of public success: *'That thought excites me more than if everyone was just waiting for it,'* he says, grinning.

He prefers popcorn to crisps, bakes home-made bread and loves to 'pickle'. His favourite Morrissey album is *Vauxhall and I*, which he describes as *'a masterpiece … with a hanging atmosphere.'*

J: Please say your full name.

S: Samuel Dylan Murray Preston.

J: Where do the names come from?

S: Samuel is after my grandpa, Samuel Hynes. Dylan is Dylan Thomas; my grandpa is a big fan of his. Murray is a family name. There are a lot of writers in our family—my brother has a new novel out, my grandpa is a writer and Professor Emeritus of English at Princeton University and my mum wrote a book about autism.

J: Really? That's fantastic.

S: Yeah, she specialises in it.

J: Can you describe yourself in a sentence?

S: The most interesting people can't!

J: Are you 'happy knowing nothing'?

S: The absolute opposite of that. The Ordinary Boys was meant to be a slightly ironic name. We were so young when we started the band. It was the same with me dropping my first name. I just so loved Morrissey I wanted to copy everything he did.

J: Did you consider other Morrissey-inspired band names?

S: Well, I managed a band and we were called This Charming Management, I was in a hardcore band called Viva Hate I had a previous band called True To you. I still feel kind of shameless about how much he influences me. He has always been such a big part of my life and always will.

J: Do you think he knows the extent of his influence?

S: Yes, I think he does. He put us on a compilation of bands he was interested in.

J: 'Little Bubble' is a glorious song. Why didn't you release it as a single?

S: It was a B-side and we weren't very precious about our early B-sides at all. A lot of them are better than some of our later album tracks. I'm very fond of 'Little Bubble'.

J: How old were you when you got into Morrissey?

S: I got into him at the tender age of twelve, when my brother bought me 'Boxers' for my birthday. Alex is a huge Morrissey fan. Then I moved to Philadelphia when I was a teenager and found this whole group of kids who liked hardcore, and The Smiths were included in that. I still feel closest to that group of friends, even though they're so far away. It's always interested me, the hardcore music, and all those kids seemed to like The Smiths too.

J: I don't think you're alone in being a fan that liked to copy Morrissey, the quiff, the oversized blouses …

S: Yes! It's fine to do it, because we're all doing it! But when you're in a band, you're expect to have at least *some* original content.

J: Morrissey has influenced you quite heavily. The name of your band, your surname as first name …

S: That was so flippant! It was our very first *NME* interview, and I thought, '*I'm just gonna be Preston.*' No one had ever called me that before and it's what I wanted to be.

J: What do your family call you? Sam?

S: Yeah. No one calls me Preston. It's such a pretentious nod to Morrissey! The *NME* put it in the article, then it stuck.

J: I've even seen a tour picture of you holding a cat …

S: The picture of Morrissey with the cat on his head cheers me up whenever I feel down. I have it bookmarked on my phone, so if I'm a little bit blue, I'll look at it. The two main things that cheer me up are: the picture of Morrissey with the cat on his head, and I like to think about the fact that Paul McCartney called his last album *Kisses on the Bottom*. That cheers me up!

J: When I listen to The Ordinary Boys, I can hear all of your musical influences in your work; Morrissey, The Smiths, The Jam, The Specials, Madness. Your sound is a bit of a mix of those influences, isn't it?

S: Yeah. I think that's true. It's funny as well, because I managed to meet all of my heroes. I got to perform with Terry Hall; I'm almost as big a Terry Hall fan as I am a Morrissey fan.

I think at the time people were grumpy about the fact that we wore our influences so heavily on our sleeves. It was just a product of so much love for that music. I still listen to the same music. I'm planning on doing a new record this year, with the band. I'm not sure on what level yet. Just because I feel like it all went a bit off-piste with the third record and I feel like I got a bit too

… well … I just tried so desperately hard to make something 'new' that I had lost sight of what music I can enjoy playing. This new record will be closer to hardcore stuff, faster, louder.

J: Your voice is quite gentle on 'Seaside'.

S: Yeah, well, maybe my voice over proper hardcore would be quite an interesting contrast. These beautiful, almost quite Bing Crosby-esque melodies with harder rock 'n' roll is something that Morrissey embraced in his later albums. Maybe as we grow old we soften the edges a little bit.

J: When you pick up your guitar, what do you like to play?

S: I love The Stray Cats. I'm best at playing rockabilly guitar.

J: So you must have enjoyed Morrissey's rockabilly band, then.

S: I did, very much, yeah.

J: Tell me about your meeting with Morrissey.

S: I remember the day so clearly, I have no idea how I managed to take it all in my stride. I asked what music he was listening to at the moment, and he said, 'I've been listening to a lot of Partridge Family.' I was just, like, *that's* why I love you.

J: What excited you the most during that time?

S: I think the very early days; going on *Jools Holland* and having Junior Murvin to my left, and Morrissey to my right. Knowing I was going on tour with Morrissey the next day was amazing. I got really close with Alain Whyte and I got my copy of *You Are The Quarry* signed by every band mate. I had set out to meet Morrissey, that had happened, and I was left with the feeling: *'What next*?' But Morrissey was always really nice to me, really sweet.

J: How did it feel to be asked to join him at Meltdown?

S: Meltdown was such an honour. Our drummer at the time got thrown out for trying to hug Moz during his set!

J: I read somewhere that you went up to him and said, 'Hi, I'm Preston' and he said, 'Yes, I know who you are.'

S: Yes! I can't tell if that was good or bad! There are photos of us together, but I can't find any. I have been trying to hunt down those photos.

One of my good friends is in Doll & The Kicks, so I managed to get out to see them backstage in Ireland, and I saw him again then.

J: Was he pleased to see you?

S: I think so, yes. I like to think so. We had a nod of acknowledgement. It was the same when I saw Nick Cave. I don't want to be that guy who's going up to someone and going, 'Remember me mate?' so when I saw Nick on the train, I remembered I had dinner with him and Will Self a few years ago. I just said 'Hi' and went on my way.

J: Did he recognise you?

S: Nick? He seemed to, yeah. Will Self is a huge Morrissey fan and when I was doing the third Ordinary Boys album, I had drinks at The Groucho with him to discuss lyrics for that album, which I think is why it has ... a much more ... I don't know ... that third album is a kind of a concept album. A weird album. It's a bit kind of bloopy and electronic, which is something that I have completely come out the other side of. I got into it five years ago and it was all I listened to. It seemed really progressive and creative, because there is no limits to the sound it can make.

J: What's your musical core? Is it the harder stuff?

S: I'm quite confident that I'm a strong lyricist. I enjoy it. I want to do something really heavy. I still listen to heavy stuff, and I like to go to those shows. It all goes back to the hardcore teens.

J: Is the 2013 Sam Preston different to the 2006 version?

S: Yeah, maybe. I just can't imagine back to then, because it's so different to how I am now, shy and awkward. An example of that was when I saw other bands' success as a personal attack on myself. We're all friends and I'm happy about it now, but I remember I took the Kaiser Chiefs along to the record label and was like: 'You have to sign this band, I really think they'd be great.' Eventually I persuaded my label to sign them and then they sold millions of records and I was like, 'Oh.' But now I'm really proud of them and think it's fantastic, because they are lovely guys.

J: I remembered The Ordinary Boys exploding onto the scene. You always seemed to be in a rush.

S: Yeah ... I think that's very accurate. It's true of my life in so many ways that ... I think the journey is always so much more exciting. I get bored of it in the end, when I get there. It's been long enough that if we were to bring the band back on some level then it will probably be even more of a struggle than it was the first time. That's kind of exciting though, I like that challenge.

J: Who are you working with now?

S: I'm working in songwriting and producing. I had a big number one with a song I wrote for Olly Murs called 'Heart Skips A Beat' and then having had the number one, I got bored with it again. It's a frustrating way to live your life. I appear to crash when I get there. But I do have a sense of urgency. I want to get this Ordinary Boys record done. I've written one song! I have had a bizarre request to sing for an existing band, too.

J: You can't say who?

S: No. It's a pretty weird one. I'm just excited to get somewhere. And I can never turn down anything that seems like it's going to be fun.

J: Can we talk about your tattoos? What's this one behind your ear?

S: This one is a Jean-Michel Basquiat crown. I've got Morrissey ones too. I've got 'sweet and tender' on my arm. I know hundreds of people with Smiths tattoos. I have a friend who has 'little charmer'.

J: What's the significance of the triangle?

S: My friend told me that it was the most intensely painful tattoo she had ever had, so I just did it out of curiosity. I'm not really one for worrying too much about the significance of my tattoos. Tattoos are quite silly, really.

J: And was it painful?

S: Oh my God, it was the absolute worst!

J: You sampled Siouxsie's 'Happy House' on 'Dressed To Kill'. Are you a fan of hers?

S: Yes! There's talk of Siouxsie writing with me, which would be … incredible! She did email me to say that she really liked 'Dressed to Kill'. I'm doing a project at the moment with the artist Dear Prudence, where I'm writing and producing with her. She has a song called 'Coming Apart Again' and that's very Siouxsie-influenced.

J: 'Dressed to Kill' is quite clubby, isn't it?

S: I was deep into my electronic phase then.

J: Were you producing your own stuff?

S: Yes, with a friend of mine. But I missed the guitars, I don't want to do any of that anymore. I'm glad that it was a one-off.

J: Shall we talk about your TV appearances? Do you want to/not want to?

S: I don't mind talking about them. That's fine.

J: To me, you seemed very at home in the *Big Brother* house.

S: Weirdly, it was one of the happiest times of my life.

J: You seemed contented.

S: I can't think what it is. It was just really weird, because lyrically I had always talked trash on that world, and it seemed so ridiculous for me to go in and be in it. But I learned a lot.

J: As a viewer it was great to watch the playful chemistry between you and Chantelle.

S: Yeah, it was fun, but I think the relationship was a product of that situation and it was always doomed to fail. I wish someone had told me: '*Dude, by the way, think about this for a second.'* But again, it's that urgency that I have, running at a thousand miles an hour.

J: You were put in the spotlight by the media when you left the house. Was it terrifying or did you love it?

S: The thing is, at that time, what I think is sad is that I feel I neglected the band. I think that's one of the reasons why two of them don't even pick up their instruments anymore. Will doesn't play guitar anymore. I wonder if I had done something differently and taken their musical careers into consideration a bit more, what would have happened, rather than getting caught up in the *Big Brother* press. But then, they both have careers that they love now.

J: What do they do?

S: Will works for *The Guardian* and James is a sound engineer.

J: Do you still keep in touch with Chantelle?

S: Yeah. We talk on the phone.

J: Was it reparative going back into the house for the second time?

S: Well, I just felt that I had done some damage since I left the first time, so I wanted to remind people that I am a nice guy really.

J: Would you go back in for a third?

S: It's a weird thing to imagine now. I couldn't do it again. I've become agoraphobic and misanthropic with age! I never really think things through much further than one or two steps. I think it's a wise thing to do. It stops you doing things that would be fun adventures if you think too much about it. It's much better to just go for it: 'That cake looks good so I'm going to eat it. It doesn't matter if it makes me fat!' Just do things!

J: I liked it when you walked off *Buzzcocks*.

S: I regret doing anything where there's video evidence of me at my worst. I didn't handle it too well.

J: Do you have regrets about your TV appearances?

S: I think if there's anything that plays on my mind that would be near to a regret is that there are Ordinary Boys records that could exist that just don't, because other things distracted me for so long. I've had recent conversations with my label that look after me for my songwriting. I'm still making them money, but they all say: 'You're going to struggle to get a new Ordinary Boys record, it's going to be hard to get radio plays.' I just think that excites me more than if everyone was just waiting for it.

J: You've got the fan base.

S: That's true. I did put a little tweet up about it and everyone was really positive.

J: The Ordinary Army seem very loyal. Do you shout them out at gigs?

S: Yeah! I know them all! All the real hardcore ones I know well.

J: Do they turn up to gigs looking like you?

S: Yeah! I guess so. Maybe they should skip the middleman and go straight for looking like Morrissey!

J: Have you still got that gold jacket you wore on *Buzzcocks*?

S: Somewhere, yeah.

J: If you don't need it anymore …

S: Yeah! You can have it! I should get rid of it! It was funny that I wore the most absurd thing of my entire life!

J: It reminds me of what Morrissey wore in the Dallas tour. I did wonder if it was a nod to that.

S: Yeah! Not a conscious one …

J: Did you keep in touch with anyone from Morrissey's band?

S: I kept in touch with Gary Day for a long while. It was always fleeting moments with Morrissey. He'd get whisked up to the stage and whisked back. It was conversations in hallways. Or if I was in the dressing room with the band, he'd come in. He never lets people watch him from the side of the stage, and I would get a note from him saying, 'You can watch from the side of the stage.' I think it's just an irritating thing when people watch you from the side, for any band. The show that you're giving isn't there, it doesn't project to the side, but if it's someone you really love you can almost see it through their eyes a little bit, which is really exciting.

J: If Morrissey walked in here right now and said, 'All right Preston?' What would you say?

S: Again, it's that thing when you meet somebody, it's horrible to be that nagging guy, but I feel that we would have a really long nice conversation. I feel like he did guide me through the early part of my career by talking about us in interviews, taking me on tour. Maybe because I feel through his lyrics he was some kind of surrogate father figure, which is true for a lot of people, I think.

J: What's your favourite Morrissey album?

S: *Vauxhall and I* is his masterpiece. PG Wodehouse's masterpiece was *Right Ho, Jeeves*, and *Vauxhall and I* is Morrissey's. I think that record has such an atmosphere ... such a lot of sounds on it, with a hanging atmosphere.

J: If Morrissey came to your house, what snacks would you put out for him?

S: I'm actually very much into pickling at the moment. I'm a big pickler. I do nice sweet pickles. You eat them with bread and butter. It's a really fun thing to do. I'd give him some of my pickles.

J: Do you put a frilly top on the jar?

S: You don't need a jar for pickles, that's for jams. You need a seal.

J: Who got you into pickling?

S: My mum does it.

J: Did your mum knit that jumper?

S: No, I got this from a charity shop.

J: What is your favourite crisp flavour? Do you like crisps with your pickles?

S: I'm not a huge crisp fan, really. I actually would go for popcorn. The Pret a Manger popcorn is my snack of choice.

J: Would you put popcorn out with pickles, then?

S: No, I'd make home-made bread.

J: You bake bread as well?

S: I love to cook. I do a nice baked eggs with merquez.

J: You're not a vegetarian?

S: No.

J: Do you have a girlfriend at the moment?

S: [stretches arms] I have a line I'm pursuing!

J: What's your favourite Morrissey single?

S: Possibly 'Boxers' because I received it as a gift and was at the age where, once you get a record, you just play it and play it and play it. And also I think as a Morrissey song it feels kind of forgotten. It's a sad lyric. When you're really young, music is much more effective at creating images in your head. I remember hearing 'Strange Little Girl' by the Stranglers and I didn't know it was about Siouxsie Sioux at the time. I can remember the image I had in my head. I remember the images that The Beatles conjured up. I can think what I imagined when I listened to 'Boxers'. It makes the record richer.

J: What's your favourite thing that your mum says?

S: Everyone makes fun of my mum because she's American. If I ever talk about my mum, for some reason my friends will say, 'Sammy! Your meatballs are ready!' I guess maybe that, but I don't know how often she actually says it! I have a great relationship with my parents. I'm terrible at romance, you see. If I don't have the right advice, I'm just doomed to walk off on my own. So I talk candidly with both of my parents about that. My brother is grown up, married and has kids, and here they still have a thirty-one year-old son still asking them what to do about girls.

J: Do you want that for yourself? To get married and have kids?

S: I do, but I'm terribly picky. I don't think I ever really was, but because of the whole Chantelle thing, then a long distance relationship after that, it has become really important for me to have complete common interests now ... I think maybe because Chantelle and I didn't. The whole problem with that is that my interests in books, film and music are pretty weird, and I'm very passionate about all of them.

J: Who is your favourite author?

S: Roberto Bolaño. I love and I devour everything that he's written. I read a lot. I think Will Self is a great writer as well. My brother has become friends with him. I love all the hipster books.

J: Favourite movie?

S: I really love *Badlands*. I love those rich visual movies.

J: Did you get into *A Taste Of Honey* and *Saturday Night, Sunday Morning*?

S: I did! It was almost like homework! I love The New York Dolls now, too. But there was a time where I didn't 'get it'. I wonder if I conditioned myself to love them as part of my homework for Morrissey.

J: Have you got a favourite childhood toy?

S: I have a Cabbage Patch Kid, that I still have, completely bald with a plastic head, so I called it Thomas Hard-head. It's at my mum's house in France.

J: The video for 'Lonely at the Top' opens with you on a single bed. Did this resemble your teenage bedroom?

S: No. My childhood bedroom was really big, even though our house was small. There weren't enough bedrooms, so I had to be in a kind of conservatory. The rain would come down on the inside. It had a few plants in it.

J: Is this when you started your acting career?

S: I used to love acting when I was younger! I was in a movie, *Christabel* with Liz Hurley, and I was in *The Muppets* and I was in *Drowning in the Shallow End* with Paul McGann, so I saved up a little bit of money for a guitar and I bought a record player for fifteen pounds. It was in the very early nineties. It was huge, bigger than me, and took up almost all of the space in my room.

J: What were the posters on your bedroom wall?

S: When I was really young it was The Pixies and Dinosaur Jnr.

J: Do you have a favourite Ordinary Boys caper?

S: We were terribly boring and sensible as a band. There were many times when I swung from lights and cut my hands and bled. But then we'd retire to the tour bus and read books. We weren't rock 'n' roll, there was no drug taking or anything like that.

J: You were good boys, then. Were you a good boy when you were younger?

S: No, absolutely terrible, horrible, brat. It felt like I had Attention Deficit Disorder as well, so I was just a handful. I still feel like I run on this nervous energy. People have told it to me enough times and I've started to see it. I just sort of run for a little bit, then get exhausted, then start running again.

J: Could you please write a note to my mum?

S: Yes!

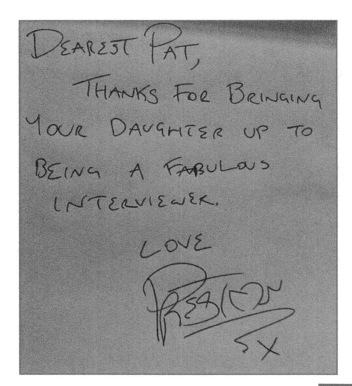

DEAREST PAT,
    THANKS FOR BRINGING
YOUR DAUGHTER UP TO
BEING A FABULOUS
INTERVIEWER.
        LOVE
        Preston
            SX

Clive Langer

Producer and co-writer with Morrissey

15 MINUTES
WITH YOU

PLATINUM producer of pop Clive Langer is best known for his work with Madness, Dexys, Elvis Costello and many other artists for his ability to effortlessly churn out top ten hits with his partner Alan Winstanley. He has achieved success over four decades with hits such as 'My Girl', 'Cardiac Arrest', 'Our House', 'Lovestruck', 'November Spawned A Monster', 'Absolute Beginners' and 'Come on Eileen'. He is the writer of the epic 'Shipbuilding,' a highly poignant ballad surrounding the social and political contradiction of the Falklands war, written for Robert Wyatt ,with lyrics by Elvis Costello. He is a founding member of the cult band Deaf School which formed in 1978 (still touring today), and he has a sharp sense of style and detail, wearing shiny oxblood wingtips, a vintage style polka-dot scarf, Buddy Holly glasses, a neatly arranged Brylcreem quiff and the cleanest, most well kept fingernails I have ever seen.

Clive became Morrissey's producer during the time of the *Bona Drag* 'Ouija Board' sessions. After co-writing 'November Spawned A Monster', he went on to take the production reigns of Morrissey's most experimental and irreverent album: *Kill Uncle* [co-written with Mark Nevin], injecting it with the more 'quirky' sound of Steve Nieve's pianos.

At the time of release, *Kill Uncle* took a pummelling from the press. Through the years, fans have had to rush to the defence of melodic and lyrical gems such as 'Driving Your Girlfriend Home', 'King Leer' and 'Our Frank', feeling that the album had been unfairly dismissed and never given proper credit during a time of 'Madchester' change. After Clive's many previous successes, the reception of this album was a bruise to his pride: *'Erm, it hurt … All the papers wrote similar things … I thought, "People just don't get it."'*

I met him in Foyle's bookshop café on Charing Cross Road, followed by a quick trip to The Pillars of Hercules around the corner for a necessary Suggs-induced hair of the dog (where I tried very hard to steal Clive's scarf). He spoke in brief sentences with a relaxed tone as he reflected on his gentle and kind friendship with Morrissey. He described his fondness for him during the Hook End days when they lived and worked together: *'We'd stay up into the early hours, walking and talking … I would look at him and say, "Are you all right? Do you want to go home now?"'*

On the chance to write together again: '*I always felt like I had unfinished business with Morrissey ... I just wanted to write more with him. I would have loved to develop a songwriting partnership with him.*'

He gets his hair cut in Camden: '*Six quid.*' His favourite Madness song is 'Our House', crisp flavour is Salt 'n' Shake and his wingtips are from Trickers.

J: Please say your full name.

C: Say my full name? Even the bits that other people don't know about?

J: Yes, please!

C: Clive William Langer, after my grandfather, who was Bill Baptist. So I was Clive William.

J: William, It Was Really Nothing.

C: I wasn't a Smiths fan. I was busy! I mean, I liked the daffodils and everything, but musically, melodically, I didn't get a lot of it, except 'How Soon Is Now' which had amazing guitar. But I appreciated them. I liked them. I was in the studio 6/7 days a week at that time. One of the guys who first produced them, Troy Tate, was in the studio with me when I was doing Teardrop Explodes. I knew Troy, so I was quite interested in what he was doing. I was aware of The Smiths, but I didn't get sucked into the phenomena. I always told Morrissey that, really. I didn't pretend to be anything I wasn't. I was so busy with Madness and we were just having hit after hit, so I didn't really listen too much, but I was aware of it. I wouldn't go home and play other bands' records unless I wanted to steal something!

J: You're not on Twitter anymore, Clive [@SirCliffHanger]. Why's that?

C: I went on Facebook for forty-eight hours and then shut it down. It was enough. All these people contacted me that I didn't really want to talk to. I don't mind saying hello to people, but I don't want a long dialogue with people from school ...

J: With Twitter, you can talk to people you don't know.

C: I don't mind strangers, I don't mind having a conversation with people. With Deaf School I have had a lot of emails from people and I enjoy talking to them.

J: I had been told that you don't do interviews, and you don't have an email.

C: I do have an email! I just don't like chatting much. Maybe I'm too hungover! I'm hungover today because of last night. We were celebrating! Madness just picked up an award from Poland yesterday. They played there in the Eighties and gave the money they earned to Solidarity (they couldn't spend it anywhere anyway, because they couldn't export the money). So they all got these medals.

J: Was it a good night?

C: Wine. Brandy. Vodka ... We [Suggs and I] are both used to drinking. We first met when he was seventeen. We've been drinking ever since. It's a quick way to get to know people, I suppose.

J: It has been a lifelong collaboration for you and Suggs.

C: Very much a lifelong friendship. Especially since he's married to Bette Bright, who is the girl singer in Deaf School, so I knew her since 1974 and I've known Suggs since 1978.

J: You went from playing in Deaf School to producing Madness.

C: I was suddenly put on a rollercoaster. After Deaf School, I had my own band, Clive Langer and the Boxes - and we toured with Madness. The first album I ever produced was *One Step Beyond* I was just a bloke in a band that had made a few albums and knew a bit. I kind of knew the process because I worked with Alan Winstanley who has the engineer expertise and is a producer as well ... It meant that we could just make these records. When 'One Step Beyond' came out ... I remember listening to it the day after, thinking 'This is a load of rubbish!' Then suddenly it was a hit, and all the singles were hits. It was a stepping stone. Then I did a Bette Bright album, Teardrop Explodes ... Record companies wanted me. I then went on to work with Elvis Costello and Dexys Midnight Runners.

J: What was Kevin Rowland like to work with?

C: Kevin wanted to work with us because he was a big Deaf School fan. He used to come and see us in Birmingham. In those days he was very strict. It was hard to get close to him, but I'm closer to him now. He worked his band like an army. They did all the moves that they do live, in rehearsal and in the studio. Everything was really choreographed. It was so different from Madness, who were flexible. Kevin's albums were kind of almost done. I've always felt guilty [about being credited as producer] on 'Come On Eileen', as Kevin did so much. I enjoyed doing the Dexys album, but it was a different experience than what I was used to.

J: Do you enjoy working with bands that have lots of members?

C: I do, yes, because it means that the arrangements can be more complex, and if someone wants to put a bit of brass on their records, or a bit of strings, then they can. With Dexys, we used brass and strings together. That was kind of a bit of a breakthrough for their sound, I suppose. To me, that was quite normal, working with Madness.

J: Do you have a favourite Madness track, or is it a bit like asking who your favourite child is?

C: I just feel pretty proud of 'Our House' when I hear that. Does that make it my favourite? Maybe. I remember 'Our House' was out in America—around the same time as Dexy's—climbing the charts, and I was very proud of it because I had done a lot to shape it.

J: Any others?

C: 'My Girl' was my original favourite track. Madness are a singles band. Their twenty-first single, got to number twenty-one and they're still selling. I went to the Palace when they were on the roof, which was just incredible! They are playing over ten thousand seaters everywhere now, including the O2; it's the biggest tour they've ever done.

J: The new Madness album is getting great reviews.

C: It was a bit too close for me to their last one. I had spent a couple of years doing the one before, and I wasn't in the right frame of mind to go in again.

J: 'Lovestruck' is another, later classic Madness pop song with unique, quirky lyrics.

C: Yeah, that's Lee (Thompson).

J: Madness have some great writers. *Wonderful* was a great era for them, as well.

C: Yeah. 'Lovestruck' was like a second coming for Madness, during the mid nineties.

J: Were there ever plans to put lyrics to 'One Step Beyond' or one of my favourites: 'The Return Of The Los Palmas 7'?

C: No. With every album we were asked to do an instrumental. It's just part of Madness, starting with 'One Step Beyond'. 'For Return Of The Los Palmas 7', Mike Barson had a book of Sixties hits—and I think, if I remember correctly—he reversed a Kathy Kirby melody.

J: Do you think that Madness get the recognition they deserve in terms of awards?

C: It will all happen now, because this year has been so big. They are seen as an English treasure. Playing all these festivals, getting through to the young kids. Everyone just sees them as an evergreen now, as opposed to old Madness. They'll get their lifetime achievement very soon.

J: Who are you working with now?

C: My son is in a band called Man Like Me and they've been supporting Madness for the last few weeks. I've been playing with them, I play guitar on one of their songs. I'm also writing stuff on my own at the moment with Deaf School. I produced three tracks for Madness this year and also worked with a guy called Eugene McGuinness, I finished his album last year. But there's not much work for me these days.

J: Why's that?

C: Well, to get me and Alan into the studio is quite an expensive experience, because we don't work computers, really. We just didn't see the end. Kids can get music for nothing now, whereas I didn't see the end of the CD, or the album. But people don't need to buy a record now, so I don't get the royalties. Our careers kind of ended, because everyone's got a laptop at home to record stuff. At home I help my son out and we do bits and pieces.

J: Describe your partnership with Alan Winstanley.

C: He's a really good engineer, and I'm more from the arranging/songwriting side. I'd just leave him to do a lot of the sound work.

J: When Langer/Winstanley produced in the Eighties, the competition was Pete Waterman and Trevor Horn. Did you pay much attention to their stuff?

C: Trevor Horn was our main competitor when we were doing really well. I think he was making 'Two Tribes' in one room and we were doing *Goodbye Cruel World* [Elvis Costello] in the other. We had finished a whole album and Trevor was still working on the drums for the single. But his records were amazing and I used to enjoy listening to them. I didn't like Pete's stuff, but I liked him because he was always a supporter of ours in the press. He seemed like a nice enough guy. I just remember once Trevor Horn won an award and we didn't, and Pete wrote a half page letter to *Music Week* as to why we should have won it. I always liked him for that.

J: When you look back at your plethora of songwriting and hits, what do you see as your finest moment?

C: 'Shipbuilding' with Robert Wyatt. It wasn't paid for, it wasn't a record company job, it was just something I wanted to do. And I dreamt that this guy would sing it. So Elvis wrote the lyrics, because I couldn't come up with anything. I said, 'I want this for Robert Wyatt,' and Elvis wrote it for Robert Wyatt, and that's why the words are the way they are. I didn't know that they were going to be as poignant as they were, but that became number one in the independent charts and when I heard it away from the studio I just couldn't believe it had happened. I was influenced by 'Strange Fruit' from the *Nothing Can Stop Us* album, and they ended up adding 'Shipbuilding' to the later pressings of that album. So I was influenced by this album and then my track was on this album! That was great, it was no music business bollocks, just something from me.

J: Do you have any regrets?

C: Not regrets, but there are certain things I shouldn't have taken on. Not really good enough. I wasn't good enough. It was tempting, though, for the money, and I never wanted to do it for the money, but we were spending, on studios, on our lifestyle …

J: Were you leading an indulgent lifestyle, then?

C: No, I was more indulgent later, only because, well, I like eating out, and I used to be happy if I could eat out and get a taxi, and I thought, that's amazing … Kind of all I wanted, really. Then I had a son, and a house, so we had a few luxuries, but I never felt really indulgent, but I never saved money. I liked to pay for bands to eat, I like to buy them dinner, I thought that was a nice thing to do.

J: Any wild nights that you remember?

C: Last night!

J: What time did you get to bed?

C: Not too late, probably one or something. I've had a few days of really late nights. We had the O2, then my wife had a party at her work, she has a gardening company and they're all young kids, so I've been indulging recently.

J: What do you think is the most important thing that a producer can do?

C: I think make the band feel comfortable, really. Make them enjoy their record.

J: So with Morrissey ...

C: We might have to go to the pub in a minute ...

J: ... the pub?

C: Yeah. Let's go to the pub. We can start again with Morrissey.

FIVE MINUTES LATER, AT THE PUB.

J: So you started with Morrissey when you picked up from Stephen Street on 'Ouija Board'?

C: Yeah. I don't know whether he wanted to go to Hook End, or EMI wanted us to work with him there. We set up and started working. I knew he was quite sensitive and so I said, 'We don't have to do this, we've been asked to work together. Let's go have a drink.' So we went and had a pint of Guinness, me and him, and sort of agreed that we wouldn't carry on, and that was all fine. And then when we got back, the band were kind of running through 'Yes I Am Blind', which sounded really good, so we kind of looked at each other and said, 'Well, let's see this through.' And that was it. I thought it sounded great.

J: So a little strange at first ...

C: It felt awkward, and then we went for a little walk, and then it wasn't awkward. I think I normally do that with people if we're halfway through an album and people are losing their confidence, or whatever, kind of talk to them, but I wasn't thinking I was going to sort the problem out, I was just thinking that I would have a nice day with him. It worked out, and when we got back things were working musically, so that was that.

J: Do you listen to *Kill Uncle* now?

C: Occasionally. I mean, that came after 'November Spawned a Monster.' We had established a relationship. He was changing from Kevin [Armstrong] to Mark [Nevin]. Kevin Armstrong was the best writer I've worked with in a way, so that was a bit difficult for me, because I relied on Kevin musically for different things.

Mark was a different kind of guitarist, he was more folky. I sort of saw the whole album as poems put to music, as opposed to trying to create the perfect pop song. I didn't think too much about its commerciality, more about the music being right. They felt like vignettes rather than big pieces. It was quite an intense experience, because we were all living together. But I really liked it. I think Andrew [Paresi] and myself were both really pleased with it. He was probably my closest ally at that time because he was there all the time and Mark was coming and going.

J: There was a notable shift from guitar to piano in this album.

C: I got Steve Nieve in and quirk it up a bit. But it was based on Mark Nevin's guitar parts that he played really well. He probably would have been more inclined to do a Fairground Attraction kind of thing, and I wasn't excited by that. Mark seemed to like everything we did, I never really argued with him. I just pushed it down the direction that I imagined the record should sound like.

J: Morrissey is a fan of Madness. Were you/ he driving this album to have more of a piano sound?

C: Well, sometimes I'd say, 'Well it sounds a bit like Madness' and he'd say, 'Good'. I knew he liked Sparks so I wrote the music for *Mute Witness* in that style. I was used to writing that kind of dink-dink-dink-dink-dink stuff for Deaf School.

J: 'Our Frank' is very Madness.

C: Yeah, 'Our Frank' is very Madness. Carl and Suggs were invited up to Hook End at that time, as well as people like Vic and Bob. I had to look after everyone.

J: Was Hook End kind of a party central, then?

C: Yeah. Well, it was a fourteen-bedroom, sixteenth-century manor house. Twenty-two acres, swimming pool, sauna. We had bought it from Dave Gilmour. It had the biggest control room in Europe. Later we sold it to Trevor Horn. It meant that we were secluded from the rest of the world, and had people running around making us too much food. So it was our own world. The weird bit of the week was going home for a Sunday, because you just felt like an alien from another world, with Andy Rourke and all the regulars. Sort of living in Morrissey's domain, no meat or fish. I think one day a week you were allowed to eat shellfish or something like that.

J: Was working at Hook End a bit like living in Morrissey's house?

C: Well, it was our house, but when he was there he set some of the rules and boundaries ... sometimes broken.

J: What are your favourite tracks on *Kill Uncle*?

C: I like 'Driving Your Girlfriend Home'. I really like the way it goes from one side of the stereo to the other. It goes 'turn left' and the musical effect is that we swing around the corner with him. It was visual, musical input that made it more 3-D. I really like the whole song, the melody, the lyric.

J: I like the drums. The brushes.

C: The good thing about all these songs is that we just put them together. They weren't a band. There were musicians around who were always there, but if we didn't like the drums we could take them off and put them on again. Andrew would hang around and say, 'I've had another idea for that song' and we could do it. So that was really quite a rare thing to happen at that time, because well, normally when you record with a band, you'd record the drummer, he'd go home, then the guitarist ... These days it's easier because of computers.

J: How did you feel when *Kill Uncle* was received less favourably by the press?

C: Erm, it hurt.

J: It must have been quite a shock for you, because you were used to producing hits.

C: Yeah, it was. I knew it was a really good album. The late Tony Wilson didn't help. Just when it came out he was key speaker at one of those new music things in America and he was part of this whole Madchester scene, and Morrissey had gone off and done this quite subtle album. He slated it, to the whole of the music industry, and just said how great the Happy Mondays were, etc., and how sh*t Morrissey had become. All the papers wrote similar things. But I knew the album was really good. What hurt was that people didn't get it. I was really pleased when I spoke to you, and you said it's a really popular album with Morrissey fans. Well, that's what it's supposed to be. I have seen it in the bargain basement a lot, but I've seen a lot of my records there!

J: It is respected for being experimental, as well as beautiful and melodic.

C: Morrissey didn't like things being worked on too much. He started to say that rough mixes should be the final mixes. After this, we lost our control. He had other ideas and moved onto more rockabilly stuff.

J: Yes, but don't you think that he has moved on with every album? No two Morrissey phases are the same.

C: Yes, especially, I suppose, by using different producers, musicians ... yeah, they're all different.

J: He went on to work with Mick Ronson. Did you follow the later work?

C: Initially I did, I liked what they were doing. My head's a bit more poppy than that, I wanted to get more pop music out of it than what he was doing. I always felt like I had unfinished business with Morrissey ... I just wanted to write more with him. I would have loved to develop a songwriting partnership with him.

J: Would you like to work with Morrissey again?

C: If he asked me. If he gave me my book back!

J: He borrowed a book from you?

C: Derek Taylor's biography. He's the Beatles' press guy. He signed Deaf School to Warner Brothers. He had limited edition handmade books, photographs and everything, all history, copies of tickets of The Beatles at Shea Stadium, pictures of Deaf School; I'm in it. All hand-signed and numbered. I was given one by Rob Dickens, who was the head of Warners at that time. Then Derek died, so that was my book, it went.

J: If Morrissey was to walk in here right now and said, 'All right, Clive?' what would you say to him?

C: Where's my book? I'd probably give him a kiss. I saw him out of a car window about ten years ago in the Parkway. Waved to him. He waved back. I doubt if we've both changed that much. I spent a lot of time with him, we had a lot of adventures. We'd stay up into the early hours, walking and talking. He wasn't used to social situations, and I'm more sociable, if you like.

J: You were quite protective of a younger Morrissey?

C: Yeah. I would look at him and say, 'Are you all right? Do you want to go home now?'

J: That's really sweet.

C: That's how close we were. That's why I was in his world. He'd do nice things, like, buy my wife some make up or give her a present.

J: There was a great fondness there between you.

C: Yeah. I'd go to his door and knock on it and say, 'It's Clive.' Sometimes he'd open it, sometimes he wouldn't.

I just remembered, it was Christmas; he wrote me a note that said, *'The only thing that's really making me happy is November.'* That was really nice. I've still got it somewhere. A special card, saying thank you.

J: Speaking of your finest pop record …

C: 'November'? Well, we recorded it, and I listened to it, and thought it was really good. I thought, what about if we split it in the middle? When I wrote music for Morrissey, I didn't know what was going to be the chorus or the verse. He knew I had an idea of what I thought, but he'd sing right over my chorus and put his chorus where you weren't expecting it. I didn't accept this with 'November'. I was more strict then. I thought, if we go into this adventure in the middle, where someone is giving birth, the music is about giving birth. It took it to a different level. We had a guide vocal on it, pulled it apart, and then he spoke to Mary Margaret O'Hara, and that was amazing to get her.

J: It all works really well. Some nice bongos while she's giving birth …

C: Well, I wrote the guitar riff on the piano [sings: 'Dong-dong-donk-a-donk-a-donk-donk']. I was probably trying to do a Stones thing or something. Maybe a bit like 'The Last Time' or

'We Love You' but slightly different. I always liked writing songs where the riff kept going but the chords would change underneath.

J: Morrissey's lyrics are a source of great hilarity.

C: He'd normally come in and do two or three guide vocals for us so that we could understand how it was laid down, which would help me. We'd just burst out laughing. Every song would move you in one way or another. That's where I became a fan. I was a late fan of Morrissey's and The Smiths. I enjoy The Smiths a lot more now than I did then. I wasn't listening hard enough. I tend not to. Lyrics come to me later. I like the whole package of pop. I'm used to 'I get around' by the Beach Boys.

J: Lyrically, not that great by comparison ...

C: Yeah, but great sound!

J: Although they did write one of the best pop songs ever in history.

C: 'Good Vibrations'?

J: 'God Only Knows'.

C: They wrote millions. 'Surf's Up' is another. Suggests the end of surf, it's over, it's amazing.

Check out *Holland*; it's a great album, some great songs on it.

J: I would imagine 'November' is quite a difficult track to do live?

C: Yeah, it is. When Morrissey was touring with the first rockabilly band, he performed it in Madison Square Garden. I was like, this is an amazing moment for me. Incredible.

J: He did 'Ouija Board' at Hop Farm. It was beautiful.

C: Johnny Marr said he liked 'Ouija Board'. I had dinner with him once. I said I'd worked with Morrissey and he said that he really liked that record. I remember walking into Warner Brothers and somebody stopping me and saying, 'Didn't you write November Spawned A Monster with Morrissey?' When I said yes, he patted me on the back and shook my hand!

J: Can I take a couple of pictures of you? Do you want your scarf on?

C: Do you want my scarf on?

J: I want your scarf!

C: I've only just got it! It was Madness merchandise, a sample; the manager had a couple and he said, 'Oh I've just been given these,' and so he gave me one about a week ago.

J: Can you get me one?

C: No. I think there were only two, sorry!

J: If Morrissey was coming to your house, what snacks would you put out for him?

C: Beef Jerky! Umm … I can't remember if he likes Marmite. I'd probably put Twiglets out. He wasn't a health freak. I might like to put out some nuts and things like that, but he might want crisps.

J: What kind?

C: Plain crisps. I'd put plain crisps and Twiglets out.

J: And for dinner?

C: I'd make him a spinach and mushroom pie with mashed potatoes and some mashed up swede.

J: What is your favourite crisp flavour, Clive?

C: I don't eat crisps. At school I used to get a packet of cheese and onion crisps and squash them up when we had double physics. My friend did the same—we'd see if we could make one packet last for eighty minutes.

J: Tiny bit by tiny bit? Did this help you concentrate on the lesson?

C: No. It just helped me get through a double period of physics. I just didn't understand physics past how a light bulb worked. I wanted to, but I couldn't.

J: Did you like school?

C: I was at a grammar school in North London. Julien Temple was one of my best friends. But by the time I got to exams, I got five O levels, one of which was art, and I had given up. I just wanted to go to art college and form a band. I went to Canterbury Art College, and one of the tutors there was Ian Dury. Then I went to Liverpool Art College, because Lennon went there. Just a week ago I found out that Liverpool are awarding me a degree. Thirty years on …

J: Congratulations!

C: Someone asked on my behalf and they didn't tell me until it was agreed. Yeah it's great. By the time I had finished college, I had my first album. I had left a term early. The album cover went on to win *Music Week* cover of the year award. I didn't design it, but I lived with the guy that did. It was an amazing piece of art, really. But as far as crisps go ... These days I'd go for something a bit more exotic. A posh plain. But not a Kettle Chip, not one that breaks your teeth. Just a nicely made crisp. I like the blue ones. Remember those? You might be too young.

J: I remember them. Salt 'n' Shake? I'm not that young. They were so unhealthy. Tudor Crisps were nice as well. Great flavours.

C: I don't know them.

J: What's your favourite TV show?

C: I like that *Borgen*. The Danish series, I thought that was really good.

J: What about soaps?

C: Well, *Borgen* is a kind of soap. My wife watches *Eastenders* and I have a little look now and again.

J: No Corrie?

C: No.

J: Any favourite soap characters?

C: No.

J: Favourite Smiths/Morrissey song?

C: 'How Soon Is Now?' for the guitar, because I'm a guitarist. 'Driving Your Girlfriend Home'. I do gravitate towards that. Whereas 'November ...' I have to be in a certain mood. 'Driving,' I can just put on and enjoy it.

J: Favourite pizza topping?

C: These are all very high carbohydrate foods you're asking. If I was going to Pizza Express I'd get a salad Nicoise.

J: Good point. What would you eat for a typical dinner, then?

C: A piece of grilled fish and some vegetables.

J: Favourite vegetable?

C: I was going to say tomato, but that's not a vegetable. I'm really happy with any green veg that's fresh. I'm happy with broccoli, but not too much. I like all vegetables, really.

J: Do you eat meat?

C: Not much, but I do eat it. I don't often order it. My wife is a vegetarian. But I cook it for my parents on a Sunday.

J: What's your favourite drink?

C: A good red wine. A good Cotes du Rhone, but at Christmas I'd go for something a bit more serious, like a Bordeaux.

J: I love Chianti Classico when it comes in the casket ...

C: Then you put a candle in it when it's finished?

J: Yes!

C: As a kid, we used to go to this restaurant that had those bottles with my parents, reminds me of that. I really like an Italian Tuscan wine called Brunello di Montalcino. I've been to the village in Tuscany a couple of times. There's about twelve different estates. It's a good wine for Christmas Day.

J: What is your favourite movie?

C: *West Side Story* comes to mind, but *Being John Malkovich* ... *Taxi Driver* ... oh ... *Blade Runner*? Too many to mention.

J: Did *West Side Story* get you into rockabilly?

C: I'm not a connoisseur of rockabilly. I like Fifties rock 'n' roll, but I'm not a fanatic. I like rock 'n' roll, blues. I love the sound of rockabilly records, but I don't go home and listen to it.

J: What do you consider to be the best pop song ever written?

C: Probably has to be 'Strawberry Fields Forever'. It's a ridiculous question, because I've probably got twenty.

J: Well, one from your top twenty.

C: 'Friday On My Mind ...' I might have had one too many now.

J: What's your favourite childhood toy?

C: Scalextric. 1962/3. You put the track together with little clips, and the car had two bits of stuff that collected dust underneath.

J: Did it come off the tracks?

C: Yeah, all the time.

J: Favourite band to see live?

C: Hendrix was pretty good. Family and Captain Beefheart. Exciting, exotic, full of energy. Going to see Family again in February.

J: Are you going to see Johnny Marr?

C: No. I don't know that much about him, but I appreciate what he does. I often go and see bands that I've worked with.

J: Were you ever into the 'synth' sound of the Eighties?

C: Well, I was brought up with Terry Riley. He started electronic sequence music. He did an album called *Rainbow in Curved Air*. It verges on modern classical music. That's what started it all off. Kraftwerk after that. I didn't like Eighties electronica much. Giorgio Moroder was really good, though. He did that amazing dance record ... 'I Feel Love' with Donna Summer. I was in the same studio when Human League were doing their record and we were doing 'Come on Eileen' at the same time. It kind of says quite a lot, cos our route was very classic and theirs more synthy.

J: I think you have a very strong idea about what you like, and what you definitely don't like.

C: Yeah, I do ... I don't know what that's all about!

J: Where do you like to eat?

C: This week I like The Empress in Victoria Park Village. Run by a really nice guy. Otherwise there's too many, Les Cornettes in La Chapelle-D'Abondance. It was exciting to go to Tribeca Grill in New York, too.

J: Who cuts your hair? It's great!

C: Thank you! My rockabilly mate Steve for six quid in Camden town. I ask for a Fifties rockabilly look.

J: Could you write a note to my mum?

C: Sure.

J: Are you sure you want to keep that scarf?

C: Yes.

Hi Pat
Happy Xmas 2012
love Clive Langer.

Grant Showbiz

The Smiths' sound engineer and producer of Rank

15 MINUTES WITH YOU

AS I approach the front door of the Showbiz house, I notice that it's decorated in many unusual and pretty door handles that Mr Showbiz later tells me are made from Balinese seashells. After a Japanese song is played in full for the doorbell, the door swings open to reveal a tall, slender, sharp-dressed man. 'You're early!' he barks, both smiley yet brisk, before he strides down the hall in such a Wonka-esque manner that I half expect his ornaments be made of chocolate.

Grant Showbiz is one of the very few who, during the short, implosive career of The Smiths, witnessed managers, producers, crew and friends come and go, while he stayed, managing to sustain his tenure as a sound man that almost completely bookended The Smiths' fertile five-year period (from fifth gig onwards through to the production of *Rank*). He is such an excitable and luminous person to talk to; the memories fizz out of him like a shaken can of coke: *'with The Smiths it was just me making what they did sound great! They didn't need any musical direction; Joe (Moss) just said to me, 'Make Morrissey's voice as loud as the rest of the band!'*

He very generously shows me around his happy home, which is filled with delicious treats because, luckily for me, all of his personal memorabilia is down from the loft as it undergoes a conversion. There's rare T-shirts, posters, singles, soundcheck tapes, postcards … Every door opens to another room of treasure: the studio is piled up with records, what used to be his upstairs bedroom is full of rolled up posters, books, tapes, videos, bags and boxes of pictures … and when he goes looking for one thing, he becomes excited to uncover another. Even his bathroom has framed gold discs and posters. He has kept every jigsaw piece of his musical life for The Smiths, The Fall, Billy Bragg or Frank Chickens, as well as his own band, Moodswings—the five artists in whom he has invested his enduring loyalty. Seeing it all laid out like this (most of it Smiths) is giving me a peculiar floating sensation, because I know I'm seeing something special, precious items that ought to be in the V&A, encased in glass, ready for a future exhibition.

On his style of working: *'You have to be receptive, dedicated and caring … I don't know the names of things. I have made a real conscious effort not to try and learn anything technical, like the model numbers of compressors. I am probably unlike most sound engineers, because most sound engineers know what they are doing. I just have my ears!'* On the sound of The Smiths: *'The Smiths were looking for the 'other'. I believe that they were looking for something that hadn't been done before, business-wise and everything else.'*

His favourite childhood toy is Action Man, he likes cheese 'n' onion crisps and for a biscuit he'll scoff a shortbread. When he's not touring with Billy Bragg or producing The Fall (or standing on a chair), he gets very busy on his free nights, reading to his little son, Taro.

J: Happy birthday! Please say your full name.

G: Grant Showbiz.

J: Why did you change your surname?

G: I dropped out of uni in 1976/77 and immediately got involved with the squat scene in London. I was working for a guy called Steve Hillage, a guitarist at Virgin Records. Through him I met a band called Here and Now a bunch of real stoner hippies. I was eighteen and I knew nothing, but even knowing so little I was still the most together guy out of all of us, because I could put the equipment on stage and set it up. That was back in the day when there was a free festival scene in the UK and we'd have three days' notice to play, so everyone would wait around for three days, no toilets, shops or places to sit. Eventually we'd play and that would be the event! Gradually, we got into the music business and I got us a record deal. I was kind of the manager and the sound man. We did a big free tour of normal venues in 1977 and I had this attaché case on the bus. When the rest of the band saw it they started shouting: 'You're just showbiz! You've turned into a complete showbiz freak!' They took the attaché case that had all the money and information about the gigs and threw it out the bus window as we were headed up the motorway and after that no one called me anything else.

J: Do you think that 'Showbiz' sums you up?

G: I do, yes. In that kind of way, I just thought, I am showbiz. As a teenager I loved to follow Bowie, Lou Reed, get the autographs, I'd try to get on stage ... All of that I loved. Everyone had a punk name in 1977 and that was mine.

J: And with that ... could you describe yourself in a sentence?

G: Yes. Loud, talkative, happy and lucky ... very lucky to walk into the Smiths.

J: You seem to maintain very long relationships with bands.

G: I'm not a career guy, working with hundreds of bands. You could sum me up as The Smiths, The Fall, Billy Bragg and Frank Chickens, and my own band, The Moodswings. It was really nice to see Mark [E. Smith] yesterday, because I've known him for thirty-five years. I've worked with Billy for nearly thirty years. I'm still friendly with Johnny [Marr] and we exchange emails occasionally. I find people that are talented and I become their friends because I love what they do, and I'm happy to work for them for as long as they like, sometimes for nothing. Billy is probably my closest male friend. We were just in Australia touring together. We played to the biggest audiences we've ever had. It was really odd, because there are very few other bands or singers from our era who aren't playing the oldies circuit for 300-400 seat clubs. We were playing to 3,000 people on our biggest tour ever! This is weird when you're in your fifties!

J: What are you doing with The Fall at the moment?

G: I just finished an album. Well, certainly yesterday's conversation indicated that had happened. But I've already finished it three times! Making a record with The Fall is unlike making a record with anyone else.

J: If you could work with anyone outside of these four acts, who would it be?

G: I'd like to work with Bright Eyes, Conor Oberst. He's really brilliant, I think he's a genius. He started releasing cassettes when he was eleven or twelve. He had a number one in America a few years ago in 2004. He has gone from being quite political to being quite mystical. I just love his lyrics.

J: Would you like to work with Morrissey again?

G: I'd love to work with Morrissey, but I don't think it's on the cards. You never know. I imagine that one day we'll get to the 'Mott The Hoople moment' when we're seventy-three and think, actually, I'm not going to be able to do this in a year's time … so let's just get together and do The Smiths one last time.

J: Who should be at that reunion?

G: Everybody really. Mike Joyce is the first guy I got to know in The Smiths. I used to sleep on his floor in Manchester. It may have just gone too far now… although who knows … age does funny things to people. I talk to people now that I thought I'd never speak to again.

J: You have an amazing record collection. Do you tend to listen to the same albums all the time?

G: I have about six thousand records. I'm always trying to find new stuff, not the stuff I've got. With my son being born, I've started to realise that I have a lot of favourite records I don't listen to anymore! So I'm going back to listen to records that I love, ones that I haven't listened to for fifteen years.

[Grant puts a tape on. Live music of The Smiths plays.]

J: Oh my, what tape is this?

G: This is one of The Smiths' soundchecks. I don't know which one ['Money Changes Everything' is playing]. I recorded a backstage video, too. I don't know why it's called *Reel Around The Fountain*, I never called it that.

J: You should make a DVD of it!

G: The quality isn't that good.

J: When you listen to these soundchecks again, are you listening as a sound engineer or as one who enjoys music?

G: Both, I think. In the beauty of things that you do there's an awful moment when you finish a record or live gig and you can see all the holes and it drives you mad. All you hear is the mistakes and eventually you have to let go. Then five years later on, after another listen there's this amazing thing that happens where you're like 'There's something really wrong with this track … What is it?' You can't remember that terrible thing that caused you sleepless nights of worry and then you're like, 'Oh, this sounds great! I did a really good job!'

['Frankly Mr Shankly' plays]

J: This sounds fantastic, even without Morrissey's voice.

G: This is when they were learning the tracks, in soundchecks. I wonder what's on every cassette I have. They're all years old. There's something totally different on the other side! When I turned it over and heard this I was like, 'Grant, what are you like?'

J: I notice that you have many collectables.

G: Yes! My downfall was the attic, because I could just put stuff in there and forget about it. Since the loft conversion, I haven't got the attic space anymore, so I'm just digging out and recovering/keeping stuff that's great. I've probably got about fifty Smiths T-shirts, all the originals. I've got this Fred Perry-style Irish Smiths tour T-shirt which says The Smiths in green with a shamrock. I've got about half a dozen of those.

J: How did you begin working with The Smiths?

G: I am blessed! Johnny and Andy were at a Here and Now gig when I was stood up at the mixing desk with my red, green and gold cardigan that I used to wear, from M&S or somewhere. I was shouting at the band on stage, trying to organize a very late soundcheck, because that's what I used to do.

J: What were you shouting? What sorts of things?

G: I would say, 'That was rubbish! Stop playing,' or 'Really, you're supposed to be off now,' or 'Actually, you should be starting … Why are you still setting up the drum kit?' or the drummer would say, 'Can you put echo on the bass drum?' and I'd be like: 'Do you really mean that?' You can talk through the monitors on stage from the mixing desk so that they can hear you, but I always thought that was boring, so I'd put my voice through the PA. I liked standing on a chair. I just wanted to be the lead singer, and I couldn't sing. Then I wanted to be the lead guitarist, but I couldn't play guitar, so I ended up as the roadie, then worked my way up to become the sound guy, and ended up doing a national tour of France with Planet Gong—who were Here and Now plus Daevid Allen—but I knew nothing.

J: You faked it with Here and Now? You must have had some basic technical knowledge …

G: No. I didn't have any technical knowledge at all. The first gig I ever did was a free gig in Hyde Park, September 1976, and it was The Steve Hillage Band supporting Queen. Fifty thousand people came, or so they say. I was the guitar tech for Steve. I went out front to look at the mixing desk and I had been getting into the different sound of records since I was a pre-teen. I knew that some records had more bass, and some other records didn't have enough bass, and other records where you couldn't hear the vocals, or some where the vocals were too loud. So I had some vague idea. Later on, I'd be sitting around smoking spliffs and talking with my mates about records. Then Steve Hillage took me under his wing and taught me little tiny bits about stereos and soldering irons and sh*t like that. Then I went out and watched the Queen gig from the mixing desk. Their sound engineer was called Patrick Humphries, who, in his day, was the go-to guy for great sound, he did Pink Floyd and people like that. So he turned up, and there were all these kind of minions and they were saying things like: 'We've got the two stereo compressors in place.' He was obviously a little bit drunk, and he sort of went: 'I've got these [points to ears], it'll be all right'. I was like [screams]: 'Oh God! Eureka! You can be drunk? And all you have to have is a pair of ears? I'VE GOT EARS!' And that was it. And Queen sounded astonishing.

J: Is that the most important thing that a sound engineer can do?

G: I am probably unlike most producers and sound engineers, because most of them know what they are doing! I have made a real conscious effort not to try and learn anything. I always wanted it to do with my ears, how it sounded, you know, and I've made some brilliant records and I'm a fantastic producer and sound engineer. But I don't know the names of things or the model numbers!

['William, It Was Really Nothing' comes on the soundcheck tape.]

J: What has kept you making these brilliant records, then?

G: Luck!

J: Talent, ears …

G: Mainly luck. You've got to be talented and not a tw*t, but luck is needed. This is what I tell the college students that I occasionally lecture. Sometimes you're in a recording studio, and you just sit back and the genius falls out, but a lot of the time it's trying to recognise a good sound and get people in the right space to create music. Being aware, accommodating and not missing that special moment. I remember when we [Billy Bragg] were doing 'Mermaid Avenue' with Wilco and we missed one take. Jeff Tweedy (from Wilco) was on my arse like a monkey! And he was right. We were still recording on tape in that session and from then on those reel to reels recorded every single thing we played in the studio.

Once I was producing in Iceland with The Fall and there's a song called 'Hip Priest' which is on Silence of the Lambs soundtrack and I had to turn round to the engineer and say, 'This is a song! This isn't them tuning up!' Cos it starts with a lot of fiddling going on. I was like: 'Start the f**king tape! This is a f**king song you know,' and that was a take and it was a brilliant take, and who's to say if we hadn't have got it then, we may never have got it. So it's being receptive, dedicated, caring. That's why I can't work with a lot of people, because I have to f**king care. I can't check in like it's my job. I never wanted a job. The last straight job I did was a postman between school and uni. I only did that to get the money to go to Jamaica to find Bob Marley. That didn't really work out, but I got back alive!

J: So you were doing a Here and Now show, and Johnny and Andy turned up to that. How did you get talking?

G: Manchester was a big area for us. They came to a gig at the Poly, we were a mess, turned up late, did the soundcheck in front of the audience. I think Johnny and Andy appreciated the deviation from the norm and the theatrical aspect of it as much as anything else. Someone doing my job should have been unnoticed and dressed in double denim, instead there's this strange maniac conducting this mad panto. Often punk bands would support us, it was free to get in, and people smoked dope in the venue.

This was how it worked: we'd phone up a uni and say, 'Look, you've got to entertain your students. We've got a PA and a band. We'll come and entertain and you don't have to pay us a penny,' and they were like: 'Yeah, great!' Then we'd go and do the gig, we were the security, and if we turned up late or if we'd found some magic mushrooms the day before, setting up the PA might take days. Sometimes we'd turn up and the kid who'd booked us hadn't got the proper permission and they'd say, 'You just can't play now,' so we would set up outside in the grounds of a college. It was wild & outlawish. There was no one looking after us and we were a f**king mess at times. We didn't get paid. We'd pass a hat round at the end of the show and go, 'If you think it's a good idea that we get to the next gig, give us some money.' God knows what happened in that gig, but I'm sure they were both there.

J: So you didn't get talking to Andy and Johnny that night?

G: No. What happened was my name came up at Rough Trade about five years later, because through Here and Now I had done the sound for The Fall. More great luck! Mark E Smith said, 'Come and produce our second album.' Imagine! It was Mark who dragged me from the squats/free festival scene into the actual music business. So I had a number one album in the independent charts in 1979. Obviously Morrissey knew about The Fall, and The Fall were on Rough Trade. Rough Trade said that The Fall can be difficult at times, but Grant is organized and can make them sound great, and he's also on time, and vaguely seems sane. I guess Scott Piering or Geoff Travis said, 'Come along and see what you think of this band [The Smiths] and if you want to work with them.' Johnny and Andy knew me through Here and Now, so there were three people in the band who knew who I was. I was a little bit of an outsider then, but capable of doing the business.

J: In what way were you an outsider?

G: I was just odd and weird. Living in squats and buses, outside the law and living on little or no money. The Smiths were looking for the 'other'. I believe that they were looking for something that hadn't been done before, business-wise and everything else. The Smiths eventually broke Rough Trade, they made it in a funny sort of way by being bigger than any band on the label... then smashed them up. Rough Trade's ambitions got so huge, on top of a crazy tottering foundation of making it up as they went along, that they crashed and burned at the end of the day.

J: You met The Smiths at ULU?

G: Yeah, it was backstage.

J: How were they? Did you get along?

G: Well yes, they were amazing. They were like The Beatles and the Stones in that they had a complete identity, language, style ... They had Andrew Berry's haircuts, who worked out of The Hacienda, very important about the hair. They had their top collars done up, beads, jackets ... and they looked unlike anything I had ever seen before. They used words like 'handsome' and 'charming'. Words that I hadn't heard ... sort of Dickensian.

J: How polite and elegant.

G: Yeah! Wonderful, wonderful! You see it in all the great bands, they're like a gang that has a language that you don't understand that you just really want to understand cos you've never heard it before. They looked great, their lovely manager was there too, Joe Moss, who seemed more like a father or older brother, and I was used to managers being quite sharky… and he was just f**king brilliant! And they really liked me! They were supporting The Sisters of Mercy, for f**k sake.

J: I love The Sisters of Mercy.

['Vicar In A Tutu' plays on the soundcheck tape.]

G: The Smiths did a clever thing which is they started off vaguely in the dark margins … There was a New York Dolls thing about them at first … I actually saw the Dolls in 1974. Johnny Thunder was playing his guitar with a rag doll at the Rainbow Rooms in Biba's—a huge outrageous department store in Kensington, everything was in black and gold, even the baked beans. Someone in drag stood on a table and fired a starting pistol into the air to start the show. Then at the end of the gig I went back to the hotel and hung out with them!

J: How did you do that?

G: I still don't know! I don't know to this day! I was with my best mate, we had hooked onto Bowie at his *Hunky Dory* stage and we couldn't get close to him, damn we tried … Somehow we lucked out with the Dolls.

J: This was just through enthusiasm and fandom?

G: Yeah! Just literally, like 'Hey, that's happening down there, let's go.' So often we'd sign into school for the afternoon then bunk off down the motorway. I've got a phial of glitter that Bowie gave me somewhere. I remember very clearly that Lou Reed came over with a band called The Tots and I had the album and I put it through the window and said, 'Can I have your autograph?' and Lou Reed autographed it and gave it back to me. I said, 'Can I have The Tots autograph?' and he said, 'Yeah, sure,' and he picked it up and wrote 'The Tots' and gave it back to me! One of the great moments of my life! So anyway, we were young, and I went to a gig where Bowie had a mime teacher. Bowie did mime every night on stage. He had a mime troop at The Rainbow Theatre and we were filmed. I would pay huge amount of money to find that footage. My fifteen-year-old self babbling about Bowie. We had older girlfriends who dressed us in drag. We must have looked so gorgeous! One of the gigs in Aylesbury was filmed for Bowie and ended up on YouTube and the guy I went to the gig with is there holding a poster! And I was stood next to him and I'm not there! Where am

I? I'm like: 'There's you! Where's me?' And he comes back three or four times! And every time I expect to see myself and I'm never there!

J: When you were working with The Smiths from virtually the beginning to the end, did you see many changes within the band over time?

G: It was so incremental. When you are inside it you don't notice changes. We didn't think it was going to end and it all seemed so natural. We were all together in the van all the time, it seemed.

J: Who was in the van?

G: Joe Moss drove the van. Oli, the swiss roadie, me … and the band. That was it. That's how it began. It was an open van, with mattresses in the back. Morrissey would sit up front most of the time and the rest of us would be in the back of the van, rolling up. I noticed that producers were always in the studio, this is why I wanted to be a live soundman as well. The producers would never get to travel to all these countries, see all these amazing gigs, meet all these girls and drink all that wine.

J: What was the banter in the van?

G: Morrissey was very funny. Everyone was very cool.

J: Did people call you Grant or Showbiz?

G: 'Showbiz'.

J: Do people still call you Showbiz now?

G: Yeah! Billy [Bragg] still calls me Showbiz. They don't call me 'Grant'!

J: In terms of gigs, what would you say was The Smiths' turning point to success?

G: I'd say Norwich was the turning point where the gigs started getting bigger. I was like, 'Hang on, there's quite a few people here and they're all going bonkers and trying to get backstage.' And I had loads of friends! Where did all these friends come from? Coach loads were coming in with the gladioli T-shirt on, and that's when I knew that the true faith started. We got some bigger gigs and Oli started to get pissed off because he had loads to do – one guy roadying for loads of people. They were like: 'Oli, where's this, where's that?' and he was like, 'F**k this, I'm going to get stoned.' He drifted away, we got a bigger van with seats in it, we got John Featherstone [lighting engineer], who was very important, he started to make it look really interesting. Johnny got a guitar tech, so gradually everything got bigger. Then we had a PA company, we had Oz McCormick, who babysat me. If I know anything technical, it comes from Oz. He was the guy that made sure everything was going well when I was going mad standing on the desk having a great time.

J: What's your favourite gig?

G: The Salford gig was great. I can't remember being pissed off with any gig. We gave good gig! Barrowlands was incredible. When the Glaswegian crowd liked you they made the same noise that was made at other gigs when they hated you! Those weird gigs in the Shetland Islands were mad, too.

J: At the Barrowlands I waved to all of you on a coach.

G: Yes, by this time we had a coach! Then there was Andy's drug problem. In Ireland I started to think, 'This is a bit odd, why doesn't somebody do something? Andy isn't playing the right riffs; oh wait, he's all right again now.' But he's your mate! What can you do? I just sort of thought it would sort itself out. As soon as Joe left, there was no management. I remember I went to Japan with Kazuko when The Smiths were starting an American tour. I phoned the agency and said, '*How am I going to get from Japan to New York*?' and they said, 'We haven't got a ticket,' and I was like: 'This is really weird!' So I just phoned up Johnny from Tokyo and told him. Half an hour later, Johnny had me a ticket. That's the sort of thing he had to do. Every moment that the record company tried to say, 'We don't want Grant involved anymore,' love their little hearts, Johnny and Morrissey stepped in.

J: What did you say to The Smiths when they were on stage? What musical direction did you give them?

G: Well, a singer is never going to be too loud, that's the first thing. But I don't like loud volume. Or cymbals. Or trebley brightness. When operating a PA, you've got the speakers on either side of the stage and then you've got the volume that's coming off the stage from the guitarist's amplifiers. I've played with guitarists that have been so loud I don't have them in the PA, which can be difficult because then they can't be controlled. The guitarist is zooming away and you need to fit everything else around that volume. There was no such problem with Johnny or Andy, it was just me making what they did sound great. They didn't need any musical direction. Joe [Moss] just said to me, 'Make Morrissey's voice as loud as the rest of the band.' I still go to so many gigs where you cannot hear the singer. With killer singers and incredible lyrics! Really, it's so easy to make a band sound great … Why don't people do it?

J: When you look back at your younger self, is there anything you would have done differently?

G: No. I think everything worked out in a really nice way.

J: Are you still in touch with Johnny?

G: Yes. Johnny is one of those genuine, nice people. I saw him last year at a Stooges gig with Angie and they were holding hands like teenagers in love. A couple of years back we met in LA and he had a '45RPM" logo from an early Tamla Motown single tattooed on his arm, and I had been wanting to get a tattoo myself for a long time; I do copy Johnny so much. Thirteen is my lucky number, there are thirteen letters in my name and I was born on the thirteenth, so I saw Johnny's tattoo, and almost within a day I had gone to the same tattoo parlour, The Shamrock Social Club on Sunset Boulevard, where Johnny has all his tattoos done.

J: Thirteen is quite a superstitious number.

G: Some people get very worried about it. When I went to India they were very concerned about it.

J: Did you bump into Morrissey while you were in Oz with Billy?

G: He was just about to come out. Following us around, funnily enough.

J: When did you last see Morrissey?

G: Probably about eight or nine years ago. He came to a Billy Bragg gig. We had a nice chat. I wish I had more time to stay and talk with him. I miss his viewpoint on the world.

J: What did you do after The Smiths broke up?

G: A lot of people were washed up on the shore by the huge tidal wave of The Smiths. Not because it was a horrible thing, it wasn't The Stones in 1972, but The Smiths were so amazing that people didn't recover from it, because they could never achieve anything like it again. Again, I was so lucky; I just carried on. I'd met Billy during The Smiths, so I just smoothed straight into producing a gold record with him and started touring, so my life was still exciting.

J: You produced *Rank*. Was this a natural evolution of your work at their live gigs?

G: Yes. In a funny way, it was a bone that they threw me. I just knew how *Rank* should sound. I would have loved to make a studio album with The Smiths as well. If you ask me what's my one regret, that's it. But I think *Rank* defines what they sounded like live. I think of it as one of the great live albums with no additional overdubs.

J: Do you consider it your personal career high?

G: One of them. The *Mermaid Avenue* stuff I did was incredible, with Woody Guthrie's lyrics being given new music by Billy and Wilco. I also loved making *Moodfood* with my own band Moodswings.

We sold half a million records in the US and I was finally on stage. At thirty-five years old, to be performing with people like Chrissie Hynde and have a record deal and do videos, I felt so lucky!

The Smiths is one of those great things that I did. My life has been blessed. I have this delightful, incredible son, and I never thought I'd have a son, or that he'd be this amazing. I've just made an album with The Fall, which is the best album they've done in years. Now I'm about to do two months in America with Billy! What's not to like?

Know what I mean?

J: I wish I knew what you mean! Can I ask you just some quick-fire questions now?

G: I don't do quick answers, do I? Let me show you a poster!

[I follow Mr Showbiz into what used to be a bedroom but is now covered floor to ceiling in memorabilia from the loft. He shows me the poster in the pic, above, and a selection of T-shirts, some of them unworn. He searches for a box of diaries, one particular diary that Morrissey gave him, but can't find it. He finds the Klaus Nomi intro music. He has the cassettes of animal noises for *Meat Is Murder*. He has the mix tapes that Morrissey made for him to play before the shows. He tells me that during the work for the loft conversion the builders took away two skip loads full of stuff. 'I am closer to getting organised,' he says, laughing].

G: Morrissey lovingly gave me an animal liberation-type diary. It says 'To Grant' and all that sort of stuff on the front. In my way, I made lists in it every day, then crossed them out. So I have a diary of things that are crossed out. I have no idea what I did on those days!

J: Did you meet Kazuko when Frank Chickens supported The Smiths?

G: No. I had a club called The Idiot Ballroom, and she turned up to do a gig as Frank Chickens and it was love at first sight.

J: Do you go to Morrissey shows now?

G: I saw him at SXSW and I just thought he was great, absolutely great. *Your Arsenal* for me is the great Morrissey album. I love that.

J: Are you a vegetarian?

G: Yes, but I eat fish. Very early on, when *Meat Is Murder* came out, the whole band became vegetarian and the catering became vegetarian, but there was secret burger eating going on amongst the crew.

J: What's your favourite drink?

G: It used to be Pernod and lemonade, but these days it's a wheat beer. I'm not drinking at the moment, though.

J: What is that you're drinking now?

G: It's orange and raspberry juice with fizzy water. Would you like some? It looks horrible, doesn't it?

J: I thought it was like a protein shake or something like that.

G: [Adopts deeper 'manly' voice] Ah, yeah! It's algae! I don't eat solid food!

J: What's your favourite pizza topping?

G: Marinara, with seafood.

J: Crisp flavour?

G: Cheese 'n' onion.

J: Biscuit?

G: Shortbread.

J: Thing to do on a Friday night?

G: Read to my son before he goes to bed.

J: TV show?

G: *Peep Show*.

J: Smiths song?

G: Changes every day ... I like 'A Rush and a Push and the Land Is Ours'.

J: Morrissey song?

G: Can't think of one at the moment.

J: Breakfast?

G: Don't usually have breakfast.

J: Childhood toy?

G: Action Man.

J: If Morrissey walked in here right now and said, 'All right, Showbiz?' What would you say?

G: 'How lovely to see you! How's life treating you?'

J: If Morrissey came to your house, what snacks would you put out for him?

G: Some Inspiral Raw Kale Chips.

J: Could you write a note to my mum?

G: Yeah!

Frankie Boyle

Comedian and Smiths fan

15 **MINUTES WITH YOU**

FRANKIE Boyle greets me with a smile and hug in the foyer of One Aldwych hotel. He holds the door open as we enter the lift. When we reach the room for the interview, he politely asks me what I'd like to drink, orders coffee with full fat milk — *'Let's go crazy!'*— then cosies himself in an armchair.

There are no pointy digs or distasteful remarks; it's just Frankie, speaking politely and plainly, and being very funny, occasionally twisting and tugging at his formidable beard, which now resembles a burning bush. His voice is quiet, just a notch above a whisper, and I'm a little discombobulated by this gentle kindness, because the Daily Rags would have me believe he's some kind of evil word wizard with a tongue that could slice bacon; but in person he's really more of a ginger Dumbledore.

On stage, he's not for everybody. To watch one of Frankie's gigs is to see freedom of speech at its most extreme. He rebels against convention and societal 'rules' of acceptability. He's crude and rude, he swears and he goes to the most forbidden places to find his material. Here is a man that dares to talk about the British 'untouchables' in a way that the media, and some of the polarised public, believe is in scandalously bad taste. No one has escaped the wrath of Frankie; politicians, celebrities, sportsmen, paedophiles, the Catholic Church and royals in particular have all fuelled his furnace: *'I'm just trying to be funny!'* He shrugs, laughing like a siren.

But millions of people in the UK who watch the shows of black-hearted Frankie find it to be a hilarious and freeing experience. They love his brutally honest comedy and the damning way in which it's delivered. They attend his sold-out gigs, watch his DVDs and read his bestsellers, welcoming his refreshing stance as one who makes jokes about typically forbidden territory that's normally only sniggered about in the pub behind a cupped hand.

Frankie will joke about whatever or whomever he likes, because he is primarily driven by an advocacy of free speech—that it should be *truly* free without constraint or judgment and not determined by mainstream media: *'It can't just be at nuclear crisis point, or at climatic crisis point where you're allowed to say anything! People need to throw off the shackles of conformity and what's acceptable, because they are living on a dying rock.'*

He explains that a joke is a proposition, a way to provoke thought: *'If I tell a joke, it's not my position on something, it's just a way of discussing serious things, and saying 'What about this, what about that?' under camouflage.'* In this controversial regard, I can't help but compare him to Morrissey. Both are language provocateurs that use shock tactics to slam home a point; whether it's the abuse of animals, or, in Frankie's case, the hypocrisy of the British press.

I met him the day before his retirement from stand-up with just one gig to go—for Comic Relief, about addiction. Frankie's final five minutes of damnation were due to be delivered: *'I'm going to implode—really badly.'*

We talked about comedy, family, his teenage years and the bands he is into: *'I was most into The Smiths at around fifteen, sixteen, especially Hatful of Hollow. They were on an arc ahead of their fans.'*

His favourite biscuit is the dainty pink wafer, and he plans to spend his retirement *'fighting off the zombie hoards from the apocalypse in three years time … or possibly this summer if it's hot enough.'*

J: Please say your full name.

F: I'm Frankie Boyle. I'm actually Francis Martin Boyle.

J: Does your mum call you Francis?

F: No, my mum calls me Proinsias. It's my name in Irish. [*The Irish form of Francis, originating from St. Francis of Assisi. Means "little French man".*]

J: Oh, I'll have to get the spelling of that.

F: Well, I had better get it as well!

J: Does she still call you Proinsias?

F: No. She calls me Frankie now. Everybody calls me Frankie. My granddad was Frank, so I'm Frankie. My parents are from Donegal. They came over when they were teenagers. It was a migration in those days.

J: Can you describe yourself in a sentence?

F: No! I'm such a complex, many-faceted jewel. Maybe that's the sentence. I'm an enigma wrapped in a riddle lowered from a window onto a horse, ridden by a child.

J: What brings you to London?

F: I'm doing a gig at Wembley tomorrow for charity, which is about addiction, but it turned out to be also part of Comic Relief. So I am going to implode ... really badly.

J: Are you going to slag off Comic Relief?

F: Yeah. That's the first thing I'm going to do.

J: Did you study to become a teacher?

F: Yeah. I did English at Brighton then I went up to Edinburgh to do teacher training. I was working in mental health. I worked in an asylum for a year and then community care homes with schizophrenics. I wanted to work with people with learning disabilities, but in mental health you can't be promoted without a mental health nursing qualification before going into social work or teaching. So that was the plan, until I started doing comedy.

J: So if you hadn't ended up in comedy, you could have been in mental health?

F: Something like that. I applied to learning disability associations and also The School for the Blind.

J: Do you look back to that time and pluck material from it?

F: I did a joke on the first DVD. It was pretty funny. But there's patient confidentiality and privacy around that job.

J: How did you end up in comedy?

F: I started as a schoolboy at sixteen. Doing open spots here and there, like a party piece, almost. On average, it went quite well. Then, when I was twenty-three and doing my teacher training, I started doing stand-up and open spots in comedy clubs, and I was compering within a couple of months for one of the nights.

J: Do you like being the compere?

F: No, but it's something you can do to get a lot of stage time. When you're starting out the average spot might be five minutes, but as a compere you can maybe get forty minutes.

J: Are most of your pals comedians? I sometimes see you on Twitter chatting to other Scottish comedians—Limmy, Greg Hemphill, Kevin Bridges ...

F: No not really, it's weird, they are friends, but I know them much more on Twitter than I would socially. It's sort of like that now isn't it? Life has got a bit like that.

J: When you were growing up, who were the comedians that you enjoyed?

F: Billy Connolly was one. I just got an album again that I love called *Bing Hitler Live At The Tron* by Craig Ferguson. I liked the English 1950s/60s thing, too—*Round the Horne, The Goon Show, Monty Python*, P. G. Wodehouse and Oscar Wilde. That was before I knew of The Smiths at all.

J: There's no other comedian like you. How would you describe your brand of comedy?

F: I hate the word 'brand', though. I think it's a big part of what's wrong with the world. There are many things I think are wrong with the world! Everybody thinks about himself or herself as something to market. Even Stewart Lee saying, 'Oh, Michael McIntyre is like this, and John Bishop is like that,' it's kind of like a weird way of saying, 'They're not like me,' and trying to market himself. People in their forties are probably the first generation who grew up with an 'advertised' life. I remember looking through those little catalogues and obsessing over objects which probably my parents never had. Before I was on Twitter—some young student at a gig said

to me, 'Oh, you should be on Twitter, it's a great way to market yourself.' I said to him, 'What do you do?' and he said, 'Nothing. I'm a student.' So he's thinking of himself as an idea. I think that's dangerous to think as yourself as a brand. What is a brand?

J: In this instance, it's just a way of differentiating your comedy from other types of comedy.

F: Sure. I just think it's a way of selling things without a salesman.

J: On the spectrum of all comedians, you're, well, you're way off that spectrum into shocking/what shouldn't be said territory ... aren't you?

F: Yes, but not on a spectrum of *people*. There are things that people would hear down the pub that wouldn't shock. What society has said is that there's a *public* order of what can be said, and there's a *private* order of what can be said. So there's this idea in Britain that 'Oh, you can't say that!' You wouldn't do a joke about a disabled celebrity child in public, right? But the reason that that idea is tolerated is because what can be *said* in public isn't *controlled* by the public. This is what's allowed: you can write a letter of complaint because of something that has been said, or you can tweet to your two hundred followers or whatever, but ultimately what's in the public domain is decided by Rupert Murdoch and by people who have a lot of power.

J: Are you trying to represent the private 'stuff' that's not allowed to be said?

F: No, I'm just trying to be funny! But what I'm also trying to do is say that you've got to be allowed to talk about anything, as a culture, intellectually or in any way. It can't just be at nuclear crisis point, or at climatic crisis point, where you're allowed to say anything! People need to throw off the shackles of conformity and what's acceptable, because they are living on a dying rock. That's the first place that I come from.

J: A few days ago, Morrissey said that the rhino is now more or less extinct because of Beyoncé's handbags. I think that there's a similar approach to your comedy, to say something controversial in order to provoke thought. Do you agree?

F: Yes. But do people look for that, or do they not? One of the reasons they don't is to do with class. If I was an Oxbridge comedian from a certain set, people would say 'Oh, I can see what he's doing there,' but I'm not, I'm a Scot, an 'ethnic', and you don't get that, and it's an advantage not to have it, because you can

surprise people more. Morrissey is such a great quote machine, and the papers have so much space to fill, people like him are used in that way.

J: Is anyone safe from your stand-up routines? Is Morrissey safe?

F: He's certainly safe from my routines, yeah. I'd pass. I don't know enough about him now.

J: You've got quite a lot in common. You both hate the monarchy, some politicians ... You might end up quite good pals! Aside from Morrissey, is there anyone you wouldn't talk about?

F: Not really. I just want to be honest. I think people fail to understand the idea that jokes are a proposition, they are not a positioning. If I tell a joke, it's not my position on something, it's just a way of discussing serious things, and saying, 'What about this, what about that?' under camouflage, really. Everything is a proposition, and under that you can talk about anything. There isn't a line, really. I don't think you're ever really funny unless there's something else in there. I never really find anything funny if it's just 'ba-boom'.

J: What does your mum think about your jokes?

F: Almost nothing. Completely disengaged.

J: She never phones you up and says, 'Frankie, you went a bit too far that time?'

F: The only time she has ever really talked to me about it was when I was a club comic and Michael Barrymore was on telly with *My Kind of People*. She went: 'Is this kinda ... what you do?' and I went: 'Yeah. It's pretty similar!'

J: Her friends must come up to her and say things.

F: Yeah. I think that does her head in. But also you must remember I was an alcoholic until I was twenty-six, so this is brilliant for them! I'm sure they thought I'd be dead at thirty. Everything is gravy for them now.

J: Well done for not having a drink during all this time.

F: Oh ... How long is it? Since 1999. It's good.

J: Do you worry about your kids seeing you on TV or picking up one of your books?

F: Not really. They literally couldn't care less.

J: They don't know that their daddy is on the telly?

F: They do a wee bit, but they just don't care. They're not interested. It's a different class of life; a middle class life for kids. It's so stimulated. They go to horse riding, karate: it's just like, I'm the guy that takes them places.

J: Do you play tricks on them?

F: No. They're too delicate. I jumped out at my son the other night in the dark. He started to cry.

J: Do you think that a Scottish accent allows you to get away with more mischief in comedy?

F: No, less. It's the way Britain works, quite a patrician system. For example, a lot of the things that Jimmy Carr says are a lot less acceptable than what I say, with a lot less point behind them, so he gets less flack, probably because he's posh. There's a whole idea of comedy about the cultural voice and versions of it. Chris Morris says stupid things in the patrician voice, but that's been about since The Goons. It's kind of important, accent. You can imagine what the character in the sitcom with my accent is going to be. It's not going to be the boss.

J: You were brought up a Catholic. Do you believe in God?

F: No, not really. Not in the sense that people mean 'God'. I think that the universe might be conscious; so the closest I've ever got to that is in Hinduism, Vedanta. I guess that's even a scientific point of view!

J: Do you experience Catholic guilt?

F: Absolutely.

J: So do you look back at stuff you've done on stage and think, 'I shouldn't have said that'?

F: No. I'm not guilty about my work, no, not at all. If you're going to feel guilty about something, then don't say it. I've definitely had that in the past, for jokes, and thought, 'Oh, that's not really on,' so I've not done them. There's very few I've regretted, because I think so carefully about everything before I do it.

J: How do you prepare?

F: I write all the time. Then I start to pull it together and do short shows. I start to do open spots, maybe twenty or thirty of those, then I try to do longer spots, like gigs.

J: Is that when you just 'pop up' in places?

F: Well, I do The Stand but I'll also do a theatre or a mixed bill when I'm not announced. Or charity gigs. If you're looking for a tough gig—i.e. does this work outside of the fans or the people that come to see you?—the charity gigs are good for that. I'm just really checking if the words work. All in all, I may do one hundred plus gigs before I start doing a tour.

J: Do you have a group of hardcore fans that wait for you at the stage door?

F: They'd have trouble catching me! Not really. If you advertise yourself, you'll get a bunch of people that are into you. If you're going to tour it, you're looking for jokes that will work in Hull on a Wednesday night. I don't really see the faces, I'm in 2,000-seaters or something like that.

J: What were you into as a teenager?

F: Joy Division, The Smiths ... I was really into *Lord Of the Rings*. I was quite, sort of, bookish. Nowadays, if you're into something it brings you together with a lot of people, so you can't really be something like a Smiths fan anymore, because that hooks you into lots of others. It could even hook you into sex! This big social group! When I was a kid, it was quite isolating being a Smiths fan. You were one of four people in the whole school … and then that thing became really important. I was into The Smiths, Talking Heads, The Fall and Joy Division. I was really f*****g depressing! It was also the Eighties, and I hated the Eighties, despite never knowing anything else. I hated Stock, Aitken and Waterman, the whole style of the thing. Everything about it appalled me. I hated The *News of The World*, Thatcher … Everything about the Eighties was appalling.

J: What was life like at school?

F: It was pretty nondescript, really. I was quite an outsider, but I had a really big pal, so I didn't really get bullied. My buddy was six foot five. I was also quite verbally aggressive, even as a little kid. I listened to a lot of comedy and read a lot of funny things, I had a good sense of humour. In our school, people were bullied into a nervous breakdown. It was brutal, like a zoo. There were two, maybe three guys that I look back on now and think: 'They were gay guys.' I think I was in my thirties when I realised that wee guy that everybody picked on and spat on … he was an outsider because he was a non self-confident gay guy, and those guys were absolutely brutalised. People used to get covered in spittle in the classes. I got taken off their wall of fame. If you ever want to know if you've

made it, get taken down off your school's wall of fame!

J: So if somebody came up to you in the playground and tried to be your pal, you'd just use a put-down to get rid of them?

F: Yeah. It's more of a protective thing. It's hard to explain to people now. School isn't like that now. I was at a school with two thousand kids, some of them educated in an annex. There was a Portakabin … a playing field. It was like a prison yard. Some of the bullies, like, died, got killed. This wee guy—his dad chopped his head off. I remember his dad, he was a drunk and somebody inked his son's jumper. He went up to the kid at the train station with his butcher knife and cut this kid's jumper open. Years later, he chopped his kid's head off.

J: He chopped his own kid's head off?

F: Aye. Cut the one wee guy's jumper in two that inked his jumper, then ended up—cut his own kid's head off.

J: That's awful.

F: There are loads of people who are dead from that time. Loads more who are dead from heroin addiction, alcoholism. I'm only forty!

J: Why did the school take you off their wall of fame?

F: I did some jokes about one of the teachers in one of my books.

J: Oh ... I won't ask. How did you get into The Smiths?

F: My brother's pal. I remember him playing it on cassette.

J: Is that your older brother?

F: Yeah. He's forty-three now. I remember I liked it, but I wouldn't say that! Then I saw 'Heaven Knows I'm Miserable Now' on *Top of the Pops* and sort of got into it then. I was most into The Smiths at around fifteen, sixteen, especially *Hatful of Hollow*. I didn't get *The Smiths* album until the end, so I had missed out on that, but *The Queen Is Dead, Louder Than Bombs*—I taped that at the library. I love them all. The Smiths were on an arc ahead of their fans. I remember listening to The Queen Is Dead at the time, and thinking, 'Well, that's not quite what I hoped it would be,' and then I came back to them, because they were all a development each time. It's almost like all art is the wrong way round. People start out doing real crisp things to prove themselves, like The Beatles in Hamburg

and James Joyce's *Dubliners*. It's only towards the end that they start to experiment. We should have a culture that supports that! James Joyce's first book should have been *Finnegan's Wake*!

J: What was it about The Smiths that appealed to you?

F: For me, it was a time I was alone in my life, a time of isolation. I just imagined that The Smiths were about this poetry of aloneness ... but it's not at all! I listen to it now and it's about disappointment and being taken advantage of! It's very funny. But I translated it into what it meant for my virgin self at that time. It's isolation when you're surrounded by people: how alone you could be when in a relationship, how alone you could be in a social situation. I think I also see the beauty of stuff like that. [sings, 'I Don't Owe You Anything'] 'Bought on stolen wine' That's a really beautiful song, but it's things he can't say to that girl or boy, it's his internal monologue. Maybe he knows that they're going to go out with someone else!

J: Did you ever see The Smiths live?

F: No. I don't like live music. I prefer the records. The things I like best live are the things that sound most like the records. That's probably no way to appreciate music, but then I've not no musical ability. I'm really into rap now. I like word-pictures and how it all works together. A comedian called Phil Kay got me into rap. He's into improvisation. He's a genius. Half the time it doesn't go well, because he literally improvises about what's in the room, every time. He got me thinking of it in terms of how words work together.

J: Have you seen any band live?

F: Yeah, The Fall, they were great. About seven/eight years ago at The Renfrew Ferry. Loads of heckling, people throwing stuff. They just played through it really loudly. At the same time, you could see that Mark E Smith was able to keep writing great stuff because of adversity. It's hard to survive being rich and loved. With Mark E Smith there is this completely unappreciated side that keeps him in that bubble where he can keep writing.

J: He has just finished another album. Supposed to be their best album ever.

F: If you'd said that about any other band, I wouldn't believe you, but the fact that it's The Fall ... That might well be true, because he's still 'out there'. I think you need to be culturally isolated to write well. It comes from the shamanic, on the edge of the village, no place in society.

J: I'm sure I've seen a picture of you with a quiff. Did you use to try to look like Morrissey?

F: Definitely. That's what I looked like anyway. I had a load of Smiths T-shirts.

J: Was there a Smiths song that you liked in particular?

F: Too many to mention, but probably 'Suffer Little Children' was a real ... well horrible ... but at the same time great piece of art. For some guys in their early twenties to write something like that! Everything off *Hatful of Hollow* resonates too, particularly 'How soon is now?'

J: I thought you were going to say 'Still Ill' because of the iron bridge.

F: Ha! I wasn't even in that ranking at that age. That seemed like an exotic dream to me, going under an iron bridge to kiss a girl!

J: When did you meet your first girlfriend?

F: At uni. I think it was that way at that time in Glasgow. If you wanted to be around girls, you had to go to parties and be in the socialization of f***ing morons! You had to expose yourself to risk. I did do that, by getting drunk. You couldn't really be as drunk at home, but by being away, you could solve your social phobias by being three drinks in when you arrived somewhere. Drinking did a lot for me! I could never go to AA, but drinking definitely helped for a few years.

J: Do you ever get the urge to drink again?

F: No.

J: What was your drink of choice?

F: Beer. Just beer. It's an interesting way to get hooked on alcohol, because you can't really keep going unless you're going to be thirty stones. Spirits are the big killer. Connoisseurship, in general. I lived in a flat with another guy, who was a dry alcoholic, and he had been into fine wines and whiskies and stuff like that. I just thought, this is never going to last, because you're addicted to luxury chocolates and I'm addicted to ... chocolate tools!

J: Chocolate tools! We used to get them off the van for the dog!

F: For the dog? Ha ha! I love that cheap, crappy chocolate!

J: The van was great. The chocolate tools were always in a box at the front.

F: Single fags! Only 10p!

J: What other bands were you into?

F: I was into Talking Heads, too. I think that the fact that things have enough gaps in the meaning for you to make your own meaning appealed to me. *Stop Making Sense* was like a huge thing, because nothing could ever mean to me what they had created. We actually had Talking Heads on in the house all the time.

J: Do you follow Morrissey's solo work?

F: I followed *Viva Hate*, *Bona Drag* and *Kill Uncle*. I started to check out after that. There's the odd flourish, but I think it's impossible to do what he did again. There's that thing in comedy, where people think audiences want Bill Hicks. But they don't really, they don't have the capacity to sit and listen to Bill Hicks. You wonder how much it would work now. Not only can noone else be Bill Hicks, but even Bill Hicks can't be Bill Hicks again. If he was about now, he wouldn't be doing Bill Hicks, he'd be doing something else, more relevant. Morrissey can't be Eighties Morrissey again.

J: Why not? Because he needs Eighties popular culture to rebel against?

F: Well, that's a point, but I think that belittles what it was. It's just hard to survive success. It's all about being in a bubble, not being integrated, being on your own, listening to it on headphones, behind the sofa, in your room on vinyl. It's not that long ago that people listened to full albums, but people don't do that anymore. We had this on *Tramadol Nights*, sketches that were such a big fight to get on, like four minutes long. They were like: 'People don't watch sketches at four minutes long,' and we were like: 'They will!' The sketch that got the most complaints was actually about the length of time. They f*****g hated it. It lasted three minutes fifty. I did an album recently with Glenn Wool. I deliberately didn't put it on SoundCloud, or even iTunes, because I don't want people to listen to it for three minutes then give up. I want folk to download it then go listen to it on a long car journey or on their earphones, or sit in the bath, where you've got them and they can get into it.

J: I downloaded it yesterday and have it saved for a long journey. I did listen to a bit, it sounds like you two had a great laugh making it.

F: We're not stoned, honest! I'd rather five hundred or a thousand people listened to it than it got podcast status. I'm a bit like that with The Smiths as well. You have to take the time to listen to it.

J: Who do you think should play Morrissey in a film of his life?

F: That's a good question. Michael Fassbender! I don't think you could do a film of his life.

J: Really? I think it would be great.

F: A film of his *real* life would be good. I'm sure that his real life would be interesting! I heard that Morrissey was about at the time of the Moors Murderers and he was scared.

J: He was born in 1959. The kids were only a few years older than him. I would imagine being quite scared too, if I lived there at that time.

F: There's a good book about it: *One of Your Own* [Carol Ann Lee]. It's like In Cold Blood - brilliant. All about their past before they met. And it goes along, and you have a lot of sympathy for Hindley, and then the murders start and you just lose it all, and then see it from both points again. You do a flip a few times in the book. It's quite an interesting story when you read her book. But it's sad. Psychopathic. I mean, Ian Brady had a motorbike, and he used to disappear for days at a time, and you think, what the f*** was he doing then? There's a mad Genesis P-Orridge song about it: *Very Friendly*. Its basically testimony read out in a weird voice over some throbbing guitar. It's horrible.

J: If Morrissey was to walk in here right now and say, 'All right Frankie?' What would you say?

F: I'd leave you to him. I can't imagine he'd be anything other than appalled at me. I can't imagine we'd have anything in common. I've always found it weird that people want to meet people that they admire. There's something a bit *Catcher In the Rye* about that. I've never felt that urge. Someone I really love—Gene Wolfe, an American Tolkien, brilliant, a real genius. Anyway, I met someone who said, 'I know Gene Wolfe, come over to Chicago and you can meet him.' I just think that would be totally intimidating. Their work is what it means to you.

J: So your interpretation of their work might change if you meet them?

F: Totally. I know Grant Morrison, best comic book writer ever. I asked him maybe one thing, about his comics, once. That was enough for me! Mark Millar said to me, 'How do you choose comics? Are you going for a new comic?' and I said, 'If I know the writer, I'll buy the comic. If the comic doesn't have the writer on the front, it must be s**t so I won't buy it. If they've not bothered to credit the writer on the front page,

f*** it.' He said, 'That's because most people don't buy it for the writer, they buy it for the artist!'

J: Have you met Billy Connolly?

F: No, not at all. I'd quite like to meet him. I'd imagine he'd be socially a lot easier than Morrissey!

J: So what would you say to Morrissey if he walked in here now?

F: I'd say, 'Would you like a cup of tea?' and I'd order some tea.

J: What if he was coming to your house. What snacks would you put out?

F: Vegetarian. Maybe some veggie sushi. I went vegetarian for a year, on the back of Morrissey, but I couldn't handle it. I can't cook. My mate that I toured with, he just ate egg sandwiches. In our lifestyle, you have to live off service stations, and it's a nightmare. But even if you're at home, you have to cook, and I can't.

J: You twist your beard a lot.

F: I want to shave it off at the minute, that's why. I do that [twist it] when I'm thinking. I don't read enough, but it means that I think more. There's a great book by Alan Watts, *The Book*. It's all about how to think about death and life, and he starts off by going: 'If you want to think about what life is about, it's not about reading.' It struck me when I read it, I just thought, that's a great point, there were whole civilisations that existed before reading came along. I've found that by concentrating more on thinking as a general concept, the downside is that I arrive at things and then read Nietzsche had thought of something five times better and managed to boil it down to a sentence before me.

J: You're quite well read and philosophical, aren't you?

F: I think I'm philosophical, but I'm not well read.

J: While we're on Nietzsche, what's your favourite biscuit?

F: Those pink wafers. My great aunt used to have tins of those and nobody else liked them except me.

J: Did you eat them a wafer layer at a time?

F: Sometimes.

J: As you get older, you're not allowed to eat biscuits that way. Society has determined that an adult with a Jammie Dodger can't eat the top bit then the jam then the bottom bit, you have to eat it 'normally'.

F: Depends if anybody's watching or not. Imagine sitting watching *The Wire*, aged forty, eating your biscuits funny!

J: What's your favourite album?

F: It's probably this collection of Bob Dylan's greatest hits that I have on CD. I thought the CD was great, because you had to carry them so you could listen to three in a row on a train. Great if you're an artist. I'd listen to this Bob Dylan album and it would skip in so many places, because I'd had it for so long. One of the places it skipped in was in the middle of the crescendo of 'Rolling Stone'. I'm writing a new book, so I might actually put some new theories in about songs l like.

J: Have you ever had any strongly worded letters: 'Dear Mr Boyle ... I was appalled ...'

F: I did a routine about Down's Syndrome that got a lot of flack. The point was that having Down's Syndrome isn't a big deal, it's probably worse if you have much older parents than if you have Down's. In a weird way, it was supposed to be an empowering routine. But this woman at a show got upset about it, partly because she wasn't listening; she and her husband were checking their phones, and I'm like, 'What are you doing?' I guess they were just not listening. The routine was about older parents buying their Down's Syndrome kids out of date presents, and they thought I was saying Down's Syndrome kids all have out of date clothes, or something. And a whole load of other people who didn't hear that routine have to relate to it by its status, 'I've heard that you said a bad thing,' which is sort of like: 'I've heard that this record isn't that good, but I've not listened to it.' That's how we relate to the world; through a web of status. It's increasingly ill-informed, because there's so much information now and so little time to process it.

J: Do you think that people need to experience something like that in order to make a joke or write about it?

F: Have you heard it? [Down's syndrome joke]

J: I've read about it, but I haven't heard it. I am a prime example of what you just said.

F: You've read a quote from the blog of a heckler. It's a joke about having older parents and them being nightmare.

J: So everything that's written in the papers is wrong?

F: Not just about this! About much more important stuff than this ... weapons of mass destruction ...

J: I know, but I think it's interesting, because you're in the paper a lot for what you say, and people speculate ...

F: Well ... that's just the starting point. Don't believe what you read in the papers. Everything is partial.

J: What's your favourite crisp flavour?

F: Cheese 'n' onion, probably, but I can't eat crisps anymore, past that point in age. I'm too old for crisps.

J: Favourite drink?

F: Coffee.

J: TV programme?

F: I don't watch TV anymore.

J: Pizza topping?

F: Tuna!

J: Thing your mum says?

F: I don't think we can print any of that!

J: Childhood toy?

F: A bear. He was called 'wee bear'.

J: Comic book?

F: *The Filth* by Grant Morrison. I just bought some comics today. I bought *Flex Mentallo* by Grant Morrison.

J: Smiths song?

F: The whole of *Strangeways*.

J: Thing to do on a Friday night?

F: Go to bed.

J: You're retiring after tomorrow's gig. How are you planning on spending your days?

F: Fighting off the zombie hordes from the apocalypse in three years' time … or possibly this summer, if it's hot enough.

J: Could you write a note to my mum?

F: Yes, sure.

Hi Pat,

I hope you're having a lovely day.

Frankie Boyle x

FAN

Steve Parish

Crystal Palace FC Chairman and Smiths fan

15 MINUTES
WITH YOU

THERE'S a lot of white in Steve Parish's office, and it suits him. White couch, white walls, a white set of earphones—one in his right ear while he finishes a call, the white wire running down past a white shirt, connected to a white Blackberry. Offset by a smart navy jacket, his blond locks have been snipped so that the hair flick sits neatly in rows of little waves. He runs his fingers through it as he talks, allowing the waves to rise and fall then relax into that signature little-twist-of-Wham!-style he has kept variations of through the years.

Lightly tanned and relaxed after a holiday in Cannes, Steve's spirit is both sunny and optimistic as he talks about the months ahead at Selhurst Park. He's about to give the Premier League '*a right go*', and it's exciting, because the club that he and his partners rescued from administration in 2010 and that he has been a fan of since the age of five is now in a position to improve, with a significant budget of sixty million: '*You never really 'own' a football club, you only look after it for a while. I want to improve the ground, bring in exciting players. I want to do something that will hopefully excite the fans.*'

It is obvious that Crystal Palace sits right in the bullseye of his heart, and this is what motivates him to immerse himself in 'emotional knowledge': '*[We're] all bound by this thing, this love for this entity that represents memories, roots, childhood and so many important things ... What I am capable of is caring about something. And when I care about something, and I enjoy it, it becomes so consuming for me, that I defy anybody to be better at it.*'

He pulls out stories like they're Russian dolls, one inside another inside another, and it's hard not to let time drift away in the loops of his very engaging '*Listen Joulee: I'll tell you what it is, righ ...*' Michael Caine jangle. So we try to hone in and spend this interview talking about his passions - the business of football: '*The most important thing about being a chairman is the ability to say no. I've never been frightened to say no to people, and I think in football people get killed by an unwillingness to say it.*'

On being a chairman: *'If you've lost a big game on Saturday then you have to talk about refurbing the bogs on Monday, it can be hard to get motivated.'*

On the music that he loves, including The Smiths: *'I'd have to go for 'This Charming Man.' It's the greatest guitar opening to any song, ever. It makes you wanna bounce up and jump around.'*

His favourite ever Palace player is Ian Wright, and he likes to snack on a lump of cheese: *'If it's got cheese on it, I'm normally in.'* His crisp flavour is Thai chilli, and after a couple of beers he likes to sit down on the floor with a few pals, turn on *The Queen Is Dead* and belt out *'Oh Mother I can feel the soil falling over my 'ead ...'*

J: Please say your full name.

S: Stephen Parish.

J: Do you have any middle names?

S: No, and it's Stephen with a 'ph.' I thought Steve McQueen was the coolest bloke in the world. I was always upset with my mum that she named me with a 'ph,' cos I wanted to be Steve McQueen and he had a 'v'. But I think you can shorten Stephen to Steve, even if you've got a 'ph,' can't you?

J: Well, you've managed it okay!

S: Exactly! And then when I want to be posh, I go for 'Stephen'.

J: What about when people are telling you off?

S: There are many, many other words for that!

J: Can you describe yourself in a sentence?

S: Oh, come on. I'm useless at things like this. I really am. I can describe myself in about ten million words, probably.

J: What would be your favourite word?

S: Is it going to be one of these interviews where it's like a quiz?

J: Yes. I love quizzes.

S: I'd like to think I was a bit different. A bit contrarian, bit obtuse maybe.

J: Where were you brought up?

S: I was brought up in Forest Hill, Lewisham, Catford, around that area.

J: How did you get into Crystal Palace?

S: At around four or five years old, I loved football. We used to play out; it was all we had to do, play in the back garden. I was born three doors down from my best mate, then we moved to the same close after that, and I was with him every day for about fourteen years, playing football. So one day I was sitting on the edge of my bed and my dad came in. I remember it like it was yesterday. I had posters on the wall of different football teams, and I said, 'Who do I support, Dad?' and in those days your dad wasn't going to take you to Manchester, the car would never make it, you wouldn't be able to get petrol after midnight ... so he said, 'You can support Palace or Millwall.' And I just thought Palace had a better kit.

J: What was the kit?

S: It was a Don Rogers kit, which is a white kit with claret and blue, because it was an old Villa director that started the club, bit like the kit that we just got promoted in, white claret and blue with two stripes down the front. I went to my first game against Chelsea. Dad took me, he wasn't a football fan, his dad was a Millwall fan. I always thought later, when I bought the club and he came to Millwall games, that sort of deep down he was a bit torn, but he wasn't that bothered about who I supported.

J: How was the game?

S: I remember it as one of the most terrifying experiences, right in the depths of football violence, before the ecstasy generation and everybody got loved up in the stands. In the Seventies it was terrible, and it was Chelsea. They let too many people in, there was no real crowd control, and I was tiny, I thought I was going to get crushed. And the swearing! I had never heard anyone swear before, my dad didn't swear, and the language was just ... incredible.

J: Where did you sit?

S: I sat in what is now the Arthur Wait Stand, cos that was where you would go if you weren't season ticket holders, or you would just stand at the front, but I think we sat. We won. It was Jim Cannon's debut and he went on to play nearly six hundred games for the club. We got relegated that year, as we always do. I remember leaving at the end, still thinking I would be getting crushed.

J: That's an exciting first game. From then on were you hooked?

S: Yes, but I couldn't go every week. I had periods where I would go a lot, but my dad wasn't that into it and there was always something else. By the time I was sixteen there were girls and nightclubs …

J: Were you still playing football when you were sixteen?

S: I played every single moment of every day when I was a kid. I was striker, winger. I wasn't very good. Once it got to organised football, I was very small and skinny and not really strong. I was all right.

J: You were wiry.

S: Yeah! Let's go with wiry!

J: Any other favourite players growing up?

S: After Don Rogers, we had a fantastic team in the Eighties, Terry Venables was manager. Malcolm Allison had come, changed the colours, changed 'The Glaziers' to 'The Eagles'. Allison made Palace sexy. There was a TV programme; 'Team of the Eighties' and a player called Vince Hilaire—one of the early black players—he was one of my favourites, and he still comes down to the club now, great bloke. Ian Wright is my favourite ever player.

Malcolm Allison did something that most don't do; he changed the image of the club, he had Page Three girls, it was all very rock and roll, and that's been there ever since. I only found out later that the Eagle was meant to represent a phoenix rising from the flames; I just thought that he thought an eagle would be better than a glass house. But we're The Eagles now, and the fans chant the nickname.

J: How would you describe the bond to your team?

S: Football is an incredible bond. People don't understand it. You don't understand it yourself. When you fall in love at four years old, before you know about anything, the first thing you fall in love with is a football team, it's an undying love. It can't be broken. You can't change football teams. I don't know anyone who's ever done that. When we were kids, footballers were gods, you didn't have this access to famous people that you do now. You didn't have this broad range of people famous for being, well, Kim Kardashian or somebody like that. You had to do something. Pop stars were massive too, because they were untouchable and you never met them. Everybody is so accessible now, there's no real mystery anymore.

J: Would you say that there's a stronger connection between the Palace fans and the club versus other fans and their clubs?

S: No, I don't think so. Probably one of the things that Palace hasn't got going for it is that it's not the name of a town. People have an unbelievable bond to their clubs, especially if it's the name of a town, and every football fan will think that their bond is the strongest. Being a football fan of any club is a relationship that was formed very young.

J: Why did you step forward to buy the club?

S: It was in trouble, you know, it was in administration.

J: Why you though?

S: Because nobody else was going to do it.

J: In the build-up, were you waiting for someone to step forward, or were you always contemplating?

S: I think … I don't know whether you post-rationalise things. I get a sense now that I knew that one day I would be involved in owning it. I don't know why. I just always thought it. It wasn't managed brilliantly over a long period of time. If you're that interested in something and you're built like me, you'll always think: 'I think I could do that better.' So when it got into trouble and people approached me, I was worried about it, because I understood exactly what's involved in it, the financial risks, all that kind of stuff, but I didn't want to do it on my own. I work quite well in groups of people, you know, it gives you that extra layer, if you're worried you've got that double-check … I wanted to try to get some other people involved. If somebody had come along and said, 'I want to buy it and I want to turn it into the biggest club in the world,' I'd have said,

'Yeah, I'll buy a box, I'll come along, enjoy the ride.'

J: What did you think that you could do better?

S: I think the ability to say no. I've never been frightened to say no to people and I think in football people get killed by an unwillingness to say no. They want to please the manager or the fans, so they do things that aren't logical, like paying big money for players. There's another thing: your football club is a reflection of you. I think all football fans feel like that. Especially when you're young, and things are going well— 'Oh, Palace will win!' Then things are going badly … It's a reflection of you in terms of when you say to people, 'Palace? Oh really?' It's a laughing stock at times, and the ground is run-down. You feel like it's doing you a disservice. We're better than that. That's how much it means to most football fans. You cannot separate yourself from it, you can't disown it. I remember going to watch games in my thirties. I would walk in to Selhurst Park, which is a dump, and my heart would be beating, you know. You're looking for that result, when you get involved with the game. People like Jim Piddock, Maxi Jazz, Eddie Izzard, Neil Morrissey, Jo Brand … as well as many, many other successful people in different walks of life like my partners, Martin, Stephen and Jeremy: all these people were all born in

that area and have all gone to the four winds and they're all bound by this thing, this love for this entity that represents their memories, roots, childhood and so many important things … When it wins it feels like you're winning. It's part of you. I remember somebody saying to me, 'Why do you want to do this?' [buy the club] In the end I think it boils down to: life doesn't mean much, nobody knows what it means, but it certainly doesn't mean whatever the microcosm of what you're dealing with at the time means, but it means something to you. It has to mean something to you. If you don't have anything that you love and care about, what have you got? You love and write about Morrissey and The Smiths.

J: They're like my football team.

S: It's not entirely rational, is it?

J: No, not entirely, but I think that's where real love exists. Are you just getting a chance to do what you love, at last?

S: Well, I'm not a spectacularly bright person. I was never going to get a First or be an amazing academic. I've met people who are astoundingly bright, but what I am capable of is caring about something. And when I care about something, and I enjoy it, it becomes so consuming for me that I defy anybody to be better at it. If you care about something, you'll worry about it. If you worry about it, you'll want to get to the right answers. And you will. So it's chicken and egg: to be good at something, I have to find something that I care about. I don't have a choice of just going: '*Oh, I'm brilliant, I'll just do that on half gas.*' Then I develop an emotional knowledge, knowledge that wouldn't work well on a spreadsheet. I try to get amongst the problems of the club to understand what everybody needs from it. The Club is a series of deals, whether it's a deal for a player or paying a builder. Life is a series of deals. I care about it, therefore it's going to be something I'm good at and I will make a difference. The beautiful thing about football clubs is that you never own one, you just look after it for a while. They are institutions, they will be going for a thousand years, so that's great, because you know that all you've really got to do is move it forward and get it somewhere better than where it was.

J: Are there other football chairmen, past and present, you admire?

S: Ron Noades was a controversial figure to some, but hugely successful and I think very similar to me in many ways. There was a lot of cash in football at the time. He was fantastically successful with the club. Anybody can go out and spend more money than anyone else, go out and buy things, but look at Huw Jenkins in the fourth division with a broken-down stadium—he created something great. Make money, don't spend all your money doing it. You have to go against popular wisdom, against all the agents that are ringing you every day, you've got to find your own path, be single-minded. There are a few people who have achieved that over the years.

J: Do you like the direct access that the fans have to you via Twitter?

S: We've got two really healthy forums—CPFC BBS forums and the Holmesdale. Of course there's Twitter and loads of social networks, I think it's fantastic, yes, I do like it, but it's a double-edged sword, isn't it? I suppose I've got a tiny idea of what it is to have any kind of public profile, how tough you have to be to expose yourself to those mediums. There's listening to the fan base and learning what they want and how to improve things, but you've still got to filter the abusive side. All those things bring out the best and worst in society. With football, everything is laid bare. Emotions are laid bare. The bloke that said you were the best thing since sliced bread on the Friday then on Sunday morning thinks you're the worst thing ever. It's a really strange business, because you're publicly tested every week.

J: Does it get to you, or have you learned to put a barrier up?

S: You can't not let it get to you. The hardest part is when you're trying to do so many things to move the club forward, and the thing in the end is all about the winning and losing. If you've lost a big game on Saturday then you have to talk about refurbing the bogs on Monday, it can be hard to get motivated.

J: When you get down to watching the games, are you watching as a chairman or as that little boy?

S: It's a combination. There's the passion of the fan, but there are differences because I know things. I know some of the secrets of football, which is there are no secrets! The psychology of a football team—what the players are thinking—is a lot more important than other things. I'm a realist. I can overcome what I want and believe the evidence with my own eyes. I get quite irritated with fans who don't see the reality, the ref's decisions, etc. During the game, I feel the tension and the excitement gets to me. If it goes wrong, I just think: 'I've got to do something, what am I going to do?'

J: You're in the public eye, now more than ever. How do you cope with that?

S: Every time you get it wrong, you publicly get it wrong, and people remind you. Imagine you've gone to a meeting to pitch a bit of business, lost, gone home and know that you screwed it up. It's not just you and the three people in the room that know. Everyone on Twitter is telling you you've done it wrong, people are ringing you up to tell you you've done it wrong … the forums are telling you …

J: Well, you're clearly not doing it wrong because in May 2013 you watched the team get promoted. Tell me the story of your experience that night.

S: I was at the game, in the royal box. Brilliant. The whole thing. On the back lawn I would relive the great games at Wembley; now, suddenly I'm in it. This kid from South London is taking a team to Wembley! Where shall we go training beforehand, what colour suits should the players wear, chatting to the manager about what we're gonna do. In whatever way, I've contributed to them getting there. All my friends, Mark, Michael, Phil, Richard, my great mates from advertising, my daughter, her boyfriend, Neil Morrissey, Elton John, Eddie Izzard. An incredible day. If you had that dinner party, can you imagine? Throw in the people that have meant the most to you in your life, chuck in a few celebs, that alone would be an amazing day! Now your team is walking out at Wembley in front of eighty thousand people. A team that you know—you know those boys, this one on a free transfer, that one from Norway for three hundred grand—you know them, remember the day they signed, you've got intimate knowledge of them. The whole day, building up to that tension of the game. We played really well. Jim Piddock at full time was like: 'How are we not in the Premier League already?'

Then in extra time the penalty goes in, and time stands still. I was watching thirty-five seconds, and it took an hour to get to thirty-six seconds … and I'm thinking things, for the club, what a difference it makes, every minute is a ten million quid minute, then one goes off the line and it looks like they're going to score … and Mark Bright is sitting next to me, a great mate, a hero of mine when he played with Ian Wright for Palace, and he sits next to me every game. I said to him, 'Brighty, I can't breathe. I literally cannot breathe.' And you *know* that the cameras are on you.

Some days just don't have a 'Yeah, but …' There was no 'Yeah, but' to that day. It was completely magical. As a football fan, the only downside was

that I could cry for the Watford fans, even now … I can't watch that penalty in case he saves it. There's a bit of me that thinks, it didn't really happen, he gets really close to the ball … Two lovely clubs. That could have been Palace, and I know it's crushing. But it's poignant for me, because the Championship is hard. Stephen Browett's working hard, trying making fifteen grand for a beer festival, Kevin Day's doing a comedy night for the academy, and make some money for Children In Need. It's those things that are getting you by, existing on that. Suddenly, some bloke from the Premier League hands you a bit of paper and says, 'We're going to give you x million on this day, x million on that day.'

J: How are you going to change the club?

S: We can change the club, we can transform the club. When I took it over, nobody expected anything. I want to improve the ground, bring in exciting players. I want to do something that will hopefully excite the fans. The problem I've got now is I've watched the Championship for over thirty, forty years. The stage we're at, I describe as the difficult third album. Most pop stars have got the first album, then enough for a second one …

J: Now you've got the deal with EMI …

S: I've got to smash it out now. But it took me ten years to write my first two! I don't really watch the Premier League; it hasn't been relevant. By the time you watch all the games then watch League One and League Two to see if there's a decent striker, there's no time. So we're in uncharted waters.

J: Will you redevelop the ground?

S: Absolutely. We have got to redevelop the ground. It's a legacy for the club. We need a modern facility. People won't accept cold, wet, cheap food. They won't take it anymore. We're all spoiled now. There's so much to do in London. In Bromley and Croydon we've got 900,000 people. Putting that into perspective, you've got somewhere like Middlesbrough with 120,000 people. We've got a huge catchment. We need to build a stadium that will keep a lot of them in there, and that will take time, money and effort to make it matter. This is where it gets tougher.

J: Very best of luck with Palace, Steve. Shall we talk about music now?

S: Yeah, let's do that.

J: Tell me about the posters on your wall, growing up.

S: Elvis was first. All those terrible movies he made, constantly on the telly. This is my first musical memory, *GI Blues*, army films. He was cool, a beautiful man. After that it was Showaddywaddy. I was just a little bit young for punk, but I remember learning all the words to Boomtown Rats' 'Rat Trap' and getting into The Who, then indie music, watching *The Tube*. *Top of The Pops* was crap.

J: I bet you watched it, though.

S: Watch it? I went to it! Somewhere there's a film of me dancing to Fun Boy Three and Bananarama. The Associates were on, maybe I went to two *Top of The Pops*. I get into bands late, because if people rave about stuff, it puts me off. The last thing you want to tell me is that a film is really great. Then I'm like, nah. Can't be bothered with that.

J: What was your first gig?

S: Madness. I'd been to Shalamar and Shakatak when I was thirteen, but the first gig that was music I wanted to go to was Madness.

J: Do you remember the year?

S: I was sixteen, so 1981. The first album. The whole thing. Two Tone suits. Ska. I massively got into that. I liked Bow Wow Wow. I got into the Pistols later, I remember watching that Bill Grundy show and thinking it was shocking.

J: What was the first record you bought?

S: Elvis. Then another rock 'n' roll band—Darts. I loved them—'Daddy Cool'. I used to go down to WH Smiths in Forest Hill and buy the records. I had an eclectic taste. My next musical coming was Dominion Theatre, Tottenham Court Road, The Style Council. The Jam had split up and The Style Council was more me. I never felt like I owned the Jam. I went back and loved them, but I wasn't there when they first came. I thought the first Style Council album was brilliant.

The support act for The Style Council was this guy with a guitar called Billy Bragg, just singing and telling jokes. I couldn't believe the balls he had. Everybody was watching him, and nobody watches support bands. He was singing stuff like: 'I love you/I am the milkman of human kindness/I will leave an extra pint.'

I've always been more into lyrics. And we were in Thatcher's Britain, so people had stuff to say and I wanted to listen to politicised lyrics. Jobs were hard to come by and he had something to say. He was funny, as well. He said, 'Weller has given me a guitar tuner. He's told me, "Billy, you've got to tune that guitar son." So I do this every now and then in a gig.' I bought the album before I went to Tenerife. *Life's a Riot with Spy Vs. Spy* and I didn't listen to anything else. This love affair with him began and never really went away. He's not everyone's cup of tea, like The Smiths. I love him singing Smiths songs. That cover of 'Jeane' was one of the first Smiths songs I heard.

Billy Bragg lived his life ten minutes before me. About his third album I had broken up with some girl and he had broken up with a girl before me, wrote a record about it, just in time for me to be breaking up with a girl!

I saw him recently . I went to get a paper and stood at the traffic lights, no one else around. Standing waiting to cross the road the other way was Billy. Who'd have thought it, this man, he wrote about his dad dying, he's the soundtrack to my life. I went to Shepherds Bush a couple of years ago and he did the whole album. Those lyrics all mean something to me. Within that was all of those bands, that whole Eighties era; even if you go to New York there are bars and it's all they play.

Then there's Morrissey, as well. I went away last week to Cannes and I made a soundtrack, and I put on 'How Soon Is Now?', 'There Is a Light', 'I Know It's Over'. I love that line: 'Oh mother, I can feel the soil falling over my head.' Again, it's poetry. Morrissey is like the modern Shakespeare. Being into lyrics, later on I got into rap, I liked Public Enemy and Eminem—all poets, really.

Then after him, The Streets, that album, so fantastic, *A Grand Don't Come For Free*. I loved that album. It has to be listened to from beginning to end. It's a complete story, isn't it? Like Smiths albums; they have to be listened to from beginning to end. Artists that can write an album of great songs should be celebrated and admired. I don't know that anybody really tries anymore; nobody's buying albums, they're just getting that track, then that track, then that track.

J: You were a Smiths fan. Did you go on to become a Morrissey fan?

S: Well, for me it was The Smiths. I saw them a few times, one time at the Brixton Academy on *The Queen Is Dead* tour. I stood on that slopey floor and there was a big punch up in the audience. I was really into The Smiths, I had my phase, but I was never one of the more hardcore fans. I'd hear one track, and that was enough for me to go and buy the album. Buying an album cost money that mattered to you, so whether you liked it or not initially didn't matter. You played it till you liked it.

J: Which album is your favourite?

S: Well, I'd say *The Queen Is Dead* but I love all the albums. I have all of them. And if we sat here and played the albums now, I'd know all the lyrics, because I have consumed them for a three/four-month period. The Johnny Marr element of The Smiths really mattered to me. I liked the Morrissey hits after The Smiths, but I really was more of a Smiths fan.

J: We once had a good conversation about cover versions. Do you still enjoy them? I love Billy's cover of 'Never Had No One, Ever'.

S: Billy does great covers. The Jackson Five, 'I'll be there', and Smokey Robinson, 'Tracks of My Tears'. Those two tracks are in the top ten tracks of my life. He did it live once. You used to be able to get bootlegs, but you can't get them anymore.

J: Do you have a favourite Smiths or Morrissey lyric?

S: Yeah. 'You go and you stand on your own, and you leave on your own, and you go home and you cry and you want to die.' I mean, it's the story of every awkward teenager. It's 'Why have I gone here? Why did I f***ing bother? There must be SOMEBODY here who might like me? No? [bangs table] I have gone here for nothing. NOTHING. I'm leaving on my own, again!' I want to sit and listen to an album now. When you leave, I'm going to have a big Smiths binge.

J: Ha ha!

S: You just reminded me of 'Bigmouth Strikes Again'. There are so many brilliant choices. The Smiths spoiled us really, didn't they?

J: Do you have any control over the music that gets played at Palace during half time? Do you ever say, 'Oh, let's shove in a bit of Smiths or Billy?

S: I don't, really, but I could do. I have to surrender to the fact that we need to cater for the younger market, get the young kids coming back.

J: Is that why you have the cheerleaders?

S: The 'Glad All Over' that they sing is up to a million hits.

J: Are you bringing the cheerleaders to the Premier League?

S: I am, but, listen, there's a fine line between something that's family and attracts girls to football and something that's not wholesome. The cheerleaders are much tamer than your average pop video. In the end, if they are dressed appropriately and fun, then it gives entertainment and something for people to look at while they're waiting.

J: If Morrissey walked in here right now and said, 'All right, Steve?' what would you say?

S: 'Wow! What are you doing here?' You get much more comfortable meeting people as you get older. One of the nice things that the football affords you is that it's the great equalizer. I was on a plane to Nice reading an interview with Arsène Wenger. There was a guy behind me talking in French, and I was like, 'God, that sounds like Arsène Wenger. Nah, I'm just reading a story about him, just imagining it.' So a bloke handed me a camera and said, 'Can you take a picture for me?' I looked round and he was with Arsène Wenger. I was just about to turn away and I thought, 'Well I'm in the same business as Arsène now, I'll have a chat to him' because we were after a couple of Arsenal players at the time. So we had a little chat, and I said, 'I've just bought Crystal Palace,' and he said 'Well good luck with that!'

I'm okay with talking to anyone, but I've never wanted to be someone because I knew someone. No matter how small your achievements are, they don't have to be public, at least they're yours and not someone else's. I feel sorry for people who are pestered all the time because they have a talent, so I try not to intrude. Instead of that moment where you want to talk to them, and you know they don't want to talk to you,

you're just another pain in the arse. You might win them over, but usually not.

I met Mick Jones, who is a QPR fan. I've never asked anybody for a picture. But I asked him. I said, 'Look,—Big Audio Dynamite, 1986, Milton Keynes Bowl, England are playing Argentina in the World Cup the same night. I still came to your gig then rushed back.' Then he went: 'I remember that gig!' It was nice.

J: Who is the most famous Palace fan?

S: Bill Wyman. He was supposed to come to a game—can you imagine that?

J: If Morrissey came to your house, what snacks would you put out for him?

S: I think he eats tofu and all that stuff, doesn't he? I'd probably say, 'Well I ain't got any of that. I've got some nuts and Walkers crisps.' I'll tell you what Julie—I'll nip to Wholefoods for him. Gimme a list!

J: What's your favourite thing to do on a Friday night?

S: Curry and a pint. But I don't do it anymore, cos I'm trying to be healthy. I race cars and I go all round England, and what I've noticed is that the only decent thing you can get to eat is curry.

J: What's your favourite drink?

S: Black tea. Black Earl Grey, lemon. Or green tea.

J: No pink champagne for Steve Parish?

S: I like Champagne! The optimum alcoholic drink would probably be lager.

J: Favourite snack?

S: Cheese. If its got cheese on it, I'm normally in. I am prone to just going to the fridge and eating a lump of cheese. I love a packet of crisps.

J: Oh! Well that's good. Favourite crisp flavour?

S: Salt and vinegar in the old days. Now I like those Thai chili ones. I'm drawn to those.

J: Pizza topping?

S: I like an American Hot. I like pepperoni and peppers.

J: Favourite Smiths song?

S: I'd have to go for 'This Charming Man.' It's the greatest guitar opening to any song, ever. It makes you wanna bounce up and jump around. That's the first ever Smiths record that I heard. I remember exactly where I was, in a flat, and somebody put that on, and I thought: 'What is that? Who is that? That's fantastic!' I was eighteen, just leaving school, and it was a really sunny day.

J: What's your favourite childhood toy?

S: I had the Evel Knievel bike. I remember doing the stunts on loop the loop. Sometimes it made it all the way around, but mainly it just fell. I also had Swingball. I spent hours and hours in the garden playing Swingball.

J: Who cuts your hair?

S: It's a bloody disaster. It happened in France. It was long and I wanted a trim. And I went in there and the woman went and cut it all off. So I came back and I went to Harry, my hairdresser, and he fixed it for me, thank God.

J: Will you write a note to my mum?

S: Of course. I can't spell, though, and I hardly ever write now.

S: How's your dad?

J: He's good. He likes it when he sees you on the telly.

S: Ha ha! 'I know him!'

Pat,

    Hope all is good. Just
here reminicing with Julie about
great times in New York with
Gerard. Seems like an age ago.
So pleased she's following a passin.
and writing. She really is a credit
to you and Jimmy.
              Its a long time since
we met inoBigger, hopefully see you
again soon.

        Lots of Love

            Stu

                    xx

Mark Bedford

Bass player with Madness and Morrissey

15 MINUTES WITH YOU

SITTING chatting on a bench in Soho Square, Mark 'Bedders' Bedford from Madness comes across as quite a private man. He's not always keen to be in the spotlight, preferring to stay as grounded in reality as he can; a typical guy in a Fred Perry and desert boots, pally with everybody from the London cabbies to the Queen ... who just happens to play bass for Britain's best-loved band. He declares himself the sensible one in Madness, but the sparkle and laughter that livens his eyes suggests otherwise; most especially when he tries to recall who was to blame for ideas like unscrewing an entire hotel with Swiss Army knives and building a giant food mountain from dressing room leftovers.

Like any family, there are times when simply being together in the same room can be a fiery experience. When members of Madness work closely together, their connection can fan a heat so intense it produces some of the most anthemic, catchy and cleverly arranged musical gems in history—like 'My Girl', 'Cardiac Arrest', 'Shut Up' and 'Lovestruck'. Sparks fly between the bandmates and fuel their creativity; ironing out quirks in rehearsal and energising on-stage performances. But there are other times when the intensity is so much, when seven colourful characters spend every waking hour together in the studio-on the road, in hotels, rehearsing, learning, playing, debating, performing, eating, drinking, creating—that the heat boils, and the relationships burn out.

'Well, everyone would call us a dysfunctional family. It's testament that we can still talk to each other now; we've had our ups and downs like any family.'

It must be love between the members of this band, as after thirty-five years the significant seven are still together, due to a healthy and respectful attitude towards individuals taking a break when they need one.

Bedders has taken a few breaks, to explore other projects and work on his graphic design business to *'stop going barmy.'* During one of these quieter, less 'Mad' periods while the band was on a hiatus in 1991, Clive Langer [Madness producer] invited him to Hook End Manor to make an album with Morrissey. At Langer's suggestion, Bedders also packed his double bass, before heading off to join Mark Nevin, Andrew Paresi and, of course, Moz: *'I thought it would be a good challenge. I thought that Mark Nevin's stuff would be really interesting, a mixture of something a little bit different—a clever collaboration.'*

Working with Morrissey was a different experience than he was used to, and he was impressed by the natural focus of the process: '*He is a man with a real singular vision. He knows exactly what he wants to do, how he wants to write, and he's very good at getting that across ... He's a clever, articulate guy ... He would more or less sing a complete vocal from start to finish. He is very together, very professional ... We did nearly every song like that, in a tightly structured way.*'

Bedders hates fairgrounds (won't go on a rollercoaster, not even for the 'House of Fun' video*)* but he likes the 2p games in the arcades. His favourite crisps are cheese 'n' onion, and drink is a cool vodka and tonic. He thinks that *Kill Uncle* is underrated, but he doesn't have much time for reviews: '*You can't let those things influence you ... If you think it's a good record, then it is.*'

On meeting Morrissey for the first time: '*He said, 'Should I call you Bedders, or should I call you Mark?' and I said, 'Call me whatever you want ...*'

J: Please say your full name.

M: Mark Bedford

J: No middle names?

M: William, after my granddad.

J: Can you describe yourself in a sentence?

M: I ... um ... bass player with Madness. Although I've a lot of other jobs as well!

J: How did you get your nickname, 'Bedders'?

M: Chris Foreman, the Madness guitarist, started calling me Bedders, from Bedford, back when we started together.

J: You've been with Madness since the start. How did you get together?

M: I've had a few breaks from the band, but since 1978 I've been there, off and on. Mike, Chris and Lee started playing in Mike's bedroom. They all lived around Kentish Town, and I went to school on Highgate Road, Woody went to school near Chalk Farm, Suggs went to school in Swiss Cottage, so everyone met in that area. Me and Woody are a little bit younger. Those three wanted to form a band, and through various friends of different friends that's how we all got together.

J: How old were you then?

M: Seventeen.

J: Did you have any idea what lay ahead?

M: When we first started to write our own songs, I thought, 'Oh, we might be onto something here.' They actually sounded quite good, and our first few attempts really weren't that bad. It's always time and place. We went to see The Specials at the Hope and Anchor, they had come down from Coventry. We said, 'Look, we're playing kind of the same music as you are—reggae, ska, whatever,' and Jerry Dammers said, 'Well we're trying to get a label together,' and everything really sprang from there.

J: What was the first Madness song you did that you thought sounded quite good?

M: Erm, like any group we did a lot of covers and learned a lot of old reggae songs. One of the first songs that was written was a song called 'Mistakes', which was the B-side of 'One Step Beyond' and I think we had written 'My Girl', quite early too, and it sounded good. When we started to hear the early songs gel, then others came along, it all felt right.

J: Growing up, did you have posters on your bedroom wall?

M: I had a fantastic Move poster, I remember that. I was only about eleven or twelve when I started buying records. I was given a bit of pocket money and was always interested in music. At around '72-74, the kids at school started buying records, and I was listening to anything from the charts to a lot of American music, people like Neil Young.

J: When did you first pick up the bass guitar?

M: About the same age, thirteen, just because a couple of mates of mine had guitars that they played at school, and they needed someone to play the bass.

J: Do you remember any of the tracks you tried to learn?

M: Oh, Beatles songs, normally.

J: In the time that you've been with Madness, has there been a favourite period for you?

M: There are lots. All with different meanings. Recording and seeing your first record.

Physically seeing it, on 2 Tone, was amazing. I was waiting for a van in Archway, because we were going off to play a gig somewhere. A friend of ours, John Hasler, showed up, carrying a box of records. He was a very instrumental figure in Madness because, although he didn't end up in the band, he played and sang at different points, he got the band together, helped organise the band. He was instrumental in kind of keeping the band together.

J: He was your manager, eventually, after drums/singing?

M: Yes, he was and he wasn't. He was a really good friend of ours, really good at getting things together, and in that early period he helped with a lot of things.

J: The band was enormous in the Eighties. What was it like to experience it from the inside?

M: It was kind of non-stop work, really. When we signed to Stiff and made the *One Step Beyond* album, I figured out that out of two years, I was away solidly for eighteen months of those two years. I wasn't at home. Just shows you the nature of the amount of work and touring that we were doing, all over the place. It was a very intense period from 1980 to 1986, constantly making records and touring.

J: And going to number one.

M: Yeah! That was really funny. When it finally happened with 'House of Fun', we were in Japan! We laughed about it, so ironic that we weren't there! It was relief, though, to be at number one at last. I think there are different things along the Madness way that please you more. Creatively, moving forward, like when songs pop out of other songs, that's kind of more satisfying in some respects.

J: How would you describe your relationship within the band?

M: Well, everyone would call us a dysfunctional family! It's testament that we can still talk to each other now; we've had our ups and downs like any family, really.

J: You must have had a lot of laughs and Madness capers?

M: We were pretty raucous when we were a bit younger, yeah!

J: Anything you'd like to share?

M: Well, being bored on the road, we got up to all sorts. We dismantled a hotel once, and everything in it. We were playing a gig in

Switzerland and the promoter thought it would be a very good idea to give us a gift of a big Swiss Army knife each. So the first thing we did was unscrew everything in the hotel. We swapped all the room numbers, systematically. We unscrewed furniture, chairs, beds, doorframes. Anything we could.

J: Did you leave it sitting together, so that if someone sat on it, it would fall apart?

M: We did. We were very good at it. We changed the room numbers on the different floors, unscrewed things and moved them around a bit.

J: How did you not get caught?

M: We were very quick. This is the kind of thing that we used to get up to in the Eighties.

J: Madness always looks naughty, like there's mischief going on, even now.

M: I think it was just being bored a lot of the time. On the road. It drives you to mischief!

J: There are seven of you in the band, and your seventh single was 'The return of the Los Palmas 7' (that you co-wrote). This went to number seven in the charts and stayed there for seven weeks. What is the significance of seven?

M: Some mystic planning? No, it's just a coincidence. A fluke, really.

J: 'The Return of the Los Palmas 7' is one of my favourite singles. What are yours?

M: I've got a few, for different reasons. When we wrote 'Grey Day' that was something completely different. A really good point along the way. We made a breakthrough there, and it's a really good sounding record, a little bit different for Madness.

J: It was a darker record for you, wasn't it?

M: Yeah. It just had a denser, heavier sound to it, which was really good. 'Yesterday's Men' was fantastic, even though it's probably not so well known by people. 'Our House' took a lot of work to get it to where it was, and is probably the most popular Madness song in different countries around the world. It took forever to get it right, and when it did, it really paid off. Some songs are written in ten minutes and it all sounds great, others take treacherous journeys; we could never get the rhythm of 'Our House' right, that was the problem; we were never really satisfied.

J: Your music and lyrics always have stories—'Bed and Breakfast Man', for example, is a great story both musically and lyrically, as is 'Cardiac Arrest' and many others—and the videos reflected this.

M: Well, that was at the time when people made videos. We used to do them really cheaply. We used simple tricks with Lee flying around. We didn't go off to some tropical island somewhere. We did them in the garage or basement of Stiff Records. Most of them were done in Hoxton.

J: How did you come up with the ideas for the videos?

M: We used to sit in a room and have a set plan. We'd meet with the head of Stiff, Dave Robinson. Some were completely unworkable, but then we'd narrow it down to a storyline and try to incorporate some of those ideas. Some were fantastic! We had an idea to build a rubber street that would all move when it was touched. That would have cost an absolute fortune. But we stuck with very simple themes, like in 'It Must Be Love', there's for the line about birds and bees, and we dressed Lee up in a bee costume. We'd always get him in a costume. I've dressed up in some weird ones—I was a nun, I've been a flower—nice easy props to do. Then we'd let the camera roll, mess around, and see what came out.

J: Is there anything that you wouldn't do?

M: Yes! I refused to go on that bloody rollercoaster in *House of Fun*. They wanted to do a shot on this really fast rollercoaster and I was like, 'No, I'm not going on that!' There is a shot of a few of the band on it, but not me!

J: What bass line are you most proud of?

M: Hard question. 'House of Fun'. It's quite mind-bending, the way it keeps circling round and round, but it creates a rhythm. That's something that me and Mike worked out together. It's rolling, rolling, rolling all the time. Technically that's quite mad, cos it keeps going and going and going. But some of the simpler ones like 'Bed and Breakfast Man' is a very simple bass line, but it's kind of Motown, so it's quite nice. That's our influences coming out. Then some of the reggae ones I was quite pleased with.

J: Can I ask you about playing the roof of Buckingham Palace?

M: It was a really good day. I took my kids. We knew what the band were going to do but weren't quite sure how it would work. We had been shown the graphics, the thirty-two projectors. We didn't realise quite how big an event it was going to be. It's one of the biggest events we've ever done.

J: Did you have to go through the Palace to get up the stairs?

M: Yes! It was mad. They had set up a village where all the bands were, dressing rooms, etc. We got there early and there was a garden party. They gave everyone a hamper with Waitrose sandwiches and drinks and a rain cape. I met my kids in there. We hung around for a while, enjoying it, and then we climbed up all these stairs, the back stairs, where all the people who work in the Palace live, right at the top. We sat in a very small room for a long time, waiting to go out onto the roof. We could hear the other bands and the crowd, but we had to wait. They opened the door, and wow—what a view, see down into the City and behind you towards the Thames and Battersea. There was a tiny platform just back from the roof's edge and we were on that. The cameraman was up there. There were snipers up there! All these people started appearing from the roof and looking. There was so much security and so many people hiding.

J: Were you nervous?

M: No. We've done it so many times before. We could just about hear the reaction, people singing along to us miming.

J: Did you meet the Queen?

M: There was a reception line after, the Queen shook my hand and said, 'What a fantastic evening!'

J: 2012 was a big year for Madness with the Olympics, too.

M: I knew that we were going to be playing at the Olympics for eighteen months, and I couldn't tell anyone. I know David Arnold, who did all the music for the closing ceremony. He's a fantastic composer, spent three years of his life getting that together.

J: How did you come to be Morrissey's bass player on *Kill Uncle*?

M: It was mainly through Clive [Langer]. He rang me and said that he was doing the next Morrissey album. He said that Mark Nevin would be writing a lot of the music for it. I had met Mark Nevin a couple of times, but had never played with him. I had done some playing with Roy Dodds, the Fairground Attraction drummer, and I'd been to see Fairground Attraction a few times, who were really good live, actually. I kind of knew them pretty well. London is a very small music village.

J: Had you heard of Morrissey/The Smiths before?

M: Yeah, I liked some of The Smiths' singles, and I was obviously conscious of Morrissey at the time.

J: So what did you think when Clive asked you?

M: Well, I thought it would be a good challenge. I thought that Mark Nevin's stuff would be really interesting, a mixture of something a little bit different. Mark is a very good songwriter, so I thought it would be a clever collaboration. I didn't know how they were going to work, but they worked completely separately. Some jobs you do and play and you never hear the songs, some you get to listen to demos, and some you rehearse and take part in the process. They had been working on this for a little bit, and the music was written quite quickly. I heard a couple of songs from Mark's tapes only a very short time before I turned up to Hook End Manor. I had never met Andy Paresi before, and he was great.

J: How did you first meet Morrissey?

M: Well, I met him at Hook End. From memory, it was really nice. He said, 'Should I call you Bedders, or should I call you Mark?' and I said, 'Call me whatever you want!' I can't remember what he ended up calling me!

J: What do you like to be called?

M: I don't mind. I always just say 'Mark'—it's my name, naturally. But I don't mind. Some people call me Bedders.

J: What did you and Morrissey chat about?

M: What was really nice about meeting Morrissey is that we talked about different things other than music. This put us at ease, you know. I remember talking to him about film quite a lot, about Alexander Mackendrick, the director of *The Man in the White Suit* and *The Sweet Smell of Success*. He did a lot of films connected with Ealing. Sometimes it's nice not to talk about music, makes it a bit more comfortable.

J: What was your daily routine at Hook End?

M: It was a sprawling place, amazing. It was residential, so we all had our own rooms. We got up in the morning and had breakfast, like a hotel almost, then had a little stroll around, then did a bit of work, then did some playing. Then we'd have a few drinks after and get up and do the same thing again the next day. There were a few TV rooms and we'd have a break in there.

J: There were a lot of Madness visitors, weren't there?

M: Yeah. Now the funny thing is that I was only there for the first part of the record, because we did the drums and bass first. I know Suggs came later on. It was Clive and Alan's place, very relaxed, like a very lovely second home somewhere.

J: What was the working atmosphere like?

M: It was a very practical working arrangement, very focused. When I did my bits with Andy and Mark, we were learning the songs on the spot. We would write out a rough chord chart for everything. Mark had sent Morrissey the tapes of these ideas, and Morrissey wrote the lyrics exactly to what Mark had sent him. Sometimes when recording, you write a bit and think, 'Well I'll just go blah blah blah here and fill the lyrics in later.' Or you might move a bit of chorus or verse here or there. But Morrissey had actually written the song lyrics, and it set the songs for how they were going to be, it was quite worked out. Madness would rehearse a lot before going into the studio, so we would get all our mistakes and everything done, 2-3 weeks beforehand. This was kind of learning the song in the studio, and there wasn't going to be much changing and movement. Clive moved the odd thing around,

but not much at all. It was a totally different way of working for me. It's a different process, because with Madness I'm there at the very beginning of the process. With Mark, he had written detailed arrangements and Morrissey wrote to them very precisely.

J: How did this work in the recording studio?

M: Morrissey had a very clear idea about what he wanted to do. At about eleven o'clock, myself, Mark and Andy would get in to the studio and have a chat about a song, try and attempt it. Clive might say, 'Can you try this or that?' until we had the song in a kind of shape that we could physically play from beginning to end. Then Morrissey would come in, and we'd say, 'Right we're ready.' He'd have the lyrics, put them down and bang, off we'd go. He'd more or less sing a complete vocal from start to finish. He was very together, very professional, and he always knew what he wanted to do. Most of it was usable. After a couple of runs through we had a very good take with a very good vocal. We did nearly every song like that, in a tightly structured way. Most of the time this is how we would work.

J: What did you do when you finished?

M: At the end we'd all have a listen, say, 'This was good, that was good, repair a little thing here and there,' but mainly the songs were in good shape, there wasn't much we had to do.

J: What surprised or excited you about *Kill Uncle*?

M: I liked playing the double bass on it. Clive said to bring it, and I liked that. There were two or three tracks, with double bass. That was a departure, I wasn't expecting to play it on a Morrissey record. But he went onto a Fifties double bass, more rockabilly stuff after that. 'Our Frank' sounded like a single straight away when we started playing it. It was up, instant, really good. It was one of the first things we attempted. 'Sing Your Life' was great. It's such an underrated album, actually! I'm biased, because I played on it. 'Driving Your Girlfriend Home' is a good song as well.

J: It never dates, does it?

M: No, it doesn't. I had a listen to *Kill Uncle,* for something else, a little while ago, and I was really surprised at how fresh it still sounds. It's a testament to Mark Nevin's writing and style.

J: Were you surprised by the reception?

M: I just thought it was a good record and we'd done our best and done really well. The sound

was great. But what can you do? There's nothing you can do about reviews. You can't let those things influence you, really. If you think it's a good record, then it is. You've done what you've done. I just think in life you have to think that some things you don't have control over, and reviews are one of those. Playing music, there are other things that can satisfy you.

J: When you think about Morrissey now, what comes to mind?

M: He's a man with a real singular vision. He knows exactly what he wants to do, how he wants to write, and he's very good at getting that across. Some people aren't good at this, they fumble around but get there in the end. He has a very good idea about where he wants to go, he thinks about it a lot and he's a very clever, articulate guy.

J: Would you work with him again?

M: Of course. It was a really enjoyable experience and we did some good work.

J: Do you keep in touch with the others? It seems amazing that there were only three of you in the band and just a few others, very intimate.

M: I have seen Mark Nevin but I haven't seen Andy Paresi, maybe just once since we did *Kill Uncle*. You're right, there were very few people on that album, compared to today's huge productions.

J: Morrissey went on to support you at the Madness reunion, Madstock, in 1992 and had to finish his set early. Did you see much of his set/what happened that day?

M: No, I didn't. And this is not a cop-out. I actually got stuck in traffic and got there late. When I did arrive, people were obviously saying that Morrissey had cut his set short. Something was thrown at him? It was quite sad that he didn't play the second night.

J: If Morrissey was to walk up here now to this bench and say, 'All right, Bedders Mark?'

M: Is that what he'd say? 'Bedders Mark'?

J: Well, he was working with two Marks during *Kill Uncle,* so he might want to distinguish between you ... but what would you say to him?

M: Who knows? I haven't seen him for a very long time.

J: Would you get up, give him a little cuddle?

M: I'm sure I would!

J: What about if he was coming round to your house? What snacks would you put out for him?

M: Oh God, I don't know! This is not something I think about ... I've never thought of this in my life! I'd be mindful that he was vegetarian.

J: What is your favourite crisp flavour?

M: Cheese 'n' onion, I suppose.

J: Favourite pizza topping?

M: Pepperoni. Not exactly original. I think it's the default position in pizzas. I don't eat pizzas that much. I do like Parma ham, though.

J: Smiths single?

M: 'Sheila Take a Bow'. I love 'Girlfriend in a Coma', and of course, 'How Soon Is Now?'. They were a very good band.

J: Morrissey single?

M: I'm going to go for 'You're the One for Me, Fatty'. Produced by Mick Ronson—which was nice.

J: Favourite drink?

M: A cool crisp vodka and tonic, if I have to, which I do.

J: Do you drink before you go on stage?

M: Not very much now. Madness have quite a hefty reputation for being able to play heavily under the influence. I don't think I'm giving too many secrets away! I did fall over four times on stage, once. I knew then I'd had a bit too much. But I got picked up, and so I just kept going. We're all pretty good now. I might have a drink after, of course, but not beforehand. You just get too tired and too grumpy with a hangover.

J: Favourite song ever?

M: That's too hard! I've got so many …

J: Favourite Nutty Boys' caper?

M: The unscrewing of a hotel in Switzerland can't really be topped, but I do remember sticking things to other things. We're quite creative. We did actually also build one of the biggest food mountains I've ever seen, out of leftover food from various dressing rooms. I think it had pizza bases that built up and up and up, then we just started to pile stuff around

it, any food that we could find. We're good at making stuff. Being stuck in places and a little bit of alcohol does that.

J: Do you still sit about and laugh about these things together?

M: There are a few stories that get rolled out, and Switzerland is one of them. It's breathtaking that we set about dismantling the place, all working together to get it done.

J: Who starts it? Who's the most mischievous?

M: Well, it's Lee, but … I did make Lee, once, in recent times … We were playing a gig with Oasis, Lee put on a monobrow, and we made Lee go in their dressing room and talk to them like that, and he followed Liam Gallagher into the toilet like that. Liam was a bit unhinged by it, I think. I said to Lee, 'You've got to keep a really straight face when you're talking to them.' Lee is always game for that kind of thing. He is mischievous, you can always get him to do stuff like that.

J: You're blaming Lee, but it sounds like you started it.

M: Well, yeah, I did send him in … but I blame Chris, actually. He starts these things off. Chris gets Lee to do things.

J: Favourite restaurant?

M: Mangal near the Rio Cinema. I like to go to St John in Spitalfields, too.

J: Favourite fairground ride?

M: None!

J: The Teacups?

M: I hate them all. I really don't like fairground rides. I do like those cascade things, with the 2ps. I spend hours doing that, putting the 2ps in and watching them fall.

J: Childhood toy?

M: A football.

J: Film?

M: *Being There*, with Peter Sellers.

J: Song to play live?

M: There are so many, really. 'It Must Be Love' is always really good, enjoyable to play. Anything that gets a great reaction. We've been playing some old reggae tunes on the road, and they're satisfying in a different way.

J: What's next for you?

M: I've been playing with Lee with his Ska Orchestra. It's a labour of love. I'm doing stuff with my friend Terry Edwards, and I'm a graphic designer, which is what I do most of the time, every day. Stops me going barmy!

J: Will you sign my two *Kill Uncles*?

M: Yes!

J: Would you write a note to my mum?

B: Yes! [Thinks for a bit, chuckles to himself]

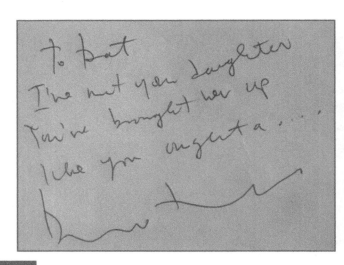

FAN

Chris Packham

Conservationist and Smiths fan

15 MINUTES
WITH YOU

CHRIS Packham sits beside me with a pot of hot chocolate and three fruity cookies. Fresh and enthused from an interview for the BBC's *Desert Island Discs*, he's looking bold in a robin-red vintage jersey that has vertical go-faster stripes running up and down the chest. He perches excitedly on the edge of the cushion in a neat, upright position, every ready with confident answers.

A conversation with one of Britain's most prominent conservationists is a nourishing experience. Mr Packham has a gift; he is able to simplify and explain complex behaviour of almost every creature on earth, and he does so in a way that is genuine and warm, easing in the facts and explanations, making it comprehensible and, above all, making it newly accessible and interesting to those of us that might just have scraped a C in science.

Throughout his life he has been a powerful crusader for animals, campaigning around the world, propelled by his own motivation and a speedy drive to preserve ecosystems. With an insistence akin to Bob Geldof at Live Aid, he fist-bangs (gently) that we are running out of time to protect endangered species, and people need to listen and act. He hasn't got time to stop for tea, and he won't do a half-ways, 'good enough' job. It has to be done right, or forget it.

I first discovered Chris Packham in 1987 when I saw him on *The Really Wild Show*. It was exciting to watch somebody on the telly doing a wildlife programme that was cool and edgy for a change. Chris was young, punky and indie and he had spiked hair, wore mad shirts (designed by his sister, Jenny) and was a captivating teacher. Seeing him years later sliding Smiths song titles into BBC's *Springwatch* was a terrific delight. His appearance and musical taste had always suggested another artistic side of him that, because of his work, remained in the shade of science.

He has great taste in music. The Damned, The Jesus and Mary Chain, The Smiths. He was raised with an appreciation for poetry, and he got an A in art for his paintings. He has two pet miniature poodles and no longer eats bread or tolerates booze in his diet, and crisps have been banished too. He does everything scientifically, properly and completely; whether it's listening to music or sanding the floors. He's all or nothing, living by his late mum's mantra: *'If a job's worth doing, it's worth doing well.'*

His favourite Smiths song is 'Reel Around the Fountain', and he doesn't eat meat: *'Well, it's murder, innit?'*

J: Please say your full name.

C: I'm Christopher Gary Packham, fourth of the fifth, nineteen sixty-one. I can't remember my national insurance number, but it begins with WC and ends in 22.

J: Are you named after anyone?

C: Not that I know of. I don't really know that much about that side of my family, really.

J: Were you happy with your names, growing up?

C: I never really thought about it growing up. There was always that middle name thing. Everybody laughed at everyone's middle names growing up, so it didn't really mean much. I remember my sister saying that she didn't like her name, once. She wanted a more pretentious name than Jenny. My family comes from Sussex. My father has recently taken an interest in genealogy and traced us back to the 1600s, but to be honest with you, I've always been a forward-looking person. What made me what I am is nothing that happened in the 1600s, it's what happened in 10 Cleveland Road when I was a kid, and that was my mum, my dad and my sister. Outside of that, my family doesn't really exist.

J: Can you describe yourself in a sentence?

C: Um. Yes, okay. I'm determined—comma, intolerant—comma, honest—comma, modest—comma …

J: You've really thought about this …

C: I'm thinking now. I am. That was in brackets. I'm hard-working. If I have any values of my own that I would hold in any regard, it would be the fact that I am honest. I tell people what I think. I am ferociously determined. I am the world's worst loser.

J: Even at Monopoly?

C: I don't lose at Monopoly. To lose would be too uncomfortable, so it's best just to win.

J: What's your strategy? Buy up Park Lane and Mayfair?

C: Anything. Anything. Cheat if I have to. Winning isn't everything, but it's the only thing that counts.

J: Did you look at the cards in the envelope at Cluedo?

C: I'd do anything to win. My sister could never figure out why I kept winning Cluedo, because I'd send her out to the kitchen to get a doughnut or something and she'd come back in and I'd be straight in there—Miss Scarlett with the lead piping. That's not a euphemism, by the way. It just came out that way!

J: You've just come from a *Desert Island Discs* interview with Radio 4. How was it?

C: I was overwhelmed to be quite honest with you, completely flattered and embarrassed. I can't imagine why they would want to interview me about the music I listen to. When I think of all the *Desert Island Disc* episodes that I've listened to in my car over the last thirty years, it includes a list of the great, the good and the bad, and to be among that list is extraordinary, and I was very flattered.

J: I know that you can't tell me what you chose, but can you give me a few 'nearly mades'?

C: Yeah, I can tell you the 'nearly mades': 'Destroy Everything You Touch' by Ladytron; I think it's got the most fabulous opening. It's a rip-roaring techno start, and I like that one. Another contemporary one that I like is 'Treats', Sleigh Bells. They make a huge amount of noise with a heavy metal guitar, but beneath it is a quite poppy lyric and sung by a girl. 'Acceleration' by The Poppy Factory. I went for pop songs, I should say. Another one was The Boys, 'Brickfield Nights'. I didn't put any Prodigy tracks in, but I like them too. I've got a list on my phone; it was very hard trying to get it down to eight. I've got to tell you—and I hope I won't be told off for telling you this—but there are no Ramones! How could you leave out the Ramones?

J: I could, quite easily ...

C: Oh no, I couldn't!

J: As a teen, what posters were on your wall?

C: My first poster was T-Rex—Marc Bolan—then Bowie, and then a hiatus until the punk time. Between Bowie and punk rock, nothing much happened for me. I couldn't stand things like ELO. Even today it makes my skin crawl. I watched the glam stuff on *Top of the Pops* and did like it. I still listen to T-Rex quite a lot. I like Sweet, 'Ballroom Blitz', that sort of stuff. I think what I liked but perhaps I didn't realise at the time, was the fact that my parents didn't like the music or the people. I remember an adverse reaction to Bowie doing 'Starman' on *Top of the Pops*. My parents just hated it. My dad hated Marc Bolan because of the glitter!

J: Did you wear make up?

C: No, I was only ten at the time. Even my sister wasn't wearing make up then! There was none to raid!

J: Were you in a band?

C: Yeah. They were called The Titanic Survivors and formed with my mate at school and his brother and various other people. We played during the punk time.

J: Do you remember any of the songs?

C: I remember them all, because I wrote them all. 'Only the Good Die Young', 'Problem Pages ...'

J: 'Problem Pages'? That sounds good.

C: My sister had a subscription to *Jackie* magazine and the problem pages were brilliant. Not that we had any sympathy at the time for the people who were writing or if they were genuine letters, although I doubt they were! They provided us with a great source of mirth.

I had a great interest in poetry. My mum was keen on poetry and read it to me as a kid. I was keen on the lyric writing but I don't have any musical aptitude at all. It's a real shame. I'm very visually orientated. I can remember people's faces and everything. If I ever see you again, in fifteen years' time, I'll recognise you. But if I hear a tune, it takes a little while to get in. I took the band very seriously. I'm not really interested in doing anything unless you do it properly. The guys in the band just weren't into it as much as I was. And true to form, it ended very acrimoniously. There's a book called *Kill Your Friends* and there's a chapter in it of a rant on why you should never start, or be in, a band. It should be read by every teenager before they make that decision. Just read that chapter first. It has good advice in it.

J: You have a strong artistic side; how did you end up in science?

C: I studied science, but given my time again, I might do differently. There's art *and* science, and that's the trouble. There was always that conflict for me. I wanted to go to art school, and I did O level and A level art. I was always really passionate about art and into it massively. My parents used to take me to galleries. Then all of that, of course, just got crushed the further I got into the academic world. There was just no time for it. By the time I graduated, it had gone, and I was desperate to get it back in again. I needed to find something creative, not just understand something but create it too.

J: You plant song titles into your *Springwatch* and *Autumnwatch* dialogue. How did that happen?

C: I was having a conversation with a guy years ago, and he said, 'I bet you can't get such and such a title into this', and I did it, and it was easy. Then when *Springwatch* came up, I thought this would be a good opportunity to broaden the audience a bit. A lot of people watch those sorts of programmes with their family and partner, and they're not into it, their partner is. So I was thinking if I could talk about football, history, art, music ... then that might get the person alongside the viewer to prick up their ears and take note. And it seems to work. The other thing is that to try and concentrate on a conversation for an hour without starting to think about something else is quite hard for me. I often talk about something but think about something completely different. To give myself a target is a good idea. So I'm constantly listening to what my colleagues are saying to see if I can get an opportunity to slip in a song title! Otherwise, I'll be thinking of the sinking of the Bismarck or something!

J: Does the director/producer know that you're doing it?

C: They don't know. If the titles were really clumsy and I really had to orchestrate it, then I can hear them all groan in my ear. Most of the time they don't know. Certainly when I was doing the Mary Chain, The Damned, The Smiths, The Manics, even the Clash, the vast majority didn't know. I also did film titles, cos I got fed up with song titles. That was fun. I did Oscar-Winning Films from 1970 onwards, and *Driving Miss Daisy* was a real highlight. I failed with *Kramer vs Kramer*!

J: How did you get *Driving Miss Daisy* in? I'll have to go and look that one up.

C: There was a beaver named Daisy, and the other beavers were driving her into the water, and so I said, 'Look, they're 'driving miss Daisy' into the water.' No one got it. They just thought I was talking nonsense. At that point I am trying to stifle a laugh. My mum always said you shouldn't laugh at your own jokes, but I've never really understood why, cos if they're funny why not laugh at them? Anyway, I was off camera and had to try very hard not to laugh.

J: Let's talk about *The Really Wild Show*, one of my favourite TV programmes as a child.

C: It was a good programme. I'd left university and started taking photos. Sold all my music gear to buy cameras and lenses, and I got a job working as a camera assistant for someone who worked at NHU [Natural History Unit at the BBC], so then they told me about *The Really Wild Show* and I wrote to them and said, 'Do you need another presenter?' and they said, 'No.' I wrote again and said, 'I think you do.' I was really quite determined to get the job. I needed something to do.

J: How did you know that you'd be okay in front of the camera?

C: I just didn't care. I had to do something. There was no failure option. I couldn't be on and off the dole all the time. I was a trained zoologist post-punk rocker with no respect for authority whatsoever, and I had to do something. I was never going to walk into a job.

J: Did you suffer from nerves, or did you get stuck right in?

C. I just got stuck right in. I've never been nervous at all, not once in my entire life. There are two reasons for that: firstly, I don't care if I make a mistake. It doesn't matter. Everyone makes mistakes. We do things again for sound, for the camera, for the animal and sometimes for me. I'm not afraid to ask, and very frequently say, 'Can I do it again? I think I can do it better.'

J: Who were your heroes—naturalists, conservationists, TV presenters …

C: As a kid, none. I didn't really watch TV.

J: What did you do?

C: I was out in the woods. I'd go home when it was dark. My mum was lucky.

J: What did your mum do?

C: She was a legal secretary for years, and my father was a marine engineer. They encouraged my interest but didn't originate it. They allowed me to make a great mess of their house with all my pets. I was very lucky.

J: What pets did you have?

C: Huge numbers of animals. Anything! An ant!

J: You'd just bring it in, give it a name …

C. There were no names. I'd put it in a jar, leave it somewhere and it died.

J: Didn't you have pet badgers at one point?

C: Foxes, badgers, buzzards … We had several foxes that lived in the garden.

J: How did you get friendly with the foxes?

C: I liked animals more than people from a very young age. I would look at them and make intense observations. I remember my mum and I were sitting in the garden once, and I put a group of lackey moth caterpillars in a flowerpot. These are processionary animals, so they follow one another. When you put them on the top, they go round and round. My mother sat watching this. My mother said, 'All those caterpillars … Look at them, they're all exactly the same!' and I said, 'No Mum, they're not the same. They're all different.' She said, 'No, no, they're all identical, just like robots going round in a circle,' and I said, 'No, they're not. I'll tell you what. I'll point out a caterpillar and then I'll turn around, and then in a minute's time I'll turn back around, look at the caterpillars and tell you which one it is.' They weren't all moving the same way. The caterpillar that I noticed was flicking his head up more than the others. When you're into animals that deeply and looking at that level of behaviour and beyond, then it's very easy to form a relationship with them. The way I live with my dogs is different to how others live with their dogs. I live with them ... not quite as a dog ... but I maximise the relationship with them, for their benefit and for mine.

J: Do they have names, or is it Dog One and Dog Two?

C. They are called Itchy and Scratchy. My stepdaughter named them. I wanted to call them Stay and Come Here. With the previous poodle there was a big fight, because I wanted to call it Help, so I'd be shouting, 'Help' and my fantasy would be that somebody would actually need help and a poodle would turn up! I was banned; they didn't want to face the embarrassment of shouting 'Help' down the park all the time. So we named it Fish instead.

J: Would you get a third dog?

C. I wouldn't get another one now, because they are ten and very possessive. We live in a triumvirate, as it were. They wouldn't accept another.

J: Do you have heroes now?

C: Alan Whicker, Sir David Attenborough. All of the presenters of the *Today* programme—I hold them in high esteem. Bill Oddie. Jeremy Paxman—I think he's a great broadcaster.

John Humphries, the backbone of the BBC-clever, manages the humour. Whicker I still think is the greatest broadcaster. He'd be in a millionaire's villa, then in a roadside shack, and would instantly be able to ingratiate himself with these people, because he wants to know the answer to his questions. Too many people ask questions on television and they don't even listen to the answers. Too much butting in to make themselves sound clever. That's rubbish broadcasting, I hate that, it's rude. How can you be an interviewer if you're not interested in the answers?

J: You've had a career that has spanned nearly thirty years on television. What has been your greatest highlight, or is it still to come?

C: Well, I hope it's still to come. Not that I haven't had highlights.

J: How about proud moments, then?

C: I don't have any pride.

J: No pride?

C. No! There have been a huge number of amazing things in my life. I grew up in a three up, three down in Southampton. Read Ladybird Books and went to a comprehensive school. We used to get second-hand *National Geographics,* and I couldn't believe that the pictures were on the same planet I was on. Now I've been able to see that world and encounter many of the animals that for me were just black and white photos in an old set of encyclopedias. I've had an extraordinarily privileged life. I could have a happy death. I think that the best way to deal with life, and death, is to be able to die at any moment happy. If someone said to me, 'You've got five minutes,' I just couldn't be churlish about it. I'd have to say, there have been so many five minutes in my life that have been awesome. It's been remarkably rich, and even now I have to walk behind the car and pinch myself. Even this year, I've been doing a series about animal intelligence and I've been working with dolphins, elephants and chimpanzees. Not animals that I've spent a lot of time working with, so this concentrated period has allowed me to have some epiphany moments.

J: Listening to you now, it sounds like animals are your real heroes.

C: Yeah, definitely.

J: You like badgers, don't you?

C: I like badgers, but no more than I like other British fauna, to be honest with you. I studied badgers for five years. I had a rescued animal—not really a pet, the RSPCA used to drop them off at my parents house—badgers, foxes, birds; at that time the RSPCA only did pets, but wild animals would still get handed in. At that time, the guy from the RSPCA would come round with a box with a kestrel in it with a broken wing. It was good.

J: How did you come to love The Smiths?

C: It was the early Eighties, and The Smiths and the Mary Chain kind of broke at the same time as the most important bands for me, personally. They're kind of post-punk and I was lucky enough to see great punk bands like The Damned, The Clash and the Pistols.

J: Did you go to a lot of gigs?

C: When I was sixteen, I would hitch round or go by train and go to gigs every week. Most bands I saw more than once; there weren't that many venues or bands, so you could go for an evening and see The Damned, The Clash and the Buzzcocks all in one night. As they matured and survived, I would continue to go and see them. I liked the whole live experience. You feel part of it. At that time, feeling part of the punk movement was something that was important to me then, something that I relished.

J: Do you have a favourite gig?

C: The Kitchens of Distinction—they did some great gigs. But my favourite gig would be the Mary Chain playing Poole Arts Centre. On the Darklands tour. They were out of control. They flooded the entire theatre with smoke. You couldn't see that far in front of your face. They had all the lights on and it was just pulsing. Then 'Sidewalking' came on, and it was a complete Mary Chain experience.

J: What did you most enjoy about The Smiths?

C: Well, when they broke up it was a disaster. I was furious with them, because I didn't think they'd finished what they needed to do. *Strangeways* had moved on, I thought they were progressing and I wanted more. Morrissey and Marr were a match made in heaven. The originality that both of them brought to the band was just ... that's what made The Smiths. Joyce and Rourke were tight, and understood what was going on in the band. The originality of Marr's guitar and Morrissey's peculiar northern, maudlin kitchen sink drama, with the Shangri-Las and The Ronnettes' type thrown in ... that was just magic beyond belief. On *Dragons' Den* no one would buy into that mixture!

J: What was the first Smiths song you heard?

C: 'Reel Around The Fountain'. I just remember thinking, 'Wow, that's the best love song since some of the Billy Bragg stuff.' It was clever and beautiful, the lyrics and everything about it. When you heard it then it was a game changer, that was the point. The relevance of that music was so pertinent at that dismal time. We were in the middle of Thatcher's Britain and you had the Mary Chain with that fantastic row, then you had The Smiths with controversial, retro, romantic songs at a time that was miserable. Everyone said they were miserable, but The Smiths made me laugh out loud! People just heard Morrissey's voice and read the titles and just thought that was bleak. They had a fantastic sense of humour. I mean, 'Girlfriend in a Coma', it's just genius, absolute genius! It's like one of those jokes where you only hear the start of the joke and don't hear the punchline. It was weird, because I didn't understand at the time that The Smiths were a classic case of English heroes— and people love to build them up and then smash them down. Doesn't matter if it's David Beckham, Paul Gascoigne—the media love to love them and then they love to tear them apart. We don't like success. When The Smiths became successful and their following was broadening and the chart success was getting okay, that's it, they turned on them. Who knows what would have happened had they continued?

J: Didn't you suffer this when you talked about the cost of the giant panda?

C: Well, yeah, it's all the time, really. Now it's badgers. It doesn't bother me; I don't care what people think about me. In those instances, I have a duty around quality conservation. If you stick your head out, sometimes you get your head cut off, but, as I always say to people, I'm not here to make friends, I want to make a difference.

J: Can you tell me about your tattoos? I know you have them, but I can't see any.

C: I've got five or six. They're all designs.

J: Are they all hidden? Can I see one?

C: You could if you looked. No one has ever seen it.

J: Is it a freckle or something?

C. No, it's not, it's cryptic.

J: Will I see it from this angle?

C: You could do.

J: Is it behind your ear?

C: No, it's not there. I did it to see if anyone would ever notice it. To this date, no one has ever noticed it, only people who know what it is.

J: This is unfair! Where do I have to look to see it?

C: I'm not telling you! It will spoil the game. It's very subtle. The others are pictorial, they all mean something. I'm not a casual collector of tattoos. It has to mean something.

J: Where are they all?

C: Well, the trouble with tattoos is, if they are in areas where the sun shines, they will fade badly. And I never take my shirt off, because there's nothing to show off beneath it. I have one on my back, one on my shoulder and one on my chest.

J: Did they hurt?

C: No, it sort of tickles. But there are places where it would hurt.

J: If Morrissey was to walk in here right now and say, 'All right, Chris?' what would you say?

C: I'd engage him in conversations about his songs, because I've read the various explanations of why they were written, but that's never really satisfied me. I want to know what the songs mean to *him*. We transpose the lyrics to our own meaning, so they all mean slightly different things to all of us. However, this is quite an intensely personal thing, so I can imagine that if you were a songwriter, there might be personal reasons why a song was written and you may not want to tell someone. I mean, there are certain things I have written that I don't want to engage in conversation now. I don't want to talk about it. Make what you like of it, but don't ask me, because it's from the heart. I've given enough away just writing it down. So Morrissey may not want to talk about these things; that would be my only concession, to his privacy, really, that's what makes people like that. I don't believe that you could write those songs without personal cost. And he's continually probed about it.

J: So would you ask him?

C: I'd like to. It would be an opportunity. I just spoke about something on *Desert Island Discs* and I was very near to tears, it caused me a lot of pain from many years ago. That was a personal loss. I think that's what makes those songs successful; someone has given something of themselves, given it away, and that's hard to do. I can imagine having given it away, and people tearing it to pieces, analysing it, ridiculing it, loved it, hated it, something else, just being badgered about it would probably be a bit hard

to swallow, wouldn't it? So he would probably say, "Get lost, Chris, make of it what you want to.' And ultimately, that's what we're all going to do anyway. It doesn't really matter that Morrissey didn't have a girlfriend who was in a coma, does it? It's a sentiment that we transpose into our own lives.

J: If Morrissey was coming to your house, what snacks would you put out for him?

C: I have very strict ideas about certain things, and certain behaviours imposed upon other people. I don't eat meat, but if I go to someone's house and they cook meat, I don't make a fuss about it, I just eat the vegetables on the side. And I don't start telling them about why they shouldn't eat meat either.

J: What are your reasons for not eating meat?

C: Well, it's murder, innit? As an organism, we eat too much meat. The meat isn't produced in a way that is conducive to modern standards, in terms of animal husbandry. I don't like the way that the animals are treated at all, and I know there is meat that you can source, but I don't have time to shop for that and I never really liked the taste of it anyway, too fatty, and I don't like fat.

J: How old were you when you gave it up?

C: Oh, early twenties. I gave up when I could.

J: Do you have a favourite Smiths song?

C: I do, it's very difficult ... Again, I had to do *Desert Island Discs*, and it's very difficult to break it down, and then you think, 'Oh no what about that one?' I just think the entire catalogue ... I can't think of a Smiths song that I don't like—I don't hate any of them. I don't really like the cover versions. 'Reel Around The Fountain' started as my favourite song, and then I remember that 'Panic' was my favourite song, it was very poppy, and 'Ask' as well. 'Last Night I Dreamt That Somebody Loved Me'—you can't argue with that, can you? So I suppose over time the two favourites have been 'Reel' and 'There Is A Light'. Anyone who writes 'If a ten ton truck kills the both of us/ To die by your side/ Well the pleasure, the privilege is mine' is genius. It encapsulates everything that he did, everything down to earth, but still retained the poignancy of all the emotional context, so you've got romances and people living in council estates and working in supermarkets, and they don't have any less romantic lives than Hollywood A-listers. Where did Morrissey buy his shirts?

J: Evans.

C: Evans. The complete antithesis of fashion. National Heath specs. It was perfect. It proved it all! It was the opposite of everything I hated in music and still hate—overblown pomposity. I don't like bands that think they're important and play stadiums.

J: What about Morrissey in his solo career?

C. 'Everyday Is Like Sunday' is great. The seaside town they forgot to close down. The atomic war. I actually nicked that. I had to do a review of Blackpool once for a TV programme, and I stood up and said, 'The only thing it's fit for is nuclear war.' It didn't go down well. I won't be going back. I had a horrid time there. But I nicked that from Morrissey. He reminds me of Hemingway and Fitzgerald, the way he makes broad observations and can condense it into one line. The seaside town—it's Hastings, it's Worthing. Those songs were more Smith-y.

J: Did you ever see The Smiths live?

C: Yes, I saw them play twice in Kilburn. My sister had a place in Kilburn at the time. We saw loads of bands there. We could just walk down and see them. And then I saw them at the GLC gig that was a disaster, where there was loads of skinheads. But that wasn't anything to do with The Smiths.

J: Do you prefer to interview or to be interviewed?

C: I like interviewing, because there are lots of questions that I would have to ask. The trouble with the music press is just rumour-mongers. That must be so hard for the bands. I remember all this when The Smiths were splitting up. It must be infuriating for them to read this stuff.

J: Absolutely. Can I ask you a few favourite things before I let you go?

C: Absolutely!

J: What's your favourite crisp flavour?

C: I don't eat crisps. I haven't eaten crisps for five years. What I mean is, not one. If I say no ... I don't drink tea or coffee. I've given it up. I won't do it.

J: Pizza topping?

C: I don't eat pizza, cos I gave up bread.

J: What do you eat?

C: Fish, rice, pasta. I still eat pasta, maybe nudging giving that up. I gave up bread eighteen months ago. My girlfriend and stepdaughter ridicule me constantly, they hate my food

neurosis. It makes life difficult to them. It makes a huge difference. As an experiment, I gave it up then I re-ate it for two weeks. It was horrible. I used to eat seafood pizzas.

J: But you like biscuits, I see.

C: I do eat biscuits, but I've given up chocolate.

J: I like the way you give things up in a real scientific way.

C: Well, with the elimination of the bread, I felt better.

J: In what way?

C: I slept better. I felt my stomach to be uncomfortable.

J: Favourite drink?

C: I haven't drank since January the fourth.

J: For health?

C: I don't know if any of this is health. I'm not particularly interested in living a long time, or anything. It's more, this year; I would have done six TV series by the end of November. This means I have had very little time off, and I'm away from home. This doesn't always give me the opportunity to eat properly. I'm fifty-two and I need to get through it on top of my game. If I'm ill, no one cares. If someone flies you to the other side of the world and you've got two days to film underwater with sharks, if you've got something wrong with you, they're not interested. You've got to get under the water and get in there. I can do this; I was never off school as a kid. If one of my legs had been falling off, my dad would have gaffa-taped it back on and sent me. Not even written a note for the PE master! I continue to work when I'm ill. It's never good, and you're not maximising your potential. I want to do all six series as best I can. So I decided to cut out the things that make me feel ill, like bread, and alcohol.

J: You look younger than your fifty-two years. What's your face cream?

C: I moisturise after shaving. Clinique After Shave Balm. I wet shave, and I always use that. I haven't washed my face with soap since I was about fourteen, not once.

J: So you have a dirty face?

C: Well, it gets greasy, but I only wash it with water, no soap. And I use sunscreen. But I don't like putting that on my face, because it's alcohol-based. For a favourite drink, well, with alcohol the first glass of wine doesn't touch the sides. I'm only enjoying the wine at the end of the bottle.

J: What are you like when you're drunk?

C. Relaxed. I become ... easier. My girlfriend moans that I don't drink, because it's anti-social. She gets annoyed because we don't stop for tea. I don't stop for tea, and that's good, cos it gets in the way! Most people would think it was boring. All the people I work with drink. Only on two occasions this year have I struggled and I've literally gone out, gone to a bar, and they've all been drinking and I've just sort of thought, 'No, and gone back to the hotel. I don't need to be pissed to enjoy myself. On those occasions I felt uncomfortable anyway. The next question is, do I ever drink again? People ask me. The answer is I was just going to stop for a few months ...

J: What was your drink of choice?

C: White wine.

J: Who cuts your hair?

C: Lisa. It was the same person cutting my hair for years, from about fifteen to about thirty-something. She moved. I had to find someone else.

J: If you don't wash your face, do you still wash your hair?

C: Yeah, when it needs it. I use Neutrogena, the blue one, for shampoo, since 1980-something.

J: When you look back at the younger you, do you feel you've done him proud?

'It's a passport photo. It's the only one I've got of the badger haircut.'

C: No. Since then, the population of rhinos has probably declined by about eighty-five to ninety percent. I could reel off loads of things where I've failed.

J: You can't blame yourself for that.

C: I know, but I and other conservationists have presided over a catastrophic decline of flora and fauna. We stand on the brink of losing the mega fauna: tigers, rhinos, elephants (ish), lions in serious trouble. In my lifetime we could lose all of those as wild animals. Not in captivity, but as wild animals. To have been someone who has constantly campaigned to protect them, then that has to be a catastrophic failure. We have made positive differences. We could readdress all of these things. We know why rhino are becoming extinct. I know why skylarks and partridges have declined so rapidly. And if I know why, that means I know how to stop it. What my generation has failed to do is convince people to stop it.

J: I read on your website that you can't pick a favourite bird.

C: It's a bit like trying to choose your favourite Smiths song, except there's ten thousand birds and it's slightly more difficult! It's just impossible. But it would be a raptor and my Smiths song would always be a love song.

J: What type of bird do you enjoy seeing in your garden?

C: Sparrowhawks!

J: What's your favourite childhood toy?

C: Airfix.

J: What's the funniest thing your mum said?

C: Oh, volumes! She would come out with them all. I do love a mantra. She died a couple of years ago, but one of the ones I stick by is, 'If a job's worth doing, it's worth doing well.' I don't do anything unless it's the best I possibly can, otherwise I just don't bother. I've just been varnishing the floor at home, and I read on the instructions that you're meant to sand the floor before you put the third coat down. And I looked at the floor, sort of stretching away from me, and I thought … 'Bollocks.' I really didn't want to sand it. I just didn't feel like it. I did it before I started, and I didn't want to do it again.

J: I bet you did it.

C: Yeah, I did it.

J: And does the floor look lovely now?

C: Yeah, it does. Well, it's okay at the minute, but by tomorrow afternoon, when those poodles have been sliding across, it will have been a complete waste of time.

J: Would you write a note to my mum?

C: Of course. That's nice. My mum used to keep bits and pieces of mine.

J: What's that?

C: It's a wasp.

J: Can I photograph you now?

C: Wait till I've finished my biscuit.

J: Okay. Thank you, Chris.

C: My pleasure.

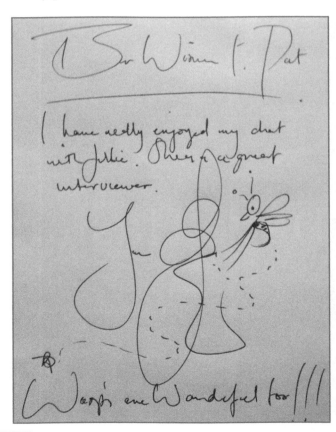

Dave Haslam

Writer, DJ and Morrissey interviewer

15 MINUTES
WITH YOU

DAVE Haslam has all the patter. After he meets me off the London train at Manchester Piccadilly, we find that the ticket machines don't work for the tram to Didsbury, so he eggs me on to jump inside and bunk the fare. Excitedly, I oblige, with one giddy eye out for the inspector. He keeps a straight face as he calls out to the packed train the wrong stops, then laughs when they shout back. As soon as the tram stops, his long legs yomp off, Bolt pace - to get to the café where we're doing the interview. 'I worry about your little legs,' he says, grinning, looking down at me as I jog along behind him.

When we get to The Art of Tea, Haslam orders scrambled eggs on a bagel. By question two, I notice how his thirty years' experience of these types of question/answer sessions have become second nature to him, as he is completely relaxed, like there's nothing he hasn't been asked before. He talks in a deep, dry drawl about experiences and interviews of the past, giving me a passenger seat account of his fond meetings with Morrissey. [From Melody Maker 1985: DH: 'This is going to be very pretentious.'/M: 'You always are, Dave.']

Looking back to a time before he was a superstar DJ, Hacienda legend, established journalist, author of several books and on-stage interviewer of the highly successful *Close Up* series, Dave Haslam began his career in 1983 as creator/editor of a fanzine: *Debris*. Fresh out of Uni, he interviewed a twenty-four-year-old Morrissey from The Smiths, and titled the piece 'Up The Garden Path with Morrissey'. The story of what happened during that interview and how it came about is very entertaining. Yes, Dave Haslam did cook cauliflower cheese for Morrissey (but he didn't eat it).

The Moz meeting was secured by Haslam in his own casual way: by knocking Joe Moss' door at Crazy Face and asking Liz Taylor (the office manager) if he could interview Morrissey. A simple and straightforward arrangement was made for Morrissey to go to Haslam's flat. They had a bit of a laugh then went to the pub. After establishing a fond respect for each other, they said goodbye. The following New Year's Eve, Morrissey then sent him a postcard from New York that refers to his fall off the stage at the Danceteria. Haslam/Morrissey continued to meet for the next few years to do interviews for various music press, until the 'fanzine panel' interview for *Melody Maker*, where Dave left in protest over a suggested photograph.

Dave Haslam's favourite drink is a Kir Royale, the pizza has to be margherita with mushroom (occasionally) and he only watches the news on TV. As a DJ, he reserves the right to play an eclectic mix of whatever he likes, and as a journalist, he once asked Morrissey his favourite colour, to which Morrissey replied:

'I think "What's your favourite colour?" is a great question.'

J: Please say your full name.

D: I'm Dave Haslam. And we're in Manchester.

J: Any middle names?

D: John. I'm D. J. Haslam. There we go, destiny calling!

J: Does everybody know that then? I didn't know that 'initial' link.

D: It's an exclusive.

J: Do you prefer to be known as 'DJ' or 'Disc Jockey'?

D: Well, since Jimmy Savile, who was usually described as a 'disc jockey', I think I'd rather be known as a 'DJ'. Fifteen years ago, when that whole superstar DJ thing happened, it was embarrassing and a bit over the top, but back then everyone wanted to be a DJ, nobody wants to be a DJ now. I like being writer/DJ.

J: Where does the 'John' come from?

D: My dad! It just slipped right in before I knew what was happening. Never saw that coming.

J: Can you describe yourself in a sentence?

D: The cat that walked by itself.

J: What do you mean by that?

D: I mean I'm quite aloof and antisocial.

J: And yet, you're married and have a family.

D: Yes, and they know this about me.

J: Do they put you out at night?

D: Ha! They don't mind that I'm kind of antisocial, it's just accepted. J.D. Salinger—he never went out the house, did he?

J: You mentioned the superstar DJ period when DJs were elevated to celebrity status. How did this happen for you?

D: I was at The Hacienda from 1986 and then I left in October 1990. In the summer of 1990 I did a Hacienda DJ tour of America with me, Mike Pickering, Paul Oakenfold and Graeme Park. In a way, that was one of the first turning points. I went to Detroit and Chicago. The idea of an English DJ going to America, to Detroit, one of the great music capitals of the world, was kind of quite presumptuous then. It was about

1992/1993 it all really took off, by which time I was DJing two nights a week at a club called The Boardwalk. I was never a superstar DJ, but I had a good thing going. I was always going for that 'I don't want to get involved' showbiz thing. I just wanted to play music and believe in what I was playing. My philosophy has always been to take my hundred favourite pieces of music out in a box for that week and play them. If you are looking to make a fortune out of DJing, there's a whole load of stuff you have to take into account: what the audience expect, what you, the DJ, represent as a brand, and I opted out of all that. I like the idea if you come to hear me DJ, you don't necessarily know what you're going to hear. I reserve the right every six months to play a totally different selection.

J: Is that what differentiates you, that you're unpredictable and eclectic with song choice?

D: I start from a perspective of 'What do I not like?', and there's lots of stuff I don't like, so I won't play it. The only challenge is to keep the audience with me. I aim to refresh the audience and I have been lucky in that respect. I DJ'd the other month at a club called Gorilla; it was the club's first birthday and the average age was twenty. I'm sure they were looking up at me, going 'Who is this old man and what does he know?' and I actually really like that challenge.

I want it to be me and my records, and 'How do I make this room magical?'

J: How does it feel when you're up in the DJ box, looking down at the crowd?

D: It's nice to get the validation for what you're doing. I don't find that I have to hold it together; I always think of the T.S. Eliot line: 'At the still point of the turning world.' Sometimes people have noticed I stay quite still and composed. I expect chaos. There's always stuff happening, you have to just stay completely in your own world, even though you're reaching out to another world. Although you're in your own world, you can't look like you are. For me, there's very rarely a moment that I'm freewheeling. I'll be thinking, madly, at two hundred miles an hour about what I should play. If I see someone in the room that's not engaged, I'll think, 'What can I play that will make them dance?'

J: What is your absolute banker record that gets everyone up?

D: It changes.

J: 'Blue Monday'?

D: I have a weird mix of 'Blue Monday' that not many people have. It has a twist! After ten or fifteen minutes on the decks, I'm thinking ahead. It's like crossing a stormy river and the records are the stepping stones.

J: I'm assuming that you play the New York Remix of 'This Charming Man' by François Kevorkian?

D: I do, yes, and funnily enough I was reading an interview that I did in 1983 with Morrissey quite recently where he really doesn't like that François Kevorkian mix! It was the first time that I had heard him say that in public.

J: Growing up, how did your music tastes evolve?

D: I grew up in Birmingham. When I was really little I loved *Top of The Pops*. I used to dance a lot, which for boys—well, a lot of boys don't, really. I can remember being aged around eleven or twelve, going to school discos and dancing. I got a nickname Disco Zombie. I guess I had some kind of mechanical/robotic dance style. I kind of had that disco thing. I remember going to see Generation X play when I was sixteen. I didn't really like Generation X, even though I probably should have, so I wandered off into the disco room and the DJ put on 'Can You Feel The Force' by The Real Thing. It felt like an enlightening moment.

That was the moment I realised I didn't have to choose between an *NME* audience's music and just jumping around on the dance floor. Generally, I was an *NME* reader and used to go to gigs. I saw Blondie when I was sixteen. I saw Magazine, Buzzcocks, bands like that. I don't know whether it's embarrassing or not, but I used to hang around bands, intrigued and fascinated. I loved a band called Fashion; I remember just being intrigued by them. The Au Pairs were the first band I used to sneak in to see at the soundcheck. I went to London to see The Au Pairs. I was passionate about music. Then I moved to Manchester. When it came to choosing a university, I just wanted to go somewhere with a great music scene.

J: What was the first record that you bought?

D: T-Rex, 'Telegram Sam', from the newsagent that had a rack of singles with all the holes cut out. A lot of my first records were bought from there. I remember being interested by David Bowie but just being slightly too young to get into his music.

J: What's your Bowie song of choice to play?

D: 'Rebel Rebel' but I also like 'Golden Years'. If I was DJing in front of an ideal audience, it would be 'Golden Years'.

J: You have written several books. How did you get started in writing?

D: I had my own fanzine. Do your readers need me to explain what a fanzine is?

J: No, we know what a fanzine is.

D: Mine was called *Debris*. It was 1983, and after I graduated from university I went on the dole, and the fanzine idea came about. The first issue of my fanzine was a collection of stuff that I liked: music, books, politics and arty films. It built up a good reputation, because it was unlike any other fanzine. Everything but the Girl was in the first issue, and then the second issue was the Morrissey interview.

J: Tell me how this interview happened.

D: I kind of didn't have any qualms about knocking on doors. Somehow I just knocked on them. I've always thought, 'You can just walk away.' 'Hand In Glove' came out, and after the fanzine started, I kind of began to know people that knew The Smiths. I decided in my wisdom that I wanted to interview Morrissey in November 1983. The band weren't that big. I found out that the building where they practiced was at Crazy Face, the clothing label run by Joe Moss. I knocked on the door and asked if I could interview Morrissey—a bit like you would do, Julie. I went in and was greeted by Liz Taylor, who ran the office and I said, 'I'd like to interview Morrissey' and she said, 'Yeah, okay, Joe's on the phone, I'll ask him. Leave a copy of your fanzine.' So I scrawled a note. I went back two days later. Liz gave me a T-shirt, and Joe said, 'Yeah, Morrissey will do it, where do you want to do the interview?'

J: What T-shirt did she give you?

D: A huge T-shirt with a red daffodil.

J: So where did you do the interview?

D: I kind of panicked, really, because I didn't know where to go and I didn't know anything about him, and there was no Internet. I knew he was a vegetarian, I knew he was celibate and I knew that he lived in Manchester, but that's all I knew. In my head I thought, 'Well, we need to go somewhere quiet.' I thought, 'I don't really go to the pub that much.' I knew the pub wouldn't be good, that was out of whack for him and me. So I said, 'Would Morrissey mind coming round to my flat?' and Joe said, 'Yeah, that will be fine,' and Liz said, 'I'll pick him up in the car and come over.' I said to Liz, 'Would Morrissey like me to cook for him?' and she said, 'Yeah, I think he'd like that.' So I made a massive bowl of cauliflower cheese, the only thing in my vegetarian repertoire at that time. Anyway, he arrived, and it turned out that his mum had already cooked him something, so he wasn't hungry. But he encouraged me to eat, so Liz and me had a bowl. It turned out that Morrissey knew the boy that lived in the flat below me.

J: It looks like you and Morrissey got along well during that interview.

D: It was really funny. Morrissey and I really did get on. I'd never met anyone like him before. He'd say something and we'd both laugh. All I can remember is that the evening was very funny. I called the interview 'Up The Garden Path with Morrissey'. I realised that Morrissey was already Morrissey. Even though it was relatively early on, he was fully formed, ready. I knew I was talking to Morrissey, not Steven, and he was ready and fully formed as a rock star, that he'd practised singing into the mirror, performing, and thought about it a lot. He gave me a great interview.

J: How old were you?

D: I was about twenty-one and Morrissey was twenty-four. We finished the interview and I said, 'Shall we go to the pub?' and he said, 'Yeah, lets!' So, contrary to my preconception, he was up for it. So we went to a pub quite near where I live called The Grants. We ordered two pints of lager and sat there, both cringing at whatever people put on the jukebox.

J: What happened after that?

D: He disappeared out of my life for a bit and the fanzine came out in the January. It was New Year's Eve 1983; they played the Danceteria in New York and Morrissey sent me a postcard. Then they went on tour Feb/March 1984 and I just started going to their gigs.

Shortly after this I got to know the little crew at The Hacienda. Since then, I've had a few little meet ups with Morrissey. I interviewed Johnny for the *NME*, too, and our paths crossed a few times. I interviewed Morrissey again in 1985 with others. He asked for a fanzine panel of his favourite fanzine writers to pose the questions.

I asked him a really good question that he was impressed by. It was basically drawing a link in *Meat Is Murder* between the cruelty of school and the cruelty of the meat industry. He said something like, 'You would ask me that, Dave.' Anyway, we fell out over a daft disagreement.

J: What happened?

D: Well, we haven't talked since, but only because he moved to London and I haven't got his email. I think we would have probably made up by now had we bumped into each other. Anyway, so at the end of the *Melody Maker* interview, they wanted to do a photo of the fanzine writers at Morrissey's feet holding up microphones to him as he sat on a throne. I said, 'Well, 'that's not really how I want to be represented, so I'm just going to leave,' and Morrissey said, 'Come on Dave, don't be like that, you should be in the photo,' and I said something like, 'It doesn't feel natural to me,' and I left. I think he wanted me to stay, but I was concerned about how I was being represented in the media, and this led me to flounce out of the moment, which is actually what Morrissey would have done!

J: Do you regret that *Melody Maker* incident?

D: I do cringe. There's a lot of stuff I cringe at from the Eighties. But I do look back and think that the weird thing around that period of 1985/86, it was a fantastic time. The Smiths had invented an alternative. The lines of demarcation had changed, that endless s**t office party atmosphere and *Top of The Pops* and mainstream politics of miners' strike, Thatcher

... then there was Rough Trade ... another way of thinking, an alternative movement, and I really valued that. I felt that it was important and a new thing that was available to people.

From 1978 right through to 1985-86, those were my formative years, for which I am forever grateful to people like Joe Moss and places like The Hacienda.

J: You knocked on Joe Moss's door, which opened a lot of other doors for you.

D: Yes.

J: If Morrissey walked in here now and said, 'All right, Dave?' what would you say?

D: These are the kind of questions you ask?

J: Yes.

D: I'd say, 'Morrissey, meet Julie.'

J: Thanks! Would you also say, 'I'm sorry I stormed off?'

D: Yeah. I'd give him a massive cuddle and say that.

J: You met him in The Hacienda another time, didn't you?

D: Yeah. I've had loads of encounters with him. Morrissey used to occasionally come in to The Hacienda. One of the jobs that I inherited from Andrew Berry was to DJ before the bands came on. The DJ box was high, overlooking the dance floor, and it was a fantastic position to see bands. I remember when Soft Cell played, Morrissey came in, and up to the DJ box, and we just stood there and watched Soft Cell and clapped at the end of every song. Another time was a normal Saturday night and I was DJing, and there was this fantastic electro record by Man Parrish called 'Hip Hop, Be Bop', and as it was playing, I started haranguing Morrissey about how he should get into stuff like this, telling him how to do his job, basically. 'Listen to this bit, listen to this next bit,' I kept saying. Of course, it was the total antithesis of what he stood for. He was looking at me, like, 'What are you going on about?'

J: Can I ask you some of your favourite things?

D: Yes.

J: What's your favourite drink?

D: Kir Royale.

J: You have quite a posh side, don't you? Do you enjoy the finer things in life?

D: Yeah. I like Prosecco too. There should be a socialist paradise where everyone has Prosecco and Kir Royale.

J: Favourite book?

D: Tao Lin, *Shoplifting from American Apparel*.

J: Favourite crisp flavour?

D: I don't eat anything like that. Occasionally I come back from the club and I'll have a Doritos sandwich. On white bread. I've never bought a packet of crisps in my life.

J: Doritos are crisps.

D: Yeah, but I never bought them. The family buys them. Cool Original.

J: Favourite Smiths song?

D: So many. That's a really bad question to ask people who like The Smiths. There's a song for every moment.

J: Pick a song for this moment.

D: For this moment? 'I Know It's Over'.

J: Why is that for this moment? Is our interview terminated?

D: Ha ha! 'I Know It's Over' and 'Asleep' are magnificent records. But the longer you live with Smiths records, the more they jostle for position on your list. I love playing 'How Soon Is Now' at the right time, in the right club. Or even at the wrong time. I've had some brilliant times playing that. I love *Hatful of Hollow*, but I'm aware it's not considered an album. Smiths songs in isolation are mini soundtracks, mini short stories. I love 'Pretty Girls Make Graves' which isn't one that people talk about. Around the time they played The Hacienda, just after the album, that was the song I was waiting to hear.

J: Favourite Morrissey song?

D: 'Suedehead'. Funnily enough, that song seems older than some Smiths songs.

J: Favourite pizza topping?

D: Anyone who has anything other than margherita with mushrooms or maybe olives—anyone who goes down a sweet corn route, basically—shouldn't be allowed *near* a pizza. It should be thin crust margarita with mushrooms, occasionally.

J: Favourite biscuit?

D: No biscuit. I quite like biscuits for cheese, but not biscuit-biscuits. The ones that I get, you can have them without cheese and they're still a treat.

J: Favourite TV programme?

D: If all I had was news, I'd be okay. I watch the news all the time. The only thing I have a TV for is news. I love the news.

J: Favourite place to eat?

D: I quite like The Lime Tree.

J: Favourite childhood toy?

D: All a boy needs is a football.

J: Please would you write a note to my mum?

D: Oh God, yeah!

Hi Pat,

① I think we'd get on

② Julie asks stuff like "Favourite childhood toy?" Rubbish questions.

③ Come listen to me DJ, i'd play 'Ain't Nobody' and we'd singalong.

Best wishes

Dave Haslam

Manchester, England.

Vini Reilly

Guitarist with Morrissey and The Durutti Column

15 MINUTES WITH YOU

THE late afternoon sun streams into Vini Reilly's living room, creating a warm and mellow low light just before it gets dark. I take a seat on the couch and imagine him here playing the guitar, creating gentle sounds that float into the air like little clouds. He is a spectacularly good guitarist (although he will deny this fervently) and has created much beautiful music with The Durutti Column, as well as contributed his own brand of guitar poetry on the incomparable *Viva Hate* with Morrissey.

It seems heart-rending and cruel, then, that three strokes have caused some paralysis to his hands, rendering him unable to tie a shoelace: *'My guitar ... I sound like a nine-year-old boy in his first guitar lesson'*, he says, despondently.

The Durutti Column was the first signing to Factory records in 1978 and released no less than thirty-seven albums, becoming known for a precise, gentle and melancholic guitar sound. This sound came to the attention of Stephen Street who, in 1988, enlisted Reilly to play on Morrissey's debut solo album. Vini recalls this time with great fondness, and cites Morrissey and Andrew Paresi as dear friends. He regrets his inaccurate and untrue comments he made towards Stephen Street, and is keen to set the record straight that comments he made were due to ill health: *'I was suffering from displaced anger. This is where you're very angry with yourself and you don't understand, you just shout at people you really care about.'*

What is surprising and slightly shocking is the violent teenage struggle he endured, a dangerous life that included guns, intense outbursts of anger and multiple attempts at suicide. It is difficult to comprehend this past life, as he is now a very gentle and giving person, with great respect for humanity and an unselfish philosophy: *'We need good things and love. It's like an energy, it stays around. Try using pure good, pure love.'*

Despite his extensive battle with depression, displaced anger and recurring illness, it is abundantly clear that Vini has retained his sense of humour, strong opinions and musical integrity. As he talks candidly about his contribution to *Viva Hate,* I feel privileged to share his gracious company this little while. *'There are so many tracks on there, classic tracks to me, very different to The Smiths, not a copy or an imitation. Nobody could copy Johnny's style, and I don't think Morrissey or Stephen wanted Johnny's style. It wasn't The Smiths, it was Morrissey.'*

Viva Vini.

J: Please say your full name.

V: I was named after my uncle Vin, one of my mother's brothers, and he was called Vincent. He was awarded the Victoria Cross. He died three years ago; we were very close; he was my favourite uncle. But my full name is Vincent Gerrard Reilly. Peter is my confirmation name; I was born and raised a catholic. I like the idea of Catholicism, of faith, but I'm not a practising Catholic. Although what the hell the pope or the Vatican has done for anybody at any time is a total mystery.

J: Could you describe yourself in a sentence?

V: I'm not a virtuoso.

J: Many would disagree with that.

V: But even when I was at my peak, I wasn't the best. Anyone who says I was—well, that was just total nonsense, written by journalists with their own agenda who knew nothing about music. I could find you two thousand players in Cordoba in Spain in bars who have never made a record who would make me look stupid. I'm not a guitar player at all now, not after three strokes.

J: How have the strokes affected you?

V: I've had three strokes. The third one is the one that did the damage. I can't even tie shoelaces now. My guitar ... I sound like a nine-year-old boy in his first guitar lesson.

J: I'm sure you don't.

V: I'm sure I do. It's a joke, man. I can play in places ... but then I fall off ...

J: You have made some very beautiful, delicate music.

V: I don't know. The thing is that I just don't know if it's good or bad or different; and I just don't care.

J: Well, your fans love it. 'Otis' is a wonderful track.

V: I nearly binned that! It was Bruce that said don't bin it! It was an experiment. I wanted to have the same base note—b flat—the whole way through a tune. If the bass note stays the same, you can do all kinds of things with harmonic progression. By shouting out in the dark; by default it will be original. I heard it in my head first of all, and thought, 'That's mad!' It had to be Otis Redding's voice; I don't know why, it just

did. It wasn't meant to be released. No kidding anybody, if I'd had the ability, I could have been better. For a long time I didn't care about myself, whether I lived or died, or what happened. I was taught martial arts by three friends from the Israeli special forces. They taught me stuff that's only used in the army. I had a weapon. I was dangerous.

J: Do you still have your weapon?

V: No.

J: Was it a gun?

V: Yes. A small gun. An 8 mm. Big enough to kill someone. I didn't care. I got held at gunpoint once, and I just said to the guy, 'Do it, man. Do me a favour.'

J: When was this?

V: Long before I worked with Morrissey.

J: Aside from your guitar playing, how would you describe yourself as a person?

V: Very, very hung up. Not hung up now, but I've led a very troubled life. I have suffered from depression since I was fifteen. I've had three attempts at suicide. My friends got weapons for me. I wanted it to end. Another friend saved me, because his girlfriend had leukemia. He asked me if I could write something for her, a tune to cheer her up. So I did two tracks, and that became my first album.

J: What are you most proud of with The Durutti Column?

V: The drummer. It was important to me that I had the correct drummer for The Durutti Column. I discovered Bruce Mitchell. If I play just me on a guitar, it's just very flat. My music in my head has certain elements to it that just arrive. It's got to be right. I asked Bruce, and he agreed. Our rehearsal was great, and within ten seconds I was playing along. For every twist and turn I made, he was already there. He had the right tones and gave it momentum. I have become part of Bruce's family. His wife Jackie is a wonderful cook and I go there for lunch every Sunday. His daughter, Zinni, wants me to be there. She's a ray of sunshine. If I did nothing else in life, I'm proud of her. The music chose me, I didn't choose the music, but Bruce and Jackie told me I was off the rails. Bruce said, 'Okay you're such a hard man, look after Zinni.' This adorable little two-year-old child. Sometimes we'd sit on the floor with crossed legs, and talk; we never sat on chairs. She used to sit with us. She's a flower. We babysat her for hours and hours and hours when we were writing, and she used to tag along.

It was fantastic and demanding and exhausting. I can understand that a mother's love for a child is the purest, most beautiful love in the whole world. The entire experience validated my life a little bit. She's now thirty-four with two adorable sons and a fantastic husband, a very fine man, a very dear friend of mine, Jamie. They saved my life.

J: Your guitar playing is beautiful on *Viva Hate*.

V: I want to talk about Stephen Street, about whom I've said wrong things in the past; this is not an excuse, this is fact; I have suffered from what they call 'displaced anger', and this is where you're very angry with yourself and you don't understand, you just shout at people you really care about. Stephen Street—I've got to tell you, you will never find a nicer man. He is one of the nicest people I've ever met in my life. Endless patience, his skills are astonishing, his ability to hear ... all those skills, a fabulous result. I loved the guy.

J: Did you have a good time recording that album?

V: Yes! They used to play great jokes on me. Morrissey had a special chef. He brought in this lady who cooked wonderful creative food. The food was to die for. I couldn't eat very much, because I suffered from post-traumatic stress disorder because of all the violence I couldn't escape from in my past. I could never finish a meal, no way. As soon as my back was turned, Morrissey and Stephen would scrape their plate leftovers onto my plate. This poor lady used to come in just as I realised what they had done, and we'd fall about giggling and laughing. Andrew would laugh; his laugh is such a delightful thing. That whole time was magical for me. Stephen is the best producer I've ever worked with. I always wanted to work with Morrissey anyway. I didn't want to step on Johnny's [Marr] toes, cos Johnny was such a nice guy. He's another brilliant bloke, great guitarist.

J: Were you a fan of The Smiths?

V: I was! I was a huge fan. It would have been world domination if they had continued. It was pure magical.

J: Did you feel the pressure, being the first guitarist after The Smiths broke up?

V: I did feel the pressure. I was astonished when Stephen suggested that the guitarist should be me for Morrissey's first album. Stephen gave him a solid foundation to write songs from, his demos. He asked me to come down and meet Morrissey. Stuart James told me that I didn't need to worry. I was a bit worried about whether I was going to like Morrissey. I thought, 'What if I don't like him?' I didn't know him! He didn't know me. We had the Irish connection, I just liked him. I thought, this is a good team, a fantastic project to be involved in. I was thrilled to bits. The whole thing was beautiful.

J: Did this continue in the recording studio?

V: It did. No compromises on either side. It was fantastic. Stephen Street produced it how he wanted to produce it. He had written it down, how he knew it should be, what he wanted it to sound like. He is very exact; we'd work until he got the performance he wanted. Same with Morrissey, if he didn't like it, he'd re-sing it. He wanted it done right. I see now that he was chasing for what he was looking for, and he got it. The sound was good, the words were fantastic and the production was second to none.

J: Do you remember the first track you worked on?

V: I don't remember. I know I was into a heavy track, I was right into it. It was pure fun.

J: What was it like when you first heard the completed 'Suedehead'?

V: It was a thrill! It was Stephen's style of guitar, and I just tried to copy it as best I could. Hopefully it is what he heard, he seemed pleased with it. It was a bit of a buzz. 'Everyday Is Like Sunday' was such a simple chord sequence but so perfect; just right for Morrissey to sing to, just right for me to play guitar to, and Andrew Paresi was a fabulous drummer. Incredible! Talk about Phil Collins-standard? Andrew was good, I'd say he was better than Phil Collins at his peak in terms of technique and feel. He's a fantastic musician. And the nicest man.

J: What were you doing when you heard the album went to number one?

V: I don't listen to the radio. It didn't surprise me in the least that it went to number one. There are so many tracks on there; classic tracks to me—very different to The Smiths, not a copy or an imitation. Nobody could copy Johnny's style, and I don't think Morrissey wanted Johnny's style. It wasn't The Smiths, it was Morrissey.

J: Do you have any favourite songs off the album?

V: 'Late Night, Maudlin Street'. I used to play it late at night. I still do. The way it all hangs together, it's beautiful. I have been in that kind of environment and Morrissey has too and we did it at night-time. It had a resonance, very moving. It was a drum machine, and we tried to recreate that poor unstable situation. He wrote the perfect lyrics for the music in that song.

J: I have read that you and Morrissey were great friends during that time.

V: Yeah. We used to hang out together. There was a little team of us, Pat Nevin the Glaswegian footballer. He was a centre forward for Scotland from the Gorbals. I've got a number seven shirt of his upstairs. We used to play kickabout, me and him and Morrissey, then hang out and chill together. Morrissey is of astonishing intellect and Pat Nevin is very clever, and then there was me. It was a nice little trio. Pat Nevin has a lovely wife—Annabel. He played small, fast and tough, so skillful, the Scottish George Best, without a doubt.

J: Do you keep in touch with Morrissey?

V: I don't know where Morrissey is now. He's always changing his location and I've never got his number. I don't keep it in my phone, anyway, just in case anyone goes through it.

J: What would you say if he knocked on the door now and said, 'All right, Vini?'

V: We'd give each other a big hug and there would be a lot of good Irish jokes going around! He used to take great delight in laughing at me. He has a sharp sense of humour. Stephen used to set it up for Morrissey to knock me down. We had a book where we'd leave comments about each other! Jokey stuff, you know.

J: Can you tell me about the day you did 'I Know Very Well How I Got My Note Wrong' with Morrissey?

V: It was eventually released with the first thousand copies of the *Vini Reilly* album. I just wanted people to know that Morrissey is human and not a prima donna. We were playing along, and all of a sudden I go and hit a wrong note. Morrissey's take was just to laugh his head off. The whole session was like that—fits of giggling.

J: Can I ask you a few of your favourite things?

V: Absolutely!

J: What's your favourite book?

V: My favourite book is by Graham Green, called *The Quiet American*. Wherever I go in the world, that's the book I'm taking with me. I also love an audio book, *Just William*. It makes me so happy, the beauty and the innocence. It is special to me. They are so cleverly put together. Genuine subversive literature.

J: What's your favourite crisp flavour?

V: It's a shame, but I can't eat things like crisps since the last stroke.

J: Who should play you in a movie of your life?

V: Someone who is not very nice, really, at all. My life story has been violent and I have hurt people physically. It should be someone who is angered. Someone who has been destroyed by physical abuse then goes on to wreak havoc with other gangsters, because that's the only place fit for him until he gets saved by very special people who keep him on the straight and narrow.

J: Are you in a relationship?

V: I don't have any girlfriend. I have nothing, at all, to offer any woman. There's no woman would want me. I'm not good enough for any woman now. It has been five years, and I haven't bothered.

J: What's your favourite song?

V: It has got to be 'All You Need Is Love'. They should rip down all those places of worship. They're evil and they cause trouble. Its just love that we need. We need good things and love. It's like an energy, it stays around. Try using pure good, pure love.

J: Favourite Smiths song?

V: It has got to be 'How Soon Is Now'. That's the one when I first heard it I couldn't believe what I was hearing. Johnny's style and Morrissey's voice and how they interwove. It was so perfect.

J: Favourite Morrissey song?

V: Well, there's so many! Not necessarily one that I've played on. He's done songs since that have been quite extraordinary. He has become more confident through the years. I listen to all of his albums. I listen to rap, too. It has the same poetry. I don't like gangster rap. I like Labirinth.

J: I saw you in a café earlier. Do you like to go out to eat, if you can?

V: Yes, but I've had a lot of trouble eating since I had the first stroke. It damaged my body and I'm only just starting to eat a tiny bit now. Physically, it has taken so much from me.

J: What's your favourite childhood toy?

V: A football. I played football all the time. My team is Man Utd. I love Fergie. Moyes is going to settle in. Fergie's not daft. Moyes is doing the right thing, taking chances.

J: Recently, fans of The Durutti Column came to your rescue, didn't they?

V: They did, via my nephew, unbeknownst to me. I don't have the Internet. He put something on Twitter? He told them that it was eighteen months since I was declared officially disabled and it took eighteen months for the benefits that I'm entitled to to be recognised, and they sent money. It was very beautiful and incredibly generous. Bruce Mitchell also helps me out, but he knows he'll get every penny back.

J: And you have royalties?

V: No, I haven't sold something for four years or more.

J: Who looks after you now, Vini?

V: Bruce. Bruce Mitchell always has. Wonderful man. Tony Wilson looked after me when I was at Factory. I used to shout at Tony and tell him I was a hard case, and he told me to shut up. He used to shout back, 'If you have learned to fight, then the first thing you do is you don't tell people about it!'

J: Please could you write a note to my mum?

V: Yes, of course I will. How is your mum?

J: She's fine, thank you. She keeps all her notes in a folder.

V: Tell your mother I'm wearing my mother's watch, given to her by my dad during the Second World War. It doesn't have the original strap on it. At the time it was given, it was very valuable.

J: I will tell her. Is there anything else you'd like to add?

V: I want my ashes scattered in the Isle of Skye. I love it there. I watched otters play and birds fly in the sky. My feet were cold in the autumn. It's ever so beautiful.

Note from Vini:

Since this interview was conducted, Stephen Street has had the good grace to contact me. After twenty-three years we have begun to try to find our way back to being good friends, thanks to Stephen's big heart. Vini.

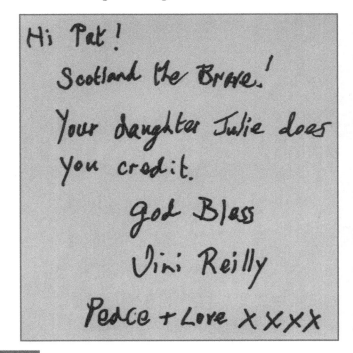

Hi Pat!
Scotland the Brave!
Your daughter Julie does you credit.
god Bless
Vini Reilly
Peace + Love x x x

Julie Hesmondhalgh

Actress and fan of Morrissey

15 **MINUTES WITH YOU**

**A**T the Corinthia hotel in London, the high lamps of the lobby bar shine down on Julie Hes' blonde crop and girlish frame, placing her in the spotlight as she swings her DMs to and fro in a big posh armchair. She orders drinks and insists to me that she's paying for them whilst she simultaneously chit-chats with the waiter: *'Don't take it yet, there's two quid fifty worth of wine left in that glass.'*

She is a gloriously gifted, award-winning British actress with a vibrant presence, and in person I doubt very much if she's changed since she was fourteen. She's 100% herself, a chat-fuelled Lancashire lass brimming with mirth and warmth, and her batteries never run dry. She nods toward the one green olive in the bowl. *'I've left you that -'* she points - *'and you're lucky to get it.'*

Julie has spent sixteen years playing Hayley, one half of *Coronation Street*'s inseparable salt-and-pepper-pot set Roy and Hayley Cropper. In soap's first ever transgender role, Hayley was portrayed as a fun loving, Lady Di-shy, more-mumsy-than-most character, who fell charmingly and awkwardly in love with Roy, an intensely routined, Dickensian and matter-of-fact traditionalist. Against all odds of prejudice, bullying, lies and complexity, the odd couple conquered all and blossomed, to go down in soap history as the exemplary pair that showed the rest of us how it's done.

Having recently left the soap (after dramatic and emotional suicide end scenes), Julie has hung up the wig and red anorak and put down the éclairs in Roy's Rolls to explore her love of theatre, only pausing to collect a National Television Award along the way. Julie's first post-Corrie role has seen her master something very dark and different, playing a mother of a troubled teen in the Simon Stephens play *Blindsided* Her intense acting amongst an incredible cast triumphed with a deserved sell-out run at Manchester's Royal Exchange.

As a lifelong fan of The Smiths, Julie was delighted to film dance scenes in the Salford Lads' Club for *Coronation Street,* and her picture hangs in the Smiths room. She met Morrissey on an escalator in Kendals one lunchtime, and lost composure after seeing her idol by dropping to her knees and shouting, 'ALL ME LIFE!' loudly in his direction. *'You have never seen a more uncool performance in your life.'*

She has her big brother to thank for her excellent taste in music, but part of her is still unable to resist a bit of cheese in the form of S Club 7's 'Reach'. Her favourite drink is tea, and she once won *All Star Mr and Mrs.* with her husband—writer Ian Kershaw—who clinched it with a 'There Is a Light' answer.

She says of Hayley, *'She's a lot better a person than I am.'* I agree. Hayley would have left me loads more olives.

JHam: Please say your full name.

JHes: My full name is Julie Hesmondhalgh. My middle name is Claire, with an 'I'. I was named after my paternal grandmother, and my brother is named after my dad's dad, who died when he was a teenager. There's a nice symmetry to it. But my mum wouldn't call me Claire, because she thought everybody would call me 'Clere'. Instead, everyone calls me 'Joolah!' Hesmondhalgh is an old Lancashire name. I always hoped it might be Scandinavian or German, but no, it's one of those old English names. There's loads of them in the phone book in Lancashire!

JHam: Did you move to London for a while?

JHes: I went to drama school in London in '88, to LAMDA. I set up a theatre company with a bunch of friends and worked there for years. I didn't really officially move back up north until I met my husband. We bought our house on the Derbyshire border, just outside of Manchester, near Glossop, in the countryside, and I sold my London flat in 2005. I have no regrets, because we have a nice little house up there. Also, I hadn't had my formative years in Manchester, so I didn't do The Hacienda or anything like that. I went to London when I was eighteen, so I missed it all, really. Now I really feel like it's a fantastic city. It's very accessible. I feel like I know everybody there and where I'm going and what I'm doing. London still excites me, too.

JHam: Can you describe yourself in a sentence?

JHes: Physically?

JHam: Any way you want to.

JHes: Christ, this is harder than I thought ... um ... Okay. I would say ... Let me let that fester in my mind. Okay, I've got it: desperately needs to be liked but hates that in herself. Pretty much can fit into any social situation and can stand astride lowbrow and highbrow with great aplomb. (I pride myself on that.) Wants to be cooler than I am. More than one sentence for you there.

JHam: Did you enjoy the experience of drama school?

JHes: I loved it. It was absolutely fantastic. Total culture shock. My brother is a professor of cultural studies at Leeds University and his specialist subject is music. He's just written a book called *Why Music Matters*. It's very accessible and about why every culture connects with music. He was a big influence on me, growing up—big into punk, and on the night

before I went to LAMDA I was conflicted about going into acting, because it's very frivolous and I wondered if I'd be better doing a job like a social worker or something. He said to me, 'I know you've got a real sense of yourself as a woman and a feminist, but have you got any sense of yourself in terms of class?' and I was really naïve about that. He said, 'You won't know where you're from as soon as you're in that environment. If anyone mocks your accent, spit in their face!' which I didn't! I had children of extremely famous actors in my year from Eton and Sandhurst. It shook my world up.

JHam: How did you get your audition for *Coronation Street*?

JHes: I started a theatre company after drama school with a teacher from LAMDA called Brian Astbury. He had set up the first multiracial theatre company in 1970s apartheid South Africa. He had a very non-British can-do attitude and persuaded a group of us to write to every famous person we could think of, asking for help, and with the money we raised we built a theatre under a block of flats in Paddington, which we ran together, and put on plays while we were signing on. It was an amazing time, a real apprenticeship. I left there in my mid-twenties and went on to do tiny bits of telly and other bits and bobs. Then I got a job in Manchester at the Royal Exchange, doing *Much Ado About Nothing*.

JHam: Is that where the Corrie producers noticed you?

JHes: Yeah. I was doing comedy male and female. So they must have thought, 'Oh, she can do both.'

JHam: How did you feel about playing a transgender character?

JHes: I knew Hayley was transgender from the get-go. The casting people were nervous about how I would feel about that, but I was thrilled to be dealing with an issue that people knew so little about. I went straight to Frontline Books in Manc, a radical bookshop, and learned a lot, but not really how to play this very particular shy and ordinary woman, and I couldn't talk to anyone in the early days because it was all top secret. I went back and met the producer the week after, read a bit, made it clear I was serious about playing her properly, and they rang while I was on the train back to London to tell me I'd got the part! It was amazing. I found out subsequently that Hayley was meant to be the first in a series of disastrous dates for Roy, and it was a bit of a joke, but it was never a joke for me. Years before, I'd done a sort of exercise about future dreams, and mine had been to play a character with an 'issue' in a soap.

JHam: You have played the character brilliantly. Do you remember how Hayley was initially received?

JHes: There was an inevitable backlash from the trans community when I got the part. They quite rightly felt a trans actress should have been cast, and were concerned that the story would be a joke at their expense. I would never be cast now. But I do feel that back then, in the Nineties it would've have been too much pressure on a trans actress in that role, too much intolerable press intrusion. And the various groups eventually realised that I was serious about it, and embraced Hayley as a good role model.

JHam: Could you feel that people were sitting up in their chairs a little as they watched you on telly?

JHes: Luckily, I didn't feel that the eyes were on me; I didn't take it on at all, I just played the character. I just played what I feel like it would have felt like to be in love with somebody and have to tell them this secret about myself. That was always at the heart of it. From day one there was such chemistry between David, who plays Roy, and myself. And that's something that you just can't account for. We had a very similar way of looking at the part. And because of the part he was playing, he was subject to mockery as well. He never saw that as a joke. We are both very protective of Roy and Hayley and their love story. What I saw in the few months that followed was absolutely extraordinary. People started watching it as a love story.

JHam: Hayley is one of the most loved characters ever created. How does that make you feel?

JHes: Well, thank you. I think she is. I get the impression from the feedback I get, because she's such a lovely person; and more than that because of the characters, because of who they are; the writers and the producers never really messed with us. They couldn't really give us the usual soap stories of affairs and all that.

JHam: Why did you feel that Hayley had to die when you left?

JHes: Well, when I decided to leave, I knew that Hayley would have to die. I know that has been a disappointment for a lot of people, but it would be much more of a betrayal of what we've done. That has been the perfect end for me. This has been a love story with a sensational beginning, a lovely middle, and a tragic end. To start with

this issue, and really make a difference to what people think about transgender people, has been amazing. People used to come up to me in the street in the early days of Roy and Hayley and say, 'When are you getting married?' and I'd say, 'Well, they're not allowed to because of the law,' and they'd be like 'Oh, forget that!' That's how you change the world. Letting someone in and then they're rooting for the character, even though there was an uncomfortable issue about them that was difficult to swallow for some people.

JHam: You have also petitioned for signatures to get more pancreatic cancer funds.

JHes: Yes! To end on this double whammy issue of a pancreatic storyline has been really interesting to me, because I didn't know anything about it. I had lost somebody that I knew to pancreatic cancer, but I didn't know that it had this terrible low survival rate that hasn't improved for forty years. Then I got involved with this e-petition and got thousands of signatures on that.

JHam: I think it was beautifully and truthfully written, encompassing all the new medical terms that a person has to learn when faced with a terminal illness.

JHes: I think it's the feelings, too. Feeling really strong sometimes and then at other times feeling desperate.

JHam: The arguments that Hayley and Roy have had have been terrific and accurate.

JHes: The most moving thing, for me, has been hearing from people who have lost people or who are dealing with cancer right now. I would have thought that people would have just turned off, and that was my big fear. From the messages I'm getting people have seen their experiences mirrored, and that's down to the writing, which has been spaced out brilliantly, because the schedule at Corrie is so manic, like you're just in it all the time. There's a lovely bit over Christmas where they do have a happy Christmas and afterwards she gets told that it's spread, and that, for me, is a real key moment, because she loses it. She absolutely loses it, because she has been so strong, then she completely goes a bit bonkers and she trashes the Christmas tree and stuff. It's a big moment for her and she's embarrassed about it, but she's glad she's done it. I'm proud of it. The 'right to die' stuff is another topic where real debate can be had.

JHam: You are very warm, friendly and open, Julie. Do you think you share qualities with Hayley?

JHes: She's a good influence on me!

JHam: How much of you is in her, and how much of her is in you?

JHes: We have melted into each other over the years. She's a lot better a person than I am; she makes me want to be a better person, and I see her as someone totally separate from me. When I did *Paul O'Grady* he asked me what it was like to hang up the anorak and leave the wig behind. I said, 'It must be the same as you leaving Lily Savage behind, a similar thing.' I find bits of her around the house, and I think, where is she now? What keeps happening is people are sending me pictures of Hayley, like, someone at a petrol station in a red coat with dark hair, or on a train … It's so amazing. It's like she lives on. I love that. Her dying is a terrible thing for her but a great thing for me. I'm so sorry, Hayley, that I've done this to you!

JHam: When you get the tough scripts, how do you prepare for the acting?

JHes: It has been difficult lately. I go through my lines with my husband, and he loses it when we're just running lines. It's so beautifully written. She might say something like 'I don't want to die, I'm not ready', and he just loses it. Then the dying scenes, I can't even ... It was like an out of body experience, so horrendous, and yet beautiful.

JHam: How did you know it was time to leave the Street?

JHes: It was a process. I did this play in Manchester last year that was about Sophie Lancaster, the young woman who was murdered in a park because she was dressed in a goth-like way. I would never have taken time out of Corrie to do any other piece, but this was so close to my heart. It was a really big success, it won awards and sold out. It was an absolutely heartbreaking story. It made me realise that there were other stories I wanted to tell. But I didn't make any snap decisions. I knew how seductive theatre could be. I thought long and hard about it, talked to my husband and friends about it, some of whom are struggling as actors, and they were like, 'You've got to do it, you've got to leave.' I thought, 'If I don't do it now, I'll never

do it.' Then I had this incredible week ... I told Corrie just before Christmas on the day that they changed over producers, then I got a message from the press office saying that they were going to release it today, and could I write a statement, and my dad was in a care home at the time. It went bonkers. Facebook and Twitter went mad, and that was the Friday afternoon. On Monday morning I got a phone call saying my dad had been taken into hospital, and he died on the Wednesday. So everything about leaving just got shunted to one side, last January 2013.

JHam: I'm so sorry for your loss. What did your mum and dad think about your role and you leaving *Coronation Street*?

JHes: It was funny, because all any northern actor ever gets asked is, 'When am I going to see you on Corrie?' It was a relief to be able to finally say, 'Next week!' My dad was dead proud. He was like, 'Oh my god!' but he loved it. My mum is worried about me leaving, she loves me being in it. She doesn't want me to do Simon Stephens plays with all that effin' and jeffin'! I really could have dribbled on forever as Hayley, until I got too old to do it. It was the biggest shock to everybody when I said I was going.

JHam: Who are your Corrie mates? Alison King? [Carla]

JHes: Apart from David Neilson, Ali is probably my best mate at Corrie. The Hayley/Carla love story has been the greatest love story never told. When we did the siege scenes, we fell in love with each other, because we didn't have much to do with each other before. The writers just got it and ran with it.

JHam: What's your next project after *Blindsided*?

JHes: *Black Roses* follows right after that. We're bringing that to the Southbank, too.

JHam: I will come to see you.

JHes: You'd better!

JHam: What posters were on your wall as a teen, and how did you get into The Smiths?

JHes: My brother was a massive influence on me. If you think that in 1980 he was seventeen and I was ten, I've always have a varied taste in music, so the first two albums I bought were The Smiths' first album and Wham. My husband says this sums me up.

JHam: You should describe yourself as somewhere between The Smiths and Wham.

JHes: Exactly. Did you see us on *Mr and Mrs*? We went on and won; the winning question was, 'Julie's favourite group is The Smiths. What is her favourite Smiths song?' Another question was, 'If Julie learned the ukulele for a while which song would she serenade you with?' The choices were 'Teenage Kicks', which was our wedding march; the Corrie theme tune, or 'Reach' by S Club 7. It was, of course, 'Reach', and he got it right. 'Reach' is the song that I have to dance to. You could be telling me about the most tragic events in your life, and if 'Reach' comes on, I'll be like, 'I'm sorry, excuse me.' I have a terrible naff streak. My brother despairs. On my tenth birthday he bought me three singles: 'Oliver's Army', 'Life On Mars?' and 'Heart of Glass'.

JHam: What a totally cool brother! What was the favourite Smiths song answer?

JHes: 'There Is a Light That Never Goes Out'. Oh my God, I nearly forgot to tell you this! Mike Joyce was on our train home! He had been to a City match. We had only met him once, but we were like: 'Mike! Mike!' and he was like: 'Hiya! Have you been to the match?' and we were like: 'Oh no!' We held up our trophy and said, 'This is where we've been! And we won it with a Smiths question!' He said, 'What question?' and we were like, 'There Is a Light That Never Goes Out'. I know it's a bit of an obvious choice, but not for me! I saw Chris Packham picked 'Reel Around the Fountain', which was a great choice. It's the one that I sing more than any other Smiths song. 'Pin and mount me like a butterfly ...' Oh!

JHam: Did you see The Smiths live?

JHes: I've seen Morrissey, but I've not seen The Smiths.

JHam: Have you ever met Morrissey?

JHes: Yes, I have! I was in Kendals in Manchester, and I was on the escalator going up, one lunchtime. I glanced down and he was behind me! You have never seen a more uncool performance in your life. It was unbelievable. I couldn't believe it was him. It was when he was living in LA, so I had to really think, 'It's him! It's definitely him!' So I arrived at the top, and he passed me and he went up the next escalator.

JHam: Did you follow him?

JHes: Well, I was frozen. I stood at the bottom. It had been wedged in my brain to shake his hand and say something like, 'Thank you for all the pleasure you have given me.' As he went on the escalator, he could see that I was there, and I knew he was a Corrie fan, because he tried to be a scriptwriter for a while and he went out with Sally one night, wandering around town trying to find other Corrie actors. I just thought, 'There's no way I can say this to him without sounding really pathetic.' So he was nearly at the top of the escalator and I was at the bottom, and all that came out of my mouth was:

'THANK YOU!'

He turned around and said, 'I think you've got me confused with somebody else.' I lost all sense of irony and just went, 'Oh no! It's you!' Again, I thought, 'He's getting away, he's at the top, I'm at the bottom.' He turned around and gave me a lovely smile, and I just went:

'ALL ME LIFE!'

And that was it! It was all I could manage! I went back to work in a stupor. I was star-struck. I was shaking, saying, 'I just met Morrissey in Kendals!' and somebody said 'Neil Morrissey?' and I said 'F*** off!' No disrespect to Neil, but I wouldn't be shaking with excitement over meeting him.

A lad called Lee who works in wardrobe—I told him, and he said, 'I've met him twice. The first time I was in my school uniform in the post office and he was ahead of me in the queue, and I was so overwhelmed I burst into tears. Morrissey put down his parcel and hugged me, and said, 'It's okay.' Years later, Lee is working in HMV and Morrissey comes to the counter with, brilliantly, a Siouxsie Sioux album. Lee says to him, 'I have actually met you before in the post office and Morrissey said 'I remember. You cried.' 'I was in floods of tears again!' He was so lovely to me. He could have turned his head away and acted really cool, but he didn't.

He didn't have to be nice to me. I think he's really nice when he meets his genuine fans and he can see they must be overwhelmed. I love the line in 'All the Lazy Dykes': 'When you look at me you actually see me'. This must hardly ever happen to him. It must all be hero worship. He's one of the only real stars left, like Madonna.

JHam: If Morrissey walked in here right now and said, 'All right, Julie?' What would you say?

JHes: I'd be like, 'Oh my God Morrissey, serious to God, Julie is doing a book about you, and we're doing an interview about you, what are the f***in' chances of that happening?' Then I would also ask him if he remembers meeting me on the escalator in Kendals.

JHam: You could have said, 'I'm Hayley off Corrie'.

JHes: That would have been a mistake. It was all going through my mind to do that but I didn't; I couldn't.

JHam: What if he came to your house? What snacks would you put out for him?

JHes: Oh God, I'd make him my roast veg. Aubergines, courgettes and all that. I'd be like, 'Just give me a minute!' Then I'd hide any fish fingers in the freezer.

JHam: What's your favourite Morrissey song?

JHes: I love 'You Know I Couldn't Last', it's so personal and honest. 'In the end the royalties buy you luxuries.' It gets to me ... But I love 'Everyday Is Like Sunday'. I love the build up, the chorus. I have a connection with that song. I love 'Camden' as well. I love the key change. I love 'Where taxi drivers never stop talking'. It's epic. I love 'The World Is Full of Crashing Bores'. I love the expression of it; I'm more interesting than you, I wouldn't ever want to be you. He's a proper poet.

JHam: Favourite drink?

JHes: Tea. If I had to give up wine or tea, I'd give up wine. I take my tea strong and milky. No sugar.

JHam: Favourite book?

JHes: *To Kill A Mockingbird*. I've got into graphic novels. I love them. I went to a graphic novel shop today on Berwick Street.

JHam: Crisps?

JHes: I'm not a crisp fan, and the thing is that I am a savoury girl, not a sweet one.

JHam: So what would you eat, then? Savoury snack of choice?

JHes: Cheese, cheese and cheese. I'm a bad cheese girl. You know when they bring a big wheel of Stilton? I could just eat the lot of that with a spoon. There's no bottom to my cheese pit.

JHam: Who's your favourite actor?

JHes: I'm saying David Neilson, he is amazing. What you don't realise is that when you're watching something like Corrie, there's no help—no lighting or music or angles or anything like that, what you are seeing is absolutely raw. If you do see something that is a little bit sublime, then it probably was sublime. I've seen that right through the years from the Sheila and Billy years in *Brookside* to the Bianca and Ricky years in *Eastenders*. When I'm acting with Ali King [Carla], I have no idea what she's going to do. She does stuff like that scene when she's a drunk bride and me and Chris take her into the bedroom, It was really late one night and me and Chris were so tired, and we were like, 'Just do what it says in the script!' She's picking up empty champagne glasses and drinking out of them and falling around, and she's amazing! She made a great pissed bride, the best. Jennie McAlpine, who plays Fizz—I just have to look at her face; if I have a scene where I have to get upset, I have no worries at all. I just look at that little face and she's so beautiful, such a beautiful, amazing person. She runs a mental health charity with her dad. She is more illuminating in real life than she is on telly. I love Maxine Peake, Kate Kelly; I'd love to mirror their careers.

JHam: Favourite past or present Corrie character?

JHes: Well, with Karen MacDonald I had moments with her where I just thought, 'What you're doing is incredible.' I loved Becky. Becky is as maligned as Hayley is. She made that character human. She never beautified her, changed her in any way; I love her for that. I'm going for Becky.

JHam: Do you have a soap scene that stays with you?

JHes: In the 1980s me and my dad were mad about *Brookside*. I've said this to John McArdle and Sue Johnston. There was a New Year's Eve episode where they kissed for the first time, and it did something; something that they did together I could have watched a million times. It made me want to be in a soap. It has been a privilege to work with Sue, she is a lovely person. Then in the 1990s it was *Eastenders*. The Bianca love triangle was a great storyline.

JHam: What's your favourite pizza topping?

JHes: I like Fiorentina with the egg in the middle and the spinach.

JHam: Favourite biscuit?

JHes: I'm not a big biscuit eater, despite the amount of tea I drink.

JHam: What about the biscuits in the factory?

JHes: I can eat as much as I like when I've got my wig on. Character calories don't count, that's the rule. I like the cheap biscuits. Custard Creams.

JHam: What was Hayley's preferred cake?

JHes: An éclair. And I did used to eat them as well. I'd be in there, I got to the point in Roy's Rolls where I just thought, 'Right I need to eat the cake now, rather than torture myself with doing the whole scene.' I'd shove it in my gob, done, dusted.

JHam: Favourite film?

JHes: That's hard, but, I will give you *Eternal Sunshine of the Spotless Mind*, Although recently *Blue Valentine* has been wonderful, I love that film so much. The deleted scenes in that film are like mini masterpieces.

JHam: Childhood toy?

JHes: My favourite toy was Mandy, my Tiny Tears. I played with her far too late into my life. I knew that I was reaching puberty and I didn't want to do it, so I clung to this doll. There are all these pictures of me as a twelve-year-old walking down Blackpool prom with a pram with Mandy in it. My grandma made her all these outfits, including Russian-type hats and double-breasted coats. I've still got Mandy with her full wardrobe.

JHam: Please could you write a note to my mum?

JHes: Yes, I will!

Julie and Mandy. Photo: Julie Hesmondhalgh

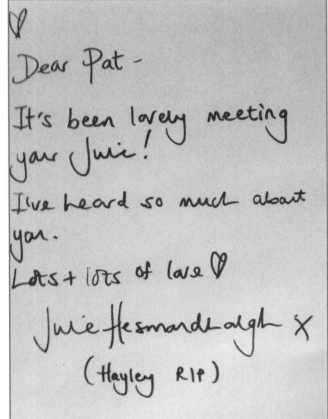

Dear Pat –

It's been lovely meeting your Julie!

I've heard so much about you.

Lots + lots of love ♡

Julie Hesmondhalgh x

(Hayley RIP)

About the Author

Julie Patricia Hamill was born near Glasgow on December 13th 1971. She became a fan of The Smiths in 1983 and saw the band from a tall, kind stranger's shoulders in the Barrowlands in September 1985 and again in July 1986. She has followed Morrissey throughout his solo career, maintaining a fascination for the singer and a continual wide-eyed and full love of his voice.

In 2012 Julie sought out people who have worked with, photographed, written about or are famous fans of the singer. In this wide and varied collection of interviews she shares the insights and personal stories of the people behind Morrissey and their connection to his work. Taking inspiration from The Smiths In Scotland tour programme of 1985, each interview also includes their favourite things.

Julie lives in London with her family and Dolly the schnoodle.

Julie founded the Twitter fan club, the Mozarmy, in 2010.

Julie Hamill's website: www.juliehamill.com

Follow Julie Hamill on Twitter https://twitter.com/juliehamill

www.fbs-publishing.co.uk